At Home Abroad

An American Girl in Africa

Nancy Henderson-James

To Ninna —
A recent friend and what a
find !
love, Nancy.

Plain View Press
P. O. 42255
Austin, TX 78704

plainviewpress.net
sb@plainviewpress.net
1-512-441-2452

ISBN: 978-0-911051-67-4
Library of Congress Number: 2009920240

Cover Art by Muriel W. Henderson
Cover design by Susan Bright

Acknowledgments

At Home Abroad could not have been written without the responses to my 1993 survey of missionary kids. And the survey would not have happened without Mary Edwards Wertsch's book *Military Brats*. Her descriptions of growing up in the discipline of military families opened my eyes to the equally strong influence growing up abroad had on missionary kids. The survey respondents stunned me with their poignant expressions of love for Africa, the advantages of growing up as they did, and their anguish about missing out on close ties to family and culture. Their words brought Africa alive again for me. In my attempts to fit into an American life, I had stuffed Africa into a hidden part of my soul. Suddenly it was stomping around my house, letting loose feelings I had forgotten. The best way to cope with them was to write this memoir.

While my children, Nathan and Noel, were young, I rarely mentioned my Angolan life to them. Coming to terms with my childhood has opened me to them in wonderful ways. Despite my early reticence in bringing Africa alive for them, they have chosen careers that commit them to embracing and bettering the world and they make me proud.

My deep thanks go to: Mary Edwards Wertsch for writing *Military Brats*; Beth Rambo who provided me with a database of missionary kids; the eighty-nine missionary kid survey respondents, including my brothers, for starting me on the path to this book; my mother for saving all the letters sent between us starting when I was nine, for lending me her journals, and for being such a champion of my work; my father, author of 3 books, for encouraging the writer in me; Chris for sitting with me for six years, for helping me find words; Ann Masur for being my first reader; Anne Vilen for always encouraging and challenging me; Norcroft, Hedgebrook, Vermont Studio Center, and the Pecos Benedictine Community for the generous gift of time, solitude, and space to write; Jana Richman and Debbie Stoddard, my writing group; Faith Eidse for including "Diving In" in *Unrooted Childhoods*; Judy Hogan for believing in my book; Charisse Coleman for an invaluable critique; Susan Bright for her interest in Africa and shepherding the book into reality; Rev. Enrique Etaungo Daniel for his wonderful compilation of Umbundu proverbs and sayings translated into Portuguese—the English translations are my own and so are any errors; Barbara Schaad Rogers for reminding me of details about Rhodesia; Nathan, Noel, Dina, and Lisa for wanting to read the manuscript; and especially Doug for love and support, taking over cooking duties to give me time to write, being a willing reader, and for working hard to sharpen up old photos and bring back slides that had mildewed.

Writing about my African life has allowed me to fall in love again with the rhythms, smells, flavors, and sounds that I grew up with and to appreciate anew the Angolans, Portuguese, Canadians, and Americans who taught me how to live.

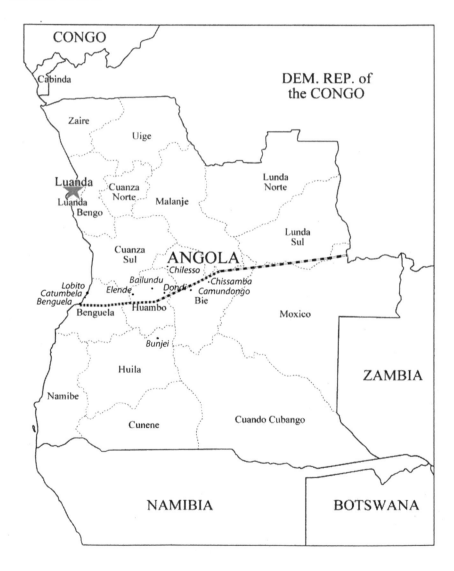

Map of Angola with mission stations indicated

Contents

Prologue — Tez

Ndimōla ocingendeleyi, ndi nekulu yocilitumbike.
Sou filha de tristes ervas e neta de aguas correntes.
I am the daughter of sad grasses
and granddaughter of running waters.
Umbundu proverb

Maria Teresa. Her birth name too long for her tiny body. At seven months, she was a wizened eight pounds, unable to hold up her head, roll over, or smile, and so she became simply Tez. I gazed at her soft brown skin, her dark eyes, and her springy curls. She grasped my finger and held on. I cradled her. I suckled her with bottles of rich milk, and watched her blossom into a sturdy grinning one-year-old, on the verge of her first step. Her legs had transformed from fragile twigs into strong saplings, planted solidly on her Angolan land. I prepared to give her, healthy, back to her family just a year before the colonial revolution against Portugal. We boarded the train, I to continue on to Rhodesia for high school, she to go home to a family she didn't know. What became of her?

I'll never completely come to terms with the audacity of handing Tez out the train window at the Bela Vista whistle stop. Wrenched from me, a 14-year-old who didn't know about repercussions, didn't understand how the body never forgets. I went on with life, moved to school 1500 miles away, learned to maneuver another culture, and left Africa abruptly when war started. But what happened to that little Angolan girl forty-eight years later, if she survived war, land mines, hunger, and flight to a neighboring country? Did she die or did she grow up a refugee—one of 300,000 who fled? After forty years, the war sputtered to a close in 2002. Has Tez returned to Angola, hoping to make her life in a devastated land, in an unfamiliar country? Whether and how she survived continues to haunt me.

Poem: I am From the Southern Cross

(After George Ella Lyons)

I am from the Southern Cross
I'm from a brilliant constellation
Smallest in the entire sky
Four points, alpha, beta, gamma, delta

I am from the Southern Cross
Revered by seers and
Followed by Wise Men two thousand years ago
Soon vanished from northern skies

I'm from the Southern Cross
Visible year round below the equator
Rediscovered by Europeans in the sixteenth century
Stars to steer by and calculate the time

Parents, missionaries, followed the Southern Cross
Seeking adventures and the Wise Men's babe
Offering precious Africa to me, their child
I'm from the Southern Cross
Jewel box of sparkling reds, blues, yellows, whites
Baby cluster, one hundred times brighter than the Sun

Chapter 1 — Chords of Energy

Ci popia oñoma, yevelela kowōlelo;
ci popia omanu limbuka apa ondaka yi pandokaila.
Para compreender a mensagem do batuque escuta-se o seu som,
e seu ritmo; para conhecer as ideias de alguém anota-se
o objectivo do seu discurso.
To understand the message of the dance,
listen to its sound and its rhythm;
to know another's ideas, note the purpose of his conversation.

Umbundu proverb

The sparkle of phosphorescence in the dark bay drew me down to the beach. From the verandah, I'd seen glints of light along the edge of the water, magical flickers that became more excited with each wavelet. My mother gave me a jar to bring water back to my bedroom, to admire up close the luminous creatures twinkling back at me. The air was soft; it stirred against my legs and arms and sent the water lapping again on the sand. Palm leaves fluttered on the trees along the road and I looked up to the sky. Stars pierced the black night.

In the city of Lobito, in Angola, Portuguese West Africa, 12° south of the equator, nights were unmarred by street lamps and back yard lights. The Southern Cross, four pulsating stars aslant in the sky, shed its light on me, an American girl, and on the mix of Angolans, Portuguese, British, and Dutch residing in that small coastal town. I like to think that the Southern Cross drew my parents to Angola, just as the same cluster of stars above the horizon drew the Wise Men to Nazareth. Shortly after Christ's birth, the Southern Cross disappeared from most of the northern hemisphere. It was only in the sixteenth century that European explorers rediscovered the Southern Cross, and used it to steer their ships. Growing up, I looked to the Southern Cross.

My mother used to wear a broach of the Southern Cross pinned to her Sunday suit. The four points, red jewels, were laid upon a gold shape of Africa. Like the Biblical searchers of the Near East, my parents followed the Southern Cross to offer their gifts to Angola. And like the European navigators, they went to explore the world.

As a missionary child, Christian beliefs and practices wove through my days. My father said grace for us before each meal, in Portuguese if we had Angolans at the table, in English when we had missionary company.

"Our Heavenly Father," he'd say, "we thank you for the food, which is before us, and we are ever mindful of those who are hungry and without food. We're grateful that you have brought the Fergusons (or whoever was there) safely to us, and ask that you watch over all our families, near and far, and keep them healthy. In Jesus' name, Amen."

Without my father's frequent reminder of our family far off in America, I didn't much think about them. Occasionally I sat cross-legged on the window seat of my mother's office and flipped through our family photo albums. I examined young incarnations of my parents, their brothers, sisters, and parents back in Tacoma, Washington, looking for a prominent nose or a crooked smile that would tell me I was related to them. I liked knowing I had tons of aunts, uncles, cousins, and even a grandma. They became real, briefly, every five years when we returned to America on furlough.

On the other hand, the hungry and needy in my father's prayers surrounded us, especially in Canata, the African section of town. My parents would steer the car through the dirt pot-holed streets, avoiding the bicyclists and pedestrians and children darting through the crowd. We would pass a long line of women and children, with enamel pitchers and tin cans balanced on their heads, waiting to get water at the pump. Scruffy, emaciated dogs slinked along the edges, sniffing for food. Pigs, ranging free, rooted in the tiny garbage dump that would have been picked almost clean.

Barefoot children, in clothes worn thin from scrubbing, their colors bleached out in the strong sun, often had the swollen stomachs and red hair of malnutrition. "*Eputa* does that to you when it's all you have to eat," Mom said. I stared at them and sighed; I was glad I had more to eat than corn meal mush. Umbilical hernias, bulges in the belly, were common among the children. I had had one when I was born. Surgically repaired, it looked like a zipper, discretely hidden under my shirt. The zipper was my secret connection with those kids. The open garbage dump and the dilapidated outhouses, perched at the end of rickety walkways over the tidal flats, seemed like good reasons for Mom and Dad to go out to meetings and services several nights a week, leaving their children in the care of Cipriano, our houseman. My parents' faith focused their attention out into the community. I knew this, but I didn't like it.

"Do you *have* to go out *again?*" I would complain to my mother when she came to my bedroom to kiss me good night and tuck in my mosquito net. I wanted her to be close by while I slept. The devotion of my missionary parents to their mission was much like the dedication of those in the military and the Foreign Service to their callings. The mission mandate controlled not simply the missionary, but the whole family. Children became miniature advocates and supporters of their parents' enterprise, ceding, without knowing it, an intimate family for the good of the organization. Sometimes, as happened in our family, the sacrifice meant extended years away from home at school. I was well into adulthood and parenthood before I fully realized how little I understood about being in a family and being a parent. I suspect the loss of family affected my stance toward religion, as well. As a child, though, I could only softly voice my complaint.

Worshipping God on Sundays was the pivot around which all missionary activities turned. Our Sunday rituals changed through the years, but when I was four, Sunday loomed long: the trip across town, the endless service at the Umbundu church, in a language whose rhythms were familiar but whose words I barely understood. I sat on a closely packed, backless bench, squished between my sister Kathy and my mother. Dad was usually up front, preaching or participating in the service. While the service rambled on, I got fidgety and cavernously hungry. I wanted food and a cooling swim. But first came the social time afterward, mingling with the congregation in the bright sun in front of the church. Behind the church the stark limestone hills, barren of trees, shrubs, or green growth of any kind, reared steeply from the salt flats. In the distance, to the right of the church, was a blue and white checkerboard of saltpans, the blue pans recently flooded with saltwater, the white pans full of salt left after the water evaporated. Beside the pans, piles of salt, some dozens of feet high, dazzled white in the sun.

As I got older, though, and understood more Umbundu and could wait more patiently for dinner, the services were comforting. The church offered refuge from the arid saltiness and the blazing sun. The brown skins of the congregation were a respite from the stark, pale colors outside. The smell of freshly scrubbed bodies and clothes mixed with the funkier odor of sweat that trickled down backs and between breasts, dampening shirts and blouses. Coughs, murmurs, the quiet suckling of babies at the breast, the shuffle of bare feet converged in my senses to mean church, friends, and warmth. Each soft sound was a stitch that bound me to the congregation. Through the years, I became intricately connected to these people whose faces and names I knew and who knew me, who asked after me when I was away at school, who enveloped my hand in theirs when we greeted each other. And when the choir raised its voices in a full range of harmonies, effortless and free, and the congregation stood to sing, our voices and bodies hummed as one, as if a chord of energy ran around the church joining us one to another.

I didn't recognize until years later how thoroughly Canata had molded me.

In 1952 when I was seven, we returned to Lobito, after a furlough year in America, to a new Sunday ritual. My father decided to reach into the Portuguese community by organizing a small Portuguese-language church in our house. The congregation included all shades from white to cinnamon to black. Mulattos the cinnamon ones were called in town, in a sneering tone that made me look at them and wonder what was wrong with being mulatto. From then till the Portuguese congregation built its own church a few years later, I never had to stray farther than the verandah for Sunday school and our living room for church. Every Sunday morning Cipriano pushed our couches and easy chairs into rows and brought in folding chairs for the two dozen members. Dona Armanda and Dona Bia festooned the makeshift altar and pulpit with flowers from their gardens. Dad stood behind the pulpit, his back to the open door that led straight out to the beach. The breeze off the water wafted in and played around our legs on its way through the room and out the door to the garden. Senhor Roëder pumped the portable folding organ, producing an altogether weaker, thinner sound than the large organ in Canata, and the tiny congregation quavered out hymns in reedy voices.

Around that time, I received an epiphany of sorts about God. I was sitting on the toilet in my parent's bathroom ruminating on what I understood about God. The *Bible* taught us to be humble. Dad had told me that was what Jesus meant when he said, "The meek shall inherit the earth." Mom told me, "Don't be a show-off." I knew I was supposed to be polite and modest in front of our guests. But something about God annoyed me. He wasn't humble at all. In fact, He was conceited because He wanted us to think about Him all the time. I remembered that Jesus said God was everywhere, a part of everything. God was just plain egotistical and self-important. As I sat on the toilet, I couldn't help wondering, If He's really everywhere, is He even occupying my BM? Of course He has to be. But, yuck, why does God think He has to prove *in that way* how important He is?

My seven-year-old bathroom revelation translated into skepticism about the divinity of God, although at the same time I accepted the formalities and teachings of Christianity as the natural course of things. The stories of the *Bible*, especially the parables of the New Testament, illustrated on flannel board in Sunday school, taught me important lessons in telling the truth and extending help to the less fortunate, but didn't convince me of God's all-powerful nature or His personal interest in me.

When the Portuguese-language congregation had raised enough funds, they built a new church across town in the area called Caponte, near the bridge to Canata. The congregation had grown over the years, but the new church remained much smaller than the Canata church, even with an apartment attached to it for the Portuguese minister they soon hired.

As the Caponte church grew, so did the youth group or *Juventude*. In my year and a half interlude at home when I was thirteen and fourteen, between returning from furlough in 1958 and going to high school in Rhodesia in 1960, our group of ten or fifteen teenagers met on Friday evenings, occasionally at our house for swimming and badminton. One evening we had congregated at the bottom of our outdoor stairway. Some of us sat on the steps leading upstairs, sheltered by the bougainvillea vine. Some sat on the couple of steps going down to the front yard. The rest of us perched on the wall that connected the steps. The Portuguese kids, the boys especially, were intrigued by stories they'd heard of fabulous wealth in America, where our family had just spent the previous year. In the dark, the boys' eyes flared with excitement as they conjured up outrageous fantasies of American streets literally paved in gold.

"*Não é.*" No, it isn't like that, Kathy and I insisted.

Not that America was poor, but I knew money couldn't be scooped up effortlessly, as they imagined. They looked skeptically at us, as if convinced we were hiding the truth from them or suspicious that we wanted to hoard the wealth for ourselves. I personally had more interest in the everyday pleasures of life. I loved to spend a day on the beach in front of our house. Or rattle off the new French my sister and I were learning at the little Portuguese school up the street. Or hang out on the beach with our cook Tomás, watching him scale and gut the fat fish he had just bought off the fishing boat as it passed in front of our house, or help my mother wrap the Christmas gifts she gave to every local teacher, nurse, pastor, and catechist, and all their large families. They were small gifts, pencils or pens, notebooks, handkerchiefs, and New Testaments, tokens of love and respect.

During that time, when I was fourteen, I decided to join the church, at least partially, I think, to bear witness to some common understanding between the church community and me. Soon after the Caponte church was dedicated, I was among a small group of teenagers who met with my father for several weeks to discuss the church's expectations of its new members.

Dad had us memorize key Scripture passages, such as the "Lord's Prayer" and the "Beatitudes." On the Sunday of our confirmation, I imagined I'd feel somehow more serious and responsible, like a young bird taking flight into adulthood. We stood, and Dad called us to the front of the church. In Portuguese, he asked if we would give ourselves unreservedly to God's service? We would. Ever mindful of the welfare of our fellow members, would we promise to walk with them in faithfulness and Christian love? We did. Dad invited the congregation to rise and welcome us. I looked out at the faces of the men and women who'd worshipped in our living room for years, the parents of my friends, Josinda, Belinha, Deolinda, Sergio, Jorge, and those who'd had us to dinner and helped celebrate birthdays. I was sure I could walk with them in love.

Then Dad led us in our first communion. For years, I'd heard my father intone the well-known phrases. This time they were for me. *O Senhor Jesus Cristo na mesma noite...* "The Lord Jesus the same night in which he was betrayed took bread: and when he had given thanks, he brake it, and said, 'Take eat: this is my body, which is broken for you: this do in remembrance of me.'" I plucked a tiny cube of bread off the tray and let it dissolve in my mouth. Dad continued, *Na mesma maneira...* "After the same manner also he took the cup, when he supped, saying, 'This cup is the new testament in my blood: this do ye, as oft as ye drink it in remembrance of me. For as often as ye eat this bread, and drink this cup, ye do show the Lord's death till he come.'" I tilted the tiny cup until the grape juice bathed my tongue. I waited. I hoped the bread and juice would be dramatically transformed into body and blood. I wanted to feel pulled, shaken and holy, into a communion of souls. Nothing happened. I was still regular Nancy.

My faith seemed to wax and wane with the intensity of the religious emotions around me. As much as anything, it was the *Bible* verses I memorized in Lobito and later at school in Salisbury that laid a spiritual foundation. I loved the cadence and rhythms of the King James' version of the *Bible*. I loved how repetition gave grace and beauty to the language. I still feel a radiant hum when I read the "Beatitudes."

"Blessed are the poor in spirit: for theirs is the kingdom of heaven.

"Blessed are they that mourn: for they shall be comforted.

"Blessed are the meek: for they shall inherit the earth.

"Blessed are they which do hunger and thirst after righteousness: for they shall be filled..." (Matthew 5:3-6)

Beyond their sheer beauty, they just seemed right. They fit my moral sense and evoked the social values of my parents. I identified so strongly with Mom and Dad's commitment to justice that I expected them to be able to solve the world's, or at least Angola's, problems. Angolan farmers constantly battled drought and infertile soil to produce a tiny subsistence corn crop. In contrast, America in 1957 had seemed like the Biblical land of milk and honey. As we drove through Iowa on our way across country, we had stopped to have our picture taken in front of a lush corn field, stretching for miles in every direction, so high we looked like midgets.

"Mom," I asked, "why can't some of that American corn be sent to Angola, to feed the hungry?"

"It's very complex," she explained. "The United States can't just send food to the hungry without affecting the economy of the receiving country." But then how, I wondered, would those who hunger and thirst be filled? I was impatient with her when she didn't have a solution.

When we abruptly left Africa in 1961 and temporarily settled in Tacoma, my mother took us to the small Congregational Church on Sundays. I resisted liking that church, as with most everything those first years out of Africa. Services droned on with boring recitation of verse and creed. Where were the emotion and the meaning, I wondered? And the way the choir and the congregation sang, they reminded me of the Portuguese church in Lobito. Their voices were wavery and thin, as if they were embarrassed to sing out with passion. In Tacoma, I had the first inkling of how naturally I had always connected music, spirit, and faith. The stirrings of joy and reverence for God I had felt in Canata, I realized, might be related more to harmonic singing and emotional ambiance than to religious belief. I have experienced a similar joy at a Benedictine abbey during vespers. The rituals of lighting incense, swinging the burner over the congregants, and bowing, combined with chanting, "Sing out, my soul, Sing out and glorify the Lord God!" have worked on me in what can only be described as a deeply spiritual way. My heart and my soul have felt as though they had opened to possibility, but the deep faith in God so obvious in the brothers and sisters has remained elusive to me. And yet, music in all its flavors, whether sacred, blues, jazz, or classical remains a source of delight and great happiness for me.

Music was everywhere in Lobito. Living as we did on open verandahs in the Portuguese section of town, the sounds of the city surrounded us. I often heard a neighbor's radio playing the mournful voice of a *fado* singer, lamenting her fate in love. *Fados* perfectly expressed the melancholy spirit of the Portuguese. They were the musical expression of *saudades*. Josinda would say, before her friend had even left, *Ja tenho saudades de Celeste*, I already miss Celeste. Missing her in anticipation brought out the sweetness of Josinda's sorrow and helped her feel it deep down. When the beginning of the war for independence drove us from Africa in 1961, I felt only loss. I often wonder if I'd had time for *saudades*, if I had been able to savor the sadness of saying good-bye to Rhodesia and Angola, perhaps I would have felt less rootless in my new life, less judgmental of America, and more open to its experiences.

From my bed on the verandah, I listened to our neighbors eat dinner with their radio on. On balmy nights they ate on their porch just beyond my shutters. Their knives and forks clinked on the plates and the smell of olive oil and garlic drifted up to me. I took a deep breath of it and I could almost taste the silky oil transforming pungent garlic into sweetness. As I drifted toward sleep, I became aware of another layer of sound, that of drumming and singing. It floated above the neighbors' dinner noises. Sometimes the drums were drowned out by laughter or *fado*, and then emerged once again during lulls. It wafted across the bay, coming from the dirt streets and bare shacks of the *sanzala*, the impoverished African part of town.

As neighborhood noises subsided, the steady beat of the drums grew stronger. Saturday night was the night for dancing, singing, and drinking. I knew that Mom and Dad disapproved of these Saturday night *batuques*.

"Alcohol goes to people's heads," said my mother. "It makes them do things they shouldn't do. And it wastes money that they don't have." But lying in bed, listening, I didn't think about its moral worth. I loved hearing the drumming, punctuated by the calls of the leader and the responses of the singers. A strong male voice chanted out a line, perhaps about the *ovindele* [the white man] and the dancers sang out their response. The music reminded me of dancing at the jubilee in Elende when I was ten.

Elende was a beautiful hilly mission up country. On the fiftieth celebration of Elende's founding, people from all eight missions had flocked to the weeklong jubilee. We stayed with our missionary "relatives," Aunt Lois and Uncle Carl Dille. (Aunt and Uncle were honorifics, bestowed on all the missionaries by missionary children. More than terms of respect, they helped create family ties in the absence of blood relatives.) After dinner, Aunt Lois plied us with root beer floats, made from homemade root beer and homemade ice cream. They told us stories about the monkeys living in the hills above their house.

At night we danced to the complex, overlapping rhythms of the drums. I joined the crowd under the vast, open-sided tent, circling with the women, including my mother, shuffling my feet in the dirt, sliding them back and forth and sometimes sideways, gradually rotating with the circle. Dust puffed up and filled the tent, hanging in fine particles in the night air. It settled on us, making the black faces ashy masks and mine streaky. Dust sprinkled on the head wraps of the women and on the babies on their backs.

At the edge of the tent, some musicians stood at their drums, beating a crisp syncopation on the skins with their hands. Others, with thick batons, squatted over their hollowed-log drums, pounding out a sonorous rhythm across the slit. The vibration of hand-plucked *ocisanji* or thumb pianos added a metallic buzz. The insistent beat of the drums propelled our shuffling feet and clapping hands. The drumming bored into me, vibrating the marrow of my bones. Suddenly over the instruments soared the voice of the lead singer, calling out his line, and we'd join in with our response. I didn't know the meaning of the words we were singing in Umbundu and it didn't matter. I was scooped up and carried along, singing at full throttle.

When I went off to school up country in Dondi and later in Salisbury, Rhodesia, music was the lifeblood for those of us living in the dorms. In Dondi, Uncle Max, the dorm father, relaxed by playing the piano and the musical saw in the evenings. Clustered around him, we sang along while he played the piano. We listened to the mellow sweetness of his musical saw. At Hatfield Girls High School in Salisbury, Miss Smith challenged the chorus with difficult pieces from "The Messiah," and through our hard work, we felt strengthened and accomplished. In the dorm, my girlfriends and I sang to the hit parade on Saturday mornings. We sang hymns to refugees; we sang in the minibus traveling around town; we sang at Billy Graham's crusade; we sang in our rooms. As Johnny Cash says, in his song "Daddy Sings Bass," "Singing seems to soothe a troubled soul." Singing made me feel joyous and sad, silly and solemn, and above all, part of a family. Singing was the glue that cleaved my friends to me.

Music had been the gift that evoked home and belonging. The music in the church in Tacoma simply left me flat.

After a year in Tacoma, my mother and brothers returned to Angola and Kathy went to Antioch College in Ohio. Alone in town, living with a family from church, I flirted with finding another church that might engage me in some deep, resonant way. The minister at the Congregational Church, unaware that I wanted to leave, asked me to teach fourth grade Sunday school. "OK, I guess I can," I said. I could almost imagine he was my own minister father, whom by then I hadn't seen in two and a half years. Even so, I was merely going through the motions of a religious life. I was spiritually ravenous, but I think now it was not a religious hunger as much as loneliness for family and home. I missed Africa. I hated the high school culture I'd been thrown into, where I felt estranged from everyone else. I was uncertain about the future, the decisions I'd have to make about college. The idea of drawing strength from God in my distress seemed inauthentic. He was, to me, impersonal and powerless, a tenuous idea at best.

When I took philosophy my senior year, suddenly a new way of thinking about the world opened up. My brain fairly sizzled to find that Socrates, Aristotle, and Kant were asking exactly the questions I'd had about myself, questions about the meaning of life and the nature of reality. What *was* my life worth? How was it valued? Who valued it? What would sustain it? How was I related to America, Africa, and the wider world? Oh my God! Christianity is just one of many paths to a good life, I realized. I could actually choose my own path. Coming from a liberal religious family that believed in individual growth and intellectual development, I didn't have to take a huge detour. My way could be a simple shift to a parallel lane. But it felt like a revelation on the order of my seven-year-old epiphany about God. I began to question not just God's divinity but the entire focus of Christianity in my life. Religion had provided me a home and reason for living in Africa. Once I'd left Angola, family, and missionary community, once philosophy raised questions about my beliefs, I was set free to seek home and my essential self elsewhere.

The release I felt then was akin to the happy abandon I had experienced when I first went away to school. I was nine. As the dry season neared its end, we would notice clouds billowing in the skies that had been clear for months. One day they would persist and darken, until we heard a crack of thunder and then there'd be a downpour. It might last five minutes, or half an hour, but that first rain of the season was the sign my up-country friends had prepared me for. "Just wait for the rainy season," my friends said. "You won't believe what happens!"

"What?" I asked. "What happens?"

"Flying ants! Ants fly out of the ground. The air looks all shimmery."

"Wow." I'd never seen such a vision.

"But, then, here's the best part. We grab them and eat them!"

"Yuck," I said. "Why do you want to do that?"

"No, no, no, they're yummy and crunchy and salty. The African kids taught us how to eat them."

And so, each year, I anticipated the flying ants.

When the rain stopped, we would be poised to dash outside to witness a swarm of ants fluttering up from the newly damp red earth, released from their seasonal underground prison. The emerging sun would glint on their translucent wings.

"The ants are out," we'd yell to each other and we'd run outside to snatch the flying delicacies out of the air. Holding them by their wings, we'd munch into their black wiggling bodies.

"Hurry, quick, they're disappearing," we'd laugh, grabbing and eating them as fast as we could.

Chapter 2 — Magic and Loss: The Voyage Home

Ci pepa ci pua; ci vala ci limba.
Não há bem que sempre dure, nem mal que sempre ature. Tudo passa.
Good doesn't last forever, bad doesn't endure. Everything passes.

Umbundu proverb

First, my sister popped out in red spots in the car while we watched the movie at the drive-in. And then my brother and I did too. Measles, said the doctor. It was the summer of 1952, at the end of a furlough year in Tacoma and Boston. From the time I was two, our Angolan life was punctuated every five years by furlough in America. The bout of measles delayed our departure for home. While my mother stayed behind to nurse three sick kids, my father flew to Angola, the "press of business" summoning him. Thus a pattern was set for our traveling life that would repeat itself each time we went on furlough. At seven, I had begun to learn that my father's work life would always take precedence over his family.

My mother later told me that Dad had had to return before his visa expired. This was a real concern in the adversarial atmosphere between Protestant missionaries and the Portuguese government, where a missed deadline could have prevented him from pursuing his life's work. Despite coming to his defense, recently my mother was reminiscing about her life with my father, now deceased. "You know," she said, "I realize now that family wasn't very important to Daddy."

When the measles had run its course, my mother packed us up and we embarked for Angola on the *Ferngulf*, a Norwegian freighter. The four of us, my mother, big sister, baby brother, and I, were the only passengers on the ship carrying goods across the Atlantic. The voyage would take thirty days of endless ocean, interspersed with stops in ports along the west coast of Africa.

On board, a heap of potatoes, stockpiled for the journey across the ocean, filled the corner of the deck to its ceiling. Here I found my secret spot. The potatoes, knobby under my bare feet, slithered and tumbled onto the deck of the ship, skittering like miniature footballs, as I clambered like a monkey up the pile. I braced against the sliding potatoes, arms and legs slightly flexed till I reached the top. Nestled into the lumps, buffeted by the damp salt breeze, I looked through the porthole at the endless choppy Atlantic. The ship plowed through the water, its prow slicing the waves and pushing them aside, leaving foam and white caps lapping against the sides and in the ship's wake. From my potato perch, I daydreamed about life on the blue Lobito bay and imagined the *Ferngulf* rounding the sand spit.

The lighthouse, white sentinel, would beckon us into the bay. The engines, with a grumble, would push our freighter toward the harbor. I saw myself standing on deck, straining to spot the cement factory sprawled on the arid hills, its tall stack venting white smoke, its siren marking the beginning, middle, and end of the day. Across the bay on the narrow spit of sand would lie my city, a city of pastels and whites, pines, palms, and papayas. I would see the Machados' peach stucco house and Aunt Hilda holding Sebby out on the porch. Madame Manise's white mansion would be hidden behind trees lining the bay. Madame Manise might be sipping tea in her pristine living room. The Radio Club's antenna would send out Portuguese fados, mournful songs of death and lost love.

I imagined the pilot boat meeting the *Ferngulf* right in front of our house and wondered if Daddy would be there or would he already be at the docks waiting to meet us? The pilot sent out to guide us into port would climb the steep gangplank. I could hear my father's voice explaining to a guest, "Lobito has the deepest natural harbor on the west coast of Africa." Daddy knew so much. Our house would pass too fast to hold on to its cool wide verandahs, its tile roof, the papaya and palm trees. My home, so close, would tempt me to leap off the ship, but the *Ferngulf* would churn forward, still far out at sea.

Until the year I'd just spent in America, Angola had been my measure of home. My parents, on the other hand, would say, "We are going home," referring to the United States, raising a question in my mind, perhaps for the first time, about my understanding of Angola as my native land and their allegiance to America. At six I was old enough to notice differences between their home and mine.

In Tacoma, we'd lived among aunts, uncles, and cousins I hadn't met before. My parents' relatives had talked to me as if they knew me. "Well, Nancy," they said, "how do you like being home in America?" I smiled at them, feeling a nervous twinge in my stomach about that word "home." I wasn't sure if they were teasing me or if they really didn't know where I lived.

The second half of the year, we lived on a missionary compound in Auburndale, Massachusetts, close to the Boston headquarters of the mission board. There I made friends with Rhonda, who was in my first grade class, and she invited me to her house to watch Howdy Doody. His goofy grin and "Howdy Doody Time," the song we sang along with the TV, made America thrilling and exotic. Telephones, readily available to speak to grandma across the country, escalators and elevators that magically whisked us up and down, stores that were crammed with more than I could imagine desiring, and the ubiquitous "I Like Ike" posters and bumper stickers of Eisenhower's campaign temporarily blotted Angola from my mind. Even Portuguese, the language I had learned with the facility of a native when I was two, retreated to a hidden corner of my brain.

On the ship, unmoored from America, and Angola a distant memory, I lived in a seven-year-old's world of whimsy and imagination. My mother's voice broke into my reverie on the potato pile.

"Na-a-ncy, time for lunch," she called.

I scooted off the pile, potatoes drumming behind me onto the deck.

My mother was below in the officers' dining room, a windowless room with space for two metal tables, bolted down so they wouldn't slide with the pitching of the ship. We ate with the captain, the first mate, and two stewardesses. Mom was settling my twenty-month-old brother David into his seat while my sister Kathy, who was eight, and I sat down to another Norwegian smörgåsbord.

The cooks treated us well. They always served potatoes, sometimes cold, sometimes hot. Cold herring and salmon. Cold liver pâté and ham with vegetable salad. Hot meatballs, omelets, and sausages. Cheese, fruit and pastry for dessert. The quantities of food reminded me of my Norwegian grandma, my father's mother, whom we'd visited in Tacoma. Kathy and I stayed overnight with her in the same tiny house where she'd raised five children during the Depression after her husband died. Out of her wood-fired stove, she fed us fresh bread, chocolate cake, roast beef and potatoes, stirring memories of Tomás, our cook in Lobito who also cooked on a woodstove.

The ship's smörgåsbord was fancy and so sophisticated that it brought out the divas in us. My sister and I draped Mom's dressing gowns over our shoulders, tied our hair in ribbons, and clumped into the dining room in her high heels. Some days we impersonated Queen Elizabeth and her lady-in-waiting, traveling to America to visit the Queen's husband and ten children. Other days Kathy took the guise of a high ranking lady and I her son Timothy. We were often sirens of the theater, gaudily made up with a bright splotch of rouge and a smear of red lipstick. After dinner, with snippets of popular American music still running around our heads, we slouched on the coffee table in the passenger lounge, blouses falling suggestively off our shoulders, as we belted out, à la Rosemary Clooney, "Come On' a My House, My House" for the Captain and any crew we could lure in.

My mother, always well organized, was prepared for her long voyage with two small girls and a toddler. At home, her practical side had to hold sway if she was to keep our complicated amalgam of home, guest hostel, and mission headquarters going. But for the ship, she had allowed whimsy to rule. She stuffed a sack with fabrics of all textures—remnants of velvet, satin, silk, and brocade—for Kathy and me to sew into doll clothes. Our dolls, Raggedy Ann and Susan, celebrated their birthdays on board. I stitched a hanky and shawl, silk pants, and a flowered silk dress for Susan's party. The stewardesses served us pastries and tea, on paper napkins and doilies whose flowery raised patterns we had colored in, choosing from our 64-hue Crayola box. Burnt Sienna, a rosy, rich brown, reminded me of home. It said: warmth, suntanned with a hint of burn. We invited the Captain to our party, and he played an innocent version of spin the bottle with us.

The Captain, whom we called Captainy, sometimes invited Kathy and me up to the bridge for Cokes in the afternoon. He was elfin and balding, with a smile on his moon face and a willingness to participate in our games. The bridge was the Captain's preserve, a place open to others by invitation only. We climbed the clangy metal stairs to his high room, where he surveyed the ocean from windows on all sides. I sat on the edge of the roomy wooden chair, trying to tame the swing out of my feet, waiting primly for Captainy to pour me some sweet fizzy Coke. Maybe we reminded him of his children at home in Norway.

"And how are your lessons coming?" he would ask in English.

"Oh, fine I guess," we'd say. Since we had missed the earlier ship home recuperating from measles and it was now early fall, Mom had started us on Calvert Correspondence lessons.

Early in the trip, I stepped out of my cabin, grabbed the thick steel door by its edge, and pulled it closed. The door swung shut and smashed the middle finger of my left hand. I howled over the thrumming of the ship's engine. My mother found me writhing in the narrow hall between our cabins, my bloodied finger held up away from my body. I didn't want anyone to touch it, but the first mate, the ship's medical officer, was summoned to wash and wrap it. Every day he came to the cabin with a bowl of warm salt water to soak the bandage off my mutilated flesh and wrap a fresh bandage. My dangling hand became one giant throbbing finger. Mom fashioned a sling out of one of David's diapers. With the arm elevated, the pain in my finger subsided, and the slung arm became my badge of courage.

Some evenings I peered down through the railings at the crew, relaxing on deck. Tall guys with crew cuts would laugh and shout at each other in Norwegian. It lilted like Portuguese, but sounded harsher, full of hard Ks. Occasionally one of the men would climb part way up the mast, and then swing out onto a guy line, doing calisthenics. He'd hang, arms extended. Then suddenly he'd pull himself up, twirl around the guy line, and leap down to the deck. Everyone would cheer and the next man would strut over to the mast to show off.

One evening as I was watching the competition, one of the crew slipped off the guy line and tumbled to the hard deck. The laughter stopped. Everyone waited, silent and expectant.

I know he'll get up, I thought. I willed him to his feet.

He rolled over, rubbed the back of his head, and seemed overcome with nausea and the shock of the sudden blow. Still holding his head, he sat up and walked unsteadily to his room below deck to sleep off his pain. I blew a small puff of relief. The first mate wasn't summoned. There wasn't even any blood.

But the next morning at breakfast Captainy and the first mate looked strained and sad. Their brows creased, they spoke in hushed voices.

"Girls, come here a minute," my mother called.

With an arm around each of us, she half-whispered, "One of the crew died in his sleep last night, after a gymnastics accident."

I stared at my mother, transfixed with shock. I felt my heart would split open and bleed. I remembered how the man had turned white and shaken his head. But how could he have died? He had gotten up and walked after he fell. He'd been alive just like me! Maybe if I hadn't been watching through the railing, he wouldn't have fallen and died.

Such guilty thoughts persisted throughout my childhood. A couple of years later, I felt waves of remorse and responsibility for the death of our dog, Peter, though realistically I could not have prevented it. As I grew older, I adopted a strong moral sense of right and wrong, holding myself, and others, to a rigid code of behavior, of shoulds and should nots. I often interpreted remarks by others as disparaging. My inflexible stance may explain why I felt so relieved, as a teenager, to discover I could lead a good and moral life outside of Christianity.

The day after the sailor's death, they buried him at sea. We stood on the upper deck, the four of us, David in Mom's arms, Kathy and I leaning against her to gather comfort. I tipped forward on my toes to take in the funeral on the deck below. Captainy stood near the railing beside a long canvas sack, playing my father's role as minister. He read solemnly and fluently from a prayer book cradled in his palm, the type of book my father used for christenings and funerals.

The wind snatched the words from his mouth and blew them away. The first mate stood at the captain's side and the stewardesses behind him. The rest of the crew formed a ragged circle all round. Their heads were bowed. Captainy finished his reading. Several of the crew wrapped a Norwegian flag around the canvas sack and secured it with cord, emphasizing the shape of the body within. The bright red flag, with a blue cross outlined in white, riveted my attention on the still man. The crew picked up the sack and tipped it into the cold ocean. Out of view, I wondered if the sack immediately sank into the frigid Atlantic. Under a chilly, overcast sky, I returned to the solid warmth of my mother, suddenly aware of how my hurt finger throbbed at exactly the pace of my own heart.

From her bag of tricks, one day my mother pulled out an illustrated book of fairy lore, poems, and stories. Delicate drawings on each page rendered fairies in wispy gowns, elves in green suits and caps, and sturdy brownies. I read about fairies by day and dreamed of them by night. Perched on my upper bunk, I imagined I could hover over the cabin just as the fairies did and spy brownies and elves in the dark corners. No matter that good-humored brownies, in cloaks and hoods, usually blended with the grass and leaves around farmhouses, secretly helping farmhands do their chores. I knew they had work to do on the ship as well. Good elves, like fairies, flew, danced, and perched in trees, but bad elves lived underground and were dangerous. They were often the source of human illness. Fairies' magic powers affected us even when we weren't paying attention.

How could *that* happen? Were the fairies near? Maybe, I thought.

I read and reread the poem "When a ring's around the moon." I asked Mom to read it to me, and Kathy and I read it aloud together.

The wee folk will be tripping
In their silver dancing-shoon
Ring-around-the-meadow
When a ring's around the moon.

I dreamed of surprising them as they danced and leaped, almost invisibly tiny and shy, in their fairy rings. And their music, so haunting, so ethereal...

The pipers will be piping
Till their tiny throats are aching.
But hearken well, what time you see
A ring around the moon
And you will hear the music
Of the wee folks' dancing tune.

I lay back on my bunk in a swoon, hearing bells and the cascading giggles of the wee folk.

Each day before dashing off to breakfast I smoothed my bedspread and leaned Raggedy Ann and Andy, handmade by my grandma, against the wall. I propped Susan on my pillow.

One day after breakfast and school lessons in the lounge I returned to the cabin, startled to find that my dolls had moved. Ann and Andy lay on their stomachs looking over the edge of the bed; Susan sat at the end with that secretive smile of hers. Kathy burst into the cabin.

"The fairies came! They made your dolls alive," she said.

Was she telling the truth? I wished I knew. I wished my dolls would tell me if the fairies had enchanted them. I wanted to believe in magic, but I looked over at Kathy's dolls, sitting right where she'd left them that morning. Wouldn't the fairies have conjured her dolls to come alive, too? Kathy must be teasing me. As soon as she left, I rearranged her dolls.

When my fairy love was in full bloom, I was presented with a chance to test my belief.

Almost four weeks after leaving Boston we approached Matadi, 90 miles up the mouth of the Congo River in the Belgian Congo, just north of Angola. As we turned into the river, leaving the ocean behind, I could feel increasing tension on board. Captainy didn't notice me when he hurried back to the bridge after dinner, his shoulders hunched into his stiff neck. The crew monitored the progress of the ship up the treacherous river, systematically checked lifeboats and ropes, and reviewed emergency procedures. Later I learned that a series of falls upriver from Matadi created the whirlpools I could see in the swift current. The ship that had felt steady and safe on the open sea suddenly felt vulnerable on the Congo River. I imagined the *Ferngulf* being sucked into a giant vortex. Captainy wouldn't be able to hold the wheel. The ship would lose its forward momentum, start to turn faster and faster, then get pulled under the water. I imagined being flushed down to the river bottom and drowning. In the dark I'd think again of the sailor who had fallen and died.

But Captainy and the pilot boat steered us through the danger into port. Relieved, I stopped watching the river and noticed the full moon shedding its subtle mysterious light. As it rose in the sky a distinct ring shone around it. A ring around the moon, no doubt about it.

"Tonight's the night the fairies dance!" Kathy and I chanted, as we danced around Mom, pulling her arms, pointing to the moon. "See the ring around the moon, Mommy?"

She saw and she understood that we had to hunt for dancing fairies. She asked the stewardesses to listen for David sleeping in his cabin and we walked off the gangplank onto solid earth.

Outside the docks, Mom found a taxi to take us fairy hunting. She directed the taxi driver to take us out of the center of town since fairies danced in fields and woods away from people. In a woodsy area near a darkened restaurant, we glided out of the taxi. Mom asked the driver to wait for us, and on tiptoe, with hushed voices, we crept toward the woods looking for signs of a fairy ring. As my eyes adjusted to the equatorial dark, I was sure I saw glimmers of light flitting here and there. Perhaps fairy dust scattering in the breeze? I squatted and leaned gingerly forward, staring at an elf cap, pointed and green, lying among the dead leaves and grassy shoots. I didn't dare pick it up for fear of scaring away its owner.

I stood quietly and listened hard for the faint fairy music wafting through the trees. A whisper of leaves rustled, obscuring a delicate lilt on the breeze.

"Mommy, I'm sure those are fairies," I said.

"Yes," Mom said, "those just may be the fairies."

I knew we'd find them. I knew it as surely as anything I'd ever known in my life, so surely that I was ready to return to the *Ferngulf*.

We slid back into the waiting taxi and onto the ship. Though we were only a day or two from Lobito, the ship when it departed stopped first in Walvis Bay, South West Africa, just to the south of Angola. Much to my surprise, my father boarded the ship to join us for the last leg of the journey.

"There's Daddy," I yelled when I spied a familiar tall, thin form striding toward the gangplank. We met midstream. His first hugs squeezed stories out of me.

"Daddy, the door smashed my finger to bits—see it? And then the sailor smashed his head and he died and they had to bury him in the ocean and then we saw real live fairies in Matadi because the moon was full and had a ring around it."

And Dad replied, "Well, life has been very calm in Lobito. You'll be glad to get there."

Still besotted by fairies, I scarcely noticed the extra time it took to get home. The ship suddenly was rounding the sand spit and making its way up Lobito bay into port. As we passed our house, we were close enough to see the two royal palms on the street in front of the house and the sandy beach at the water's edge. Papaya trees snuggled, like fruity arms, against each side of the house. Through the dark shade of the verandah, I made out my playhouse on the corner outside my bedroom. I spotted the apartment building at the end of our block; closer to the docks, I saw the bar where we bought ice cream cones.

The pilot boat guided us s-l-o-w-ly into port. The docks were alive with Angolan dockhands who tethered the ship to its moorings with thick chains. Their bare chests glistened with sweat that stained their shorts. Portuguese officials, in white shirts and khaki pants, supervised them. With a cacophony of grunts, shouts, clangs, and creaks jangling in our ears, we left the ship.

Returning to Angola was like beginning anew, as if my pre-school years in Lobito had sunk beneath my imagination and had to be pulled up with all the muscles of my memory. Surrounded again by salt breezes and Portuguese floating on the air, by Dona Isaura, our Portuguese neighbor, and Allison and Cecily Gant, my English playmates, and of course by my house full of the toys I'd left behind, and the Angolan men and women who worked for us, the subtleties and details of my Angolan life resurfaced.

All the way home from the docks, I had known right away I'd head first for the playhouse, the only place in our rambling house that was mine alone, where even my mother knocked on the door before entering.

Turning from the driveway and parking on the cement slab in front of the house, I saw the familiar faces of Cipriano, our houseman, Tomás, the cook, Mãe Florença, our laundry lady, and David, the gardener, gathered to welcome us home. They softly clapped their hands in greeting.

"Akombe veya," they welcomed us in Umbundu.

"Sejão bemvindos," they said in Portuguese.

I shyly shook their hands, murmured "Hi, hello," but couldn't find the words in Portuguese. How did I say it? I was completely surprised to find I couldn't speak my almost natal language. What would happen if I popped in to the kitchen to chat with Tomás? How would I let him know what I wanted to eat? Jereminha, just about my toddler brother's age, sat on Mãe's hip gazing at us. He didn't remember me and I didn't remember Portuguese.

After my failed greetings, I bolted to the house, heading for the playhouse, kicking off my shoes as I went. There would be time later to check out the rest of the house:

The living room, where our guests sat and talked or listened to the news, where our books sat neatly on shelves behind glass doors that swung up to open, where *The Five Little Peppers*, *Little Women*, and *Little House on the Prairie* lived.

The dining room, whose table was long and wide and so high that I would still need a booster seat even though I was already seven. Sometimes that table wasn't big enough for all our guests and my mother had Cipriano set a table for the kids on the verandah outside the dining room. We liked to eat out there because we could throw our vegetables, especially carrots, over the railing into the sandy yard and no one would know.

The damp, dark laundry area, where Mãe scrubbed our clothes in the cement washtubs. She lathered the clothes with gray lye soap and rubbed them into suds on the washboard. She brought the clothes upstairs to hang them in the sunny front yard. The sheets and towels dried rigid like cardboard, but Mãe shook them and ironed them into pliant folds so that the smooth sheets felt cool against my cheek at night. She set up her ironing board under the thick shade of the tulip tree, ever blooming scarlets and yellows, and coaxed fire into black charcoal lumps, turning them red hot. She dropped the lumps into the iron. As the charcoal turned to ash, she held the heavy iron by the handle with two hands, tilted it, and shook the ashes out of the holes in the side of the iron. Then she put in more charcoal. One day she washed and the next she ironed.

Later I'd check the kitchen to see what Tomás was cooking for dinner. Would it be my favorite *caldo verde*, potato kale soup, aromatic with olive oil, or *canja*, a clear chicken soup with rice? I hadn't had his meaty baked fish, caught fresh in the morning and heaped with onions, tomatoes, and peppers, for a whole year. Or his pineapple upside-down cake. The cake got moister and sweeter just under the pineapple layer. The kitchen, with its big cast-iron, charcoal-burning stove, sat across the verandah from the dining room. I'd come sweating out of the kitchen onto the cool verandah. The breeze from the bay felt as cool as water against my skin. But I was feeling a little shy about seeing Tomás. I wouldn't know how to answer him if he asked me a question.

Instead I climbed the stairs. The frilly bougainvillea vine floated above me, its blossoms like deep red origami birds flying over my head. I walked around the upper verandah, past the guest rooms, and weaved through the guest beds crowded on the end of the verandah darkened with shutters for privacy. The southern sun filtered through the slats onto the navy and white striped mattress ticking. I flopped onto a bed and my nose filled with the musty smell of the feather pillow, impregnated with salty humidity. If our two guest rooms were full, Mom put guests on the verandah to sleep. When kids were assigned to sleep outside we liked hopping around from bed to bed, listening to the creak of the springs. Sometimes the beds became covered wagons, carrying us across the prairie along with Laura Ingalls Wilder. On the bay side of the verandah, I peered into my parents' bedroom. The next room was the bedroom I shared with Kathy. Above the sink was our old tooth-brushing chart with gold stars for the days we remembered to brush. The toy box still held our balls, jacks, and jump rope. Our books were propped crookedly on the shelves of the wobbly bookcase. Just around the corner was my playhouse.

I pushed open the Dutch door. The wood facade, partitioning a corner of the verandah, swayed momentarily. I squeezed my eyes shut, wondering if this was a dream. I'd forgotten about the painted table and chairs Mom had bought on our first sea voyage to Angola on *A Pátria* when I was three. When the ship stopped overnight at the island of Madeira, vendors in little rowboats thronged around the ship, holding up brightly painted wooden chairs, tables, mirror frames, and trays, pleading with the passengers to buy from *them*. Madeira bristled with forests on its mountainsides, and tourists could hurtle down the slick, cobbled hills in wooden sleds. I suddenly remembered *madeira* was the word for wood.

My Madeira furniture was enameled white with bright red and blue flowers. Green vines, punctuated by red and green dots, snaked up and down the legs. I sat on one of the chairs just my size. Against the wall outside the bedroom window, my empty doll beds were lined up, and beside the beds was my box of dolls. I kneeled and opened the box, thinking that my babies, packed away for a year, would be anxious to lift their heads out of the stuffy box and smell the breeze from the bay.

My dolls lay quiet, waiting for me to pull them out. I cradled my soft baby with her always-sleeping eyes.

"Your mama is home, sweet baby. You are soaking wet!"

And I eased her out of her sleeper to change her diapers. Next out of the box was my ventriloquist doll, his flimsy legs swinging from his hard body.

He looked at me and opened his mouth when I hooked my finger through the opening in his back and pulled. He wanted to know exactly where I'd been all this time. He sat on my knee listening to stories of America and the *Ferngulf*.

Mom's birthday doll lay at the bottom of the box. When we were only six and five, my sister Kathy and I had spotted two large white boxes, with pictures of dolls on the ends, stashed high on top of the wardrobe in the front guest room. They enticed us into stacking up some chairs to reach them. I handed the boxes down to Kathy. Inside we found two beautiful girl dolls with real brown curls, blue eyes that opened when we picked them up, and frilly dresses of yellow and pink. I was thrilled, but if they were Christmas dolls, Christmas had passed and wouldn't be back for a long, long, long time. We carefully replaced the boxes, leaving no trace that we had snooped. After a long day, the weight of our secret burdened us so much that we had to spill it out to Mom. Who were they for? Mom looked at us and said, "They belong to the person with the next birthday."

She must mean me! I thought. Of course. I knew they must be mine. "My birthday's next, July 13, four days before Kathy's."

But then Mom said, "Don't forget my birthday's in June."

I sighed. Why did Mom get everything? But, as time passed, the idea of my mother playing with two dolls intrigued me. Maybe she'd let me play with them sometimes. Maybe she'd let them sleep in the playhouse.

During the months leading up to her birthday, I often returned to stare at the boxes on top of the wardrobe. "How many more days to go, Mommy," I'd ask. Days and weeks became months until June arrived. At Mom's birthday party the two boxes lay under the other presents. I stood at Mom's elbow, crowding her, anxious to see the girl dolls again. She oohed and aahed and hugged the dolls when she lifted them from the boxes. I wanted to stroke their silky hair, watch their eyes pop open, but they were Mom's dolls and I had to let her hold them. Suddenly she handed one to Kathy and the other to me and said we could play with them as much as we wanted. I couldn't believe it. I held the doll, danced her around the table, and let her sit on my lap for the rest of the party. And that was how I came to have Mom's birthday doll.

My mother, of course, did not plan to give herself dolls for her birthday. My Aunt Marcia in Tacoma had sent them as Christmas presents for my sister and me, but as often happened, they hadn't arrived until after the holidays. Mom was holding them for our birthdays. When we discovered them, she shortened the long wait till July by dubbing them hers and then presenting them to us.

I sat in my playhouse for a long time, cradling my baby. I remembered the times Mom, with my baby brother on her hip, knocked at the Dutch door to my playhouse and I invited her in to tea. I felt the gentle breeze from the bay. I was like my white cat Fluffy, purring with contentment. America was huge, brassy, complicated, and scary. I had felt out of step, forever trying to figure out what was expected of me. Just when I got used to my first grade in Tacoma, we moved to Auburndale. There, though my school was next door to our house, I was afraid of being late, afraid of forgetting my lunch or my assignment.

But now I was home in Lobito, rediscovering the familiar. The cicadas in the tulip tree screamed over the buzz of mopeds speeding by the house. The breeze rustled the palm leaves and pushed wavelets lapping on the beach. Seeing a ship in the distance reminded me that as it approached my house, the calm, flat bay would turn into rolling waves. I'd hurry into my bathing suit, grab an inner tube, and roll it across the street and down the cement steps to the sand. The inner tube would race across the beach, flop in the water, and I'd jump on it to catch the waves as they swelled and washed on shore. But my first day home in Lobito, I sat in my playhouse, scuffing my bare feet against the cool cement verandah, fish and olive oil smells wafting up from the kitchen where Tomás was cooking. Mom's birthday doll sat on my lap. I listened to the voices of the neighborhood kids yelling to each other in Portuguese. I picked out "E pá! Vamos a praia." (Hey guys, let's go to the beach!)

I understood! Soon more memories would flood back, my Portuguese with them, and I'd be able to say anything I wanted.

Back in Angola, the lure of fairies still lingered. We hadn't been home long when the full moon once again rose with a ring around it. Kathy begged Dad to take her to look for dancing fairies. She seemed to require more proof. I'd had ample evidence in Matadi: the glimmers of light, the elf hat, in reality a green leaf, the faint rustlings and music. I went to bed. Kathy climbed on the passenger seat of Dad's motorbike, hitching her hands on his belt, and they putted to the end of the spit. The narrow desert coastal strip of Angola was devoid of the fields or woods that are optimal for fairies. Lacking them, the small circular park at the end of the spit with a patch of grass around the monument had to do.

When Dad and Kathy came home, I was already asleep. Mom had tucked my mosquito netting securely under my mattress. Kathy came to our room, woke me up, and blurted, "We didn't find any fairies and Daddy says they don't exist! And neither does Santa Claus."

I stared at her. Mostly asleep, I tried to grasp what she was saying. Why would Dad tell her such a thing? Didn't we have all sorts of evidence that Santa and the fairies were real? Santa had to be real. He filled our stockings and left us new baby dolls every year. The milk and cookies we left for him were always gone on Christmas morning and he signed, "Thank you, love, Santa," on the note we left him. I knew that the fairies existed, because we found them in Matadi. And hadn't Mom said so?

I lay in bed confused and angry. I hated my father for insisting that magic wasn't real. I was sure he and Kathy hadn't found the fairies because they hadn't looked in the right place. And I hated Kathy for telling me what Dad had said.

Now I can imagine what must have happened. Kathy would have insisted on searching every foot of the park. Dad would have reluctantly followed behind, enlisted by Kathy for this quest, but not that interested a participant. Maybe he even sat it out on one of the benches, leaving the hunt up to her. And when the fairies eluded her, she had to know the truth. Point blank. "Tell me, Daddy. Do fairies exist?" I imagine her standing in front of him, hands on her hips, pigtails swinging, demanding an answer. In his place, Mom might have suggested searching again at the next ring around the moon or she might have explained how shy fairies are. Years later my mother told me how angry she had been with my father for spoiling the fantasy she had so carefully nurtured.

Lying in bed that night, the bright moon, the Queen of Heaven, shone through my door, bringing back memories of the sea voyage. When I touched my still sensitive finger, I remembered writhing on the floor in pain. I recalled the sailor falling to the deck, stunned and nauseated. Dizzily, I clutched the mattress to keep from spiraling down into the whirlpool of death. But the moon, casting its light on me, evoked the fairies who danced and sang. Looking at the mysterious ever-changing moon, the moon with the ring that beckoned the fairies and lit the dark night, I didn't care what my father had said. My fairies were real.

Chapter 3 — Love Lines

Ciliva wa ipa; miti wa pumba.
A ratoeira apanhou; a armadilha malogrou. O pequeno,
por vezes vale mais que o grande.
The mousetrap catches; the snare fails.
A small thing is often worth more than a large.

Umbundu proverb

In Lobito, we resumed the life we'd temporarily put aside during our interlude in America. For my mother, that meant plunging into the care and feeding of an endless stream of guests in transit to or from America, while at the same time supervising Kathy's and my education, and keeping an eye on David. Later, the birth of my brother Mark, when I was eight and a half, definitively shifted my mother's focus to her young sons and away from her older daughters.

In the mornings, my sister and I worked on the Calvert Correspondence School lessons we'd begun on the ship. We studied at two small desks in Mom's office and piano room off the living room, on the bay side. Like my former American classmates, I continued learning to read with Dick, Jane, and Sally.

"OK, kids, study your spelling words and I'll be right back to give you your test," said Mom, as she hurried out to help Tomás make a decision about dinner. A few minutes later, I was ready.

"Mommy, I'm ready for my test," I yelled. No answer. I sat down to doodle at the piano, picked out "Mary Had a Little Lamb" and wished I knew how to read the notes in Mom's piano book. I perched on the window seat and flipped through *World Famous Paintings*. Fluffy, our cat that we'd adopted from Madame Manise, strolled in and rubbed against my legs. He was fluffy and white, just like everything in Madame Manise's mansion. Fluffy white carpet, fluffy white sofa cushions, fluffy white lady with fluffy white hair. I stared out the window at the bay. The tide was way out, leaving a wide beach striated by tiny streams meandering into the receding water. I wanted to take Rälte, our pointer dog, to the beach where he loved to stalk fish. It must be time for my morning swim.

"Mommy! Where are you?" I yelled, but this time I ran out to the front verandah in search of her. No, she wasn't in the kitchen; she wasn't with Mãe; she wasn't in the garden. I finally found her upstairs, tending to David, who was screaming mad about something, and talking to Cipriano about which beds to change and who was arriving.

"Can I go swimming?" I asked.

"After your spelling test," she said.

"Well, let's go," I said. "I've been waiting."

Beyond the household, my mother tended to the issues of the big world that occupied my father. As administrator of the mission on the coast, Dad made sure the schools had teachers and supplies, the clinics had nurses and first aid medicines, and the churches had deacons and pastors. He interceded in disputes between the Portuguese authorities and the Protestant community. As a woman in a male world, especially the colonial Portuguese culture in Lobito, my mother's voice was barely heard. Within the church, which was more open to women as leaders, she ran Sunday school, sewing, and literacy classes and brought comfort and concern to the sick.

"I saw myself as a social person with a conscience," my mother told me, when I asked how she perceived her work in Angola. "I liked the Africans and Portuguese we worked with, and thought of myself as a co-worker who helped organize things. I didn't know how to knit, but I found a teacher for the knitting group, put the group together, and found the yarn and needles. I was a good organizer of practical household routines, social events, and spiritual needs. For instance, when we raised money to build the Caponte church, I accompanied a group of Portuguese women in the congregation going door to door asking for donations."

I was surprised to learn that she solicited funds in the white part of the city. I had thought the prevailing suspicions of Protestants by the conservative Catholic Portuguese would have discouraged her from face-to-face appeals. But she said, "We had Dona Carmen and Dona Leontina in our group, women who were recognized and respected in town, so I wasn't afraid."

I'd heard stories from my mother about feeling isolated within the expatriate European community of Portuguese, English, Dutch, and white South Africans, because, she said, they didn't approve of my parent's entertaining Angolans in their house. I wasn't always aware as a child of my parents' daily small acts of courage.

My parents did much of their work from the house during the day and attended meetings and services in town many evenings. My father's study was on the front corner of the house looking toward the driveway. He was often at his huge, pigeonholed desk that formed a wall between the door and him. His tall dark bookcases were full of theology books and concordances, church histories and histories of Angola. Senhor Isaias, Dad's secretary, worked at his desk on the verandah outside the study, and they consulted each other through the open window. Senhor Isaias typed church bulletins and newsletters and ran the mimeograph machine, feeding every page in by hand as the big drum clicked and turned.

With my parents present in the house yet focused on their work, our animals, the cats and dogs, the parakeets and chickens, the tortoises and baboon, were ready sources of entertainment and affection for me. The more time I spent with my animals, the more they adored me and invited me to play with them. We belonged together. They were helpless and dependent. I loved them. Even more, nothing distracted their attention from me in the way that work preoccupied my parents and our household help.

I loved to take delicacies to our two tortoises that lived in the sandy front yard between the chicken pen and tulip tree. They were bold, not at all given to pulling in their heads and legs at the slightest move, and they were big enough for me to sit on. When I put chunks of paw paw and banana on their plates, they slowly but determinedly lumbered over to eat. They reminded me of the achingly slow and deliberate chameleon, who lived in the custard apple tree, the way they opened their mouths wide, chomped into the fruit, and chewed as if their jaws were controlled by a tight coil. Spring, sprong, spring, sprong. Their thick leathery tongues wagged the food around in their mouths. They fixed me with unblinking, reptilian stares. What were they thinking? Were they happy I'd brought them fruit?

One morning, we discovered that the smaller tortoise had been smashed and killed by someone wielding a heavy stone. "Why would someone hurt the poor tortoise?" I asked my mother. But she had no answers.

Chico, our baboon, was much easier to understand than the silent tortoises. I could tell when he was happy because he chuckled and chattered. He was full of mischief, reaching out to pull at my buttons or undo my sash. He greedily peeled and ate the bananas I pulled off the stalk for him. But when he was mad, he'd screech, bare his teeth, and jump around the stake he was tethered to under the tulip tree. Chico was given to us when he was already grown and had had to adapt to a series of owners. Maybe that's why he was temperamental. But I soon learned he was as dependent on me as the tortoises had been.

Word about Chico's arrival had flown around the neighborhood, drawing the Portuguese children to visit him. He was staked near the driveway, just as it made its final turn into our front yard. The neighborhood kids in groups of three or four would stand behind the low hedge, gawking and laughing. Colonies of baboons lived in the forested hills of Hanya inland from Lobito, but the families in town with pet monkeys usually kept them in their enclosed courtyards or on their tiny apartment porches. Our Chico was wide-open to the world. At first he ignored the kids. He picked at his belly, pulling out fleas, sat with his back to them and inspected the sandy soil for grubs, and climbed the tree. But one day, I heard Chico screeching. The kids were pelting him with sticks and pebbles to get his attention. I was painfully shy except with people I knew well, and I held back, uncertain what to do. Finally, I couldn't bear to watch the assault on Chico. "Não faz isto! Don't do that!" I commanded in a small voice. I said it again a little louder and felt braver when they quit hounding him and left.

But whenever they could catch him alone, the neighborhood children tormented him until his spirit broke. In our household of many adults concentrating on their jobs, and in a small but noisy city full of dog barks, whizzing motorbikes, and the dull roar of the ocean two blocks away, I am not surprised that Chico was left to defend himself. I imagine that our many servants, who may have noticed the sadistic teasing, would have silently deferred to my parents rather than intervene against white children. In the colonial climate of the 1950s, our servants would have risked angry retaliation by the Portuguese parents if they had chastised the children. Chico tried to hide up the tree or pulled his tether taut to get out of range of the kids' missiles. One day he broke loose altogether. Cipriano spied Chico up on our roof, completely out of reach. Everyone in the household—parents, kids, cooks, laundry lady, and gardener—craned heads to see him. We called his name, "Ch-i-i-i-co, come down!" He seemed happy to be away from people, but perhaps he tired of the barren tile landscape, because eventually he shinnied down one of the papaya trees and took off down the beach. We dashed after him, yelling, coaxing, but were unable to keep up with his erratic zigzags. Finally he gave up. Mom approached him gingerly, quietly. She crouched near him and he climbed, with a whimper, into her lap.

My mother decided to return Chico to his former owners. She had a new baby to tend to, and Chico was one too many responsibilities. I was sad to see him leave, but didn't know how I could protect him, especially since I would soon be going up country to school.

Another of our menagerie that immediately enchanted me was Peter, a boxer pup my family adopted when I was nine. I had been away at school when he came to live with us and I first met him when I came home for summer vacation. From the moment I stepped off the train, I knew he was special.

"He's a thoroughbred," my mother explained to me.

He looked like a fighter, square-shouldered, thick-necked, but his playfulness quickly erased my fear. His squished snout looked pretty silly. Still his clipped ears and bobbed tail worried me. Mom said that was what boxers were supposed to look like, but I could only think of the breeder looming over a fragile pup with his big shears. I stroked Peter's ears, running my finger along the clipped edge, imagining what he had looked like with floppy ears and a long tail. When I stroked his head, he looked up at me with eyes like pools of bittersweet chocolate. He jutted his lower teeth over his upper lip and groaned quietly. We were a perfect motley pair.

One day that summer, I sat on our back wall, keeping my eye on Peter and looking out at the ships on the bay. Peter and the neighbor's dog sniffed each other. Peter, at six months, stood tall as a full-grown dog but he acted like a puppy, insisting that the other dog play. I smiled as Peter rose on his back legs, sparring with his front legs. No wonder he's called a boxer, I thought. The dogs frisked in the street, since the sidewalk was narrow, but I wasn't worried because the few cars on that side street traveled at a sedate speed.

When a car approached, the neighbor dog broke away to bark and chase after the car. Peter watched. The next time a car drove by, he chased the car as well. The other dog, small, quick, and experienced, raced along right at the front wheel, barking, letting the driver know who was boss, but Peter was slow and awkward.

"Peter," I shouted, "come here! Bad dog! Don't chase cars!"

But he didn't listen, and I didn't know what to do. I felt as helpless as a rowboat trying to stop a ship at sea. If only I could grab hold of his collar, maybe he'd avoid the looming danger. When I leapt off the wall to run after Peter, he thought I was playing keep-away and wouldn't let me get near him. Just as I got close, he wheeled around, grinned at me, and raced back up the street. I was scared, and the more he played, the angrier I got.

"I'm going to give him what for," I steamed, "I'm going to smack his nose. I'm really going to teach him a lesson."

Suddenly I heard another car approaching and I screamed at Peter. "Come here, right NOW!"

Peter leapt into the chase. Instead of running beside or behind the front wheel, he ran right in front of it. As the car hit, Peter, my brown ball of energy, turned into a howling siren.

I didn't know whether to stay with him or run for Mom, but she had heard the commotion and ran out to see what had happened.

"Mommy," I wailed, "I told Peter not to chase the car, but he did anyway. He wouldn't listen to me. I called and called him."

She quickly hugged me then turned to help Cipriano lift Peter off the road. He seemed to be paralyzed. We placed him in a wooden box, lined with blankets, on the verandah where the stairs, kitchen, and dining room intersected so he wouldn't be lonely.

I felt sad for Peter and for myself, too. He lay helpless in the box, alert when someone passed by, but unable to move. I'd pat his head, run my fingers down his squat snout to his hot nose, hoping he would forgive my anger. I expected that any day he'd struggle up onto his feet and we could play again. Lobito had no veterinarian, so after a few days Dad consulted the doctor up the street and ascertained that Peter would never recover. My mother told me, "Peter has internal injuries. We're going to have him put to sleep."

I put my hand on the damp spot just at the tip of his nose and remembered the sailor who'd fallen from the mast on the *Ferngulf*. Outside he looked fine, no blood, no mess. The next day he was gone.

Every night I cried myself to sleep, wracked with sadness and guilt, but I couldn't speak of them to anyone, not even my mother. Images of Peter's sweet silly face, with his lower teeth jutting out, swam before me, but now his howling pain drowned out his contented groans. My once cozy bed seemed too large. I felt lost rolling around by myself. Even the mosquito net tucked in all around didn't shelter me. I wanted to feel cradled. I remembered the empty crib out on the verandah, large enough for my slight, nine-year-old body. I got out of bed and silently climbed into the crib. With the netting pulled over me, I fell asleep.

I longed to tell Mom how sad and lonely I was feeling about Peter, but I remembered a year or two earlier when I had tried to tell her some terrible news about my white rooster, and she didn't understand what I was saying. I was down listening to my animals' voices and my mother was up above listening to the important talk of the grown-ups, making decisions about how to feed all our guests and how to help the people who came to the hostel.

I had raised the white rooster, feeding and tending to him from the time he was a chick. Early one morning, a couple years before Peter's death, I heard the lapping of water on the beach and the flutter of palm fronds in the breeze before I opened my eyes. The house was still quiet with sleep.

Through the mosquito netting I saw the light blue sky with just a few puffs of clouds above the cement factory across the bay. A faint rooster crow reminded me that my chickens would want to be fed, so I slipped on my dress and started for the chicken pen.

As I walked down the stairs I spied Tomás, our cook, on the cement driveway in front of the garage, squatting in front of a white enamel basin spattered red with blood. I paused for a moment, fascinated by what I saw, and then hurried down for a closer look. A headless white chicken weaved on unsteady legs around Tomás. I couldn't understand how its legs kept moving or how it held itself upright without the head. Tomás appeared amused at the sight of blood pulsing from the chicken's neck until it keeled over dead. I clutched my neck in sympathy for his suffering, then burst into giggles. The chicken did look ridiculous, walking headless on wobbly legs. Tomás rather absently picked up the chicken, plunged it into the hot water in the basin, and started plucking off the feathers. Would I ever treat my chickens like they were just food, not animals?

To get away from the blood and mess that would be our dinner, I left Tomás and continued nonchalantly to the chicken pen beyond the garage. I pulled open the door just wide enough to slip in. The cheeping chicks rushed over to me, tickling the tops of my feet with their spidery claws. When I crouched down to pick up one of the chicks, it settled in my hands. In just a few days it had changed from a tiny adorable fuzzy yellow baby to this scraggly looking stage. Its feathers were turning to a mottled white and brown. As its neck lengthened, the ugly pasty skin showed through the feathers. But that was O.K. I didn't want to love the chicks too much because I knew we were going to eat them. Instead, I concentrated on watching them grow, from tiny chick to plump hen in no time all.

I mixed some corn meal and water into a paste and watched the chicks attack it.

"Eat up, little guys, fill your tummies," I told them.

I grabbed handfuls of corn and threw them out on the sandy floor of the coop for the grown chickens. They scurried over, with their heads down, pecking fast. One whole kernel after another slid down their throats. Then they dipped their beaks into the water dish and threw their heads back, beaks open, as dramatic as opera singers. While the chickens were off their nests, I found three eggs, streaked with dry chicken shit, to take to Tomás.

Suddenly I wondered where Henny Penny was, my favorite white rooster whom I knew we'd never eat. He couldn't have flown out the top of the coop because we kept his wings clipped. I turned around to look outside the pen for a handsome white rooster, prancing around the garden enjoying his freedom. Maybe he had slipped out when I came in. Then, through the chicken wire, I spied the flurry of white feathers settling around Tomás' feet.

I felt queasy. The dancing chicken that had made me both giggle and gag must have been my rooster. I stumbled out of the coop, wiped tears from my eyes, and then stalked angrily over to Tomás.

"O meu galo branco não sta lá. Onde sta? My white rooster isn't there. Where is he?" I demanded, afraid I already knew the answer.

Tomás, with not a hint of regret, solemnly pointed to the naked bird at his feet and said, "Vamos comer o galo hoje para jantar. We're going to eat him for dinner today."

My anger crumpled to despair.

Two steps at a time, I ran back up the stairs. My breath caught in my chest. Something squeezed my heart. I peeked through the screen door to the quiet, dark in my parents' bedroom. I didn't think I should wake them, but I had to. I walked around to Mom's side of the bed.

"Tomás has killed Henny Penny to eat for dinner," I said quietly.

The words grabbed my throat. I gagged and sobbed. With effort, she opened her sleepy eyes and scrutinized me. She listened, but she wasn't sure what I was upset about. Having chicken for dinner? Tomás killing a chicken? Tomás chopping off its head? I thought she would leap out of bed and find out why Tomás had killed my rooster. But she lay still as a mummy wrapped in linen bandages, removed from Henny Penny's and my world, as if she were dead, I thought.

Why was my mother so blind? Why couldn't she see the cords of love running all over our house and yard, from me to each feathered or furred creature I cared for? Why weren't the same lines running from her to me, entangling us, bonding us—mother and daughter? The answers lie, I think, in our family dynamics. My parents, like many of their generation, were not attuned to their children's emotional needs. We were expected to fit in to our parents' life without making messy demands. My mother was and is an eminently practical woman, dealing with life's details in a businesslike manner. She is not inclined to inquire about the feelings behind actions. She no doubt noticed the attention I paid to our animals, but would not have thought of my rooster as a beloved pet.

I didn't know where to go, whom to talk to. Everyone upstairs was sleeping and downstairs Tomás was acting calm and cheerful. He thought

I was silly to be hysterical about my rooster. I crept downstairs, trying not to let Tomás hear me and flopped on the living room couch. The morning sun filtered through the sheer curtains on the double doors looking out to the bay. A lizard scurried across the wall above the couch. Was I the only one who cared about Henny Penny?

Tomás called to me when I went back outside. He snickered in an attempt to stifle a laugh. "Look in the toilet," he said, gesturing to the small bathroom next to the living room.

Why should I look in the toilet? I didn't have to listen to him. But Tomás kept urging me to look. I walked over and stood in front of the closed door and I heard something moving. Soft scratchy sounds. A low gurgle. I pushed open the door and there facing me on top of the toilet seat, under the pull chain dangling from the tank, was a large white rooster. We stared at each other. He must have been thinking, well, finally someone is letting me out of here, and I was wondering, who are you and why are you in the bathroom? Tomás was doubled up behind me, laughing, telling me, "É o seu galo mesmo. É mesmo. That's really your rooster."

The trick Tomás played on me has puzzled friends who have heard the story. Was he sadistic and cruel? Did he hate me? Or was this a cultural oddity? Because he laughed so much when I discovered the rooster, I tried for years to find humor in it despite my anger at the time. In truth, I had never known Tomás to be mean. He was easy going and cheerful, and joked around with me when I came into the kitchen. Pressed to explain him, I think his trick was a result of the common practice among Angolans to closely observe the habits of whites in their midst, and at times to poke fun at them. He had noticed what my routines were and how attached I was to the rooster. He had probably also been the object of a few of my father's jokes. My father liked to tease with word play. In that cultural context, I believe Tomás planned his elaborate ruse as a compliment to me, to show that he knew me as a real person.

In the bathroom, I gathered the white bird in my arms, holding him tight across his chest. I could feel his heart beating fast, but his legs hung relaxed against my hip, his yellow claws extended. He had no idea how desolate I'd been about losing him. He swiveled his head and fixed me with his black eyes. I told him, "You're going back where you belong, Henny Penny."

I noticed as I walked to the coop that Tomás had cleaned up the chicken mess.

"Well, then, who *was* that other white chicken?" I asked.

"I bought it at the market," Tomás answered casually.

I let Henny Penny flutter out of my arms in the coop and gave him a handful of corn. I watched him, alive and present, gulp down the kernels.

Poem: Ten Views of Dondi

Red clay roads
Crunch, snap of eucalyptus bark
Sharp scent

Kutatu Falls gush
Over and between boulders
I leap like a goat

Acacia trees spread
Umbrellas of filtered shade
On rocky expanses

Orange mangos ripe
Yellow nespras like sun drops
Purple mulberries

Bela Vista bike rides
Fadário's store
Chewing gum and candy

School for missionary kids
Boarding with the Collins
Homesick

The terror of independence
Leaden heart
Tears

Dormitory living
The joy of best friends
Loving caretakers

Run sheep run
Kick the can
Sardines

Continued

Rebellion and war
Deforestation
Landmines

Chapter 4 — The Robbery

Cipondiya mandiya māi; si pandiya omamale.
Não há mãe como a própria mãe.
There is no mother like your own mother.
                                        Umbundu proverb

At the age of nine I left my parents and home for school in Dondi three hundred kilometers away. Dondi was a playground for children, with wide red clay avenues for riding bikes, leopard caves to explore, waterfalls to swim in, mangoes, nespras, and guavas to pick. Dondi even now evokes in me longing, tenderness, and *saudades*, the Portuguese word connoting a bittersweet aching for an irretrievable past.

Located on the mile-high plateau that rose sharply only a few kilometers from my coastal home, Dondi's crisp, cool dry season alternated with a season of daily predictable thunderstorms that came and went quickly. Delicate acacia trees covered the hills. Under their canopies, in the filtered light, red-and-yellow Christmas lilies bloomed. Like flashing traffic signals, they compelled the passerby to stop and admire them. Streams trickled through the woods and seeped from mottled, gray slabs of granite into a river that tumbled into falls. Hippos occasionally lumbered out of the river and left their tracks in the road and woods. Fast-growing eucalyptus trees towered over the settled areas of the mission, the hospital, the Institute, the seminary, and Mean's School, shedding their strips of bark, sharp aromas, and seeds that crackled underfoot.

Those images live in me despite what I now know: that the endless wars of liberation and civil conflict devastated Dondi's landscape. A few years ago a childhood friend returned to Dondi and documented the ruins on video. I forced myself to watch, despite mounting sadness. Red brick houses, schools, and hospitals are now ruins. Woods and fruit trees have been flattened by bombs and cut for firewood. Land mines are strewn throughout the area, preventing human habitation and crop tending.

Today's landscape is a fitting metaphor for my flawed memory of Dondi. Though I'll always believe in the beauty and innocence of the time, I've come to recognize the emotional land mines planted in me, the stories I constructed, and the feelings I buried to live through those three years.

On my ninth birthday, in July 1954, I believed I was old enough to leave home. Old enough to travel overnight on the train with my sister Kathy, to be independent, strong, and self-sufficient. Indeed, child development experts say that nine is an age for declaring independence from parents and for tackling new pursuits.

"Just think girls, in two months you'll be leaving for school." Mom then catalogued the benefits of going to school away from home. "Pauly and Mimi will be coming from Camundongo, Joy and Kathy from Chissamba, and all your other friends."

Pauly's freckled face and auburn pigtails came to mind. I'd get to see my best friend every day instead of writing letters to her.

"You'll have such fun playing together," Mom continued.

We talked about the swimming pool built for us, the picnics at Kutatu Falls, and bike rides into Bela Vista.

"Gosh, it's going to be such an adventure!" Mom said, perhaps trying to convince herself as well as us.

From earlier visits to Dondi, I remembered that when the frangipani bushes ("franzipanzis," as I thought they were pronounced) were in bloom, the air was laden with their honey fragrance. I never could resist picking a bouquet of their yellow, pink, and cream funnel flowers, only to find milky sap dribbling down my hand. I remembered poinsettia bushes that grew twice my height and covered themselves with an exuberance of bright red flowers. Dondi was a place so different from Lobito but just as beautiful.

"Mom, you know what we'll do?" I said. "We'll play games like run-sheep-run and kick-the-can with all those kids."

Earlier Kathy and I had taken the train to Chissamba, without Mom accompanying us, to attend the wedding of Aunt Bev and Uncle Tom, a missionary aunt and uncle. It had been a real white-dress wedding in English, with a tower of a wedding cake. I had caught Aunt Bev smiling at Uncle Tom; I was dazzled by their love. Staying with the Steeds in Chissamba had seemed like good practice for being in a dorm with lots of kids. In addition to the three Steed girls, the three Ferguson sisters had come from nearby Camundongo. I barely thought about my family at home in Lobito.

I decided, "I *would* like to go to Dondi."

"And, of course," said Mom, "you'll attend school with a lot more kids. Daddy and I think it will be good for you to judge where you stand against the others."

They thought Calvert School at home was fine for second and third grades, but now we needed competition, she said. Tommy Welch was the only other fourth grader I could think of, but my mother was convincing. It all sounded exciting. Turning nine was my best birthday, I thought, because it marked my budding independence, which I found thrilling and adventurous.

Now it's hard to remember more than fragments of the next three years, which I lived through a fog of longing and loss. I imagine a girl child wandering in a cloud, her voice muffled, losing sight of herself, and disappearing from view of parents and world. Louise Bates Ames, who has written extensively about childhood, expresses it this way: "It may indeed be a somewhat lonely business to pull free from a parent who not only is not holding on, but who is not even noticing that you have left."

In Dondi that first year, I lived with Uncle Ralph and Aunt Jean Collins. Kathy lived with the Tuckers a couple of kilometers away in Lutamo, where Angolan girls attended Mean's School. Accustomed to being the younger sister of Kathy, who radiated confidence and ease in the world, I felt adrift on my own. I was relieved to be sharing a room with Mary Collins, my surrogate sister who, like Kathy, was ten. The Collins family included Uncle Ralph and Aunt Jean, Mary, Frank who was twelve, and two absent children: Lois attended university in Canada and Stephen was in Rhodesia for high school.

Much of our family life took place at the dining room table. I sat beside Mary on one side of the table and Frank faced us. Uncle Ralph and Aunt Jean anchored the ends. The emotional life at the table tilted towards Aunt Jean, who was taller, younger, and more talkative than Uncle Ralph. Aunt Jean fielded the questions and handed down the answers in the family.

"Mummy," asked Mary, "Nancy and I want to sleep in the station wagon tonight. Is that O.K.?"

And Aunt Jean said, "Of course, you can."

The way she took charge comforted me and reminded me of my mother.

Even so, homesickness sat in my stomach like a ball of lead, dense and heavy, leaving no room for food. I hunched over at the table, hugging my chest to keep my heart from cracking. Tears that sprang from nowhere made me terrified that I would shame myself and make my mother ashamed of me. I thought I was heading for the challenge and excitement that Mom had promised me. Instead, I was lonely. Still, I was sure Aunt Jean would want to know how homesick I felt, and I imagined she would invite me into her lap, listen to me, and understand how much I missed my family.

I'd been with the Collins a couple of weeks, when we gathered in the living room after dinner to listen to Uncle Ralph practice the organ. I approached Aunt Jean, in her comfy chair, and said, my voice wavering, "I don't feel good. I think I'm homesick."

Her dark eyes scrutinized me. Then she brightened into a cheery smile and said, "Homesick? You shouldn't feel homesick. Just think about the wonderful things we're doing for you, and that'll take it all away. You just wait and see!"

As she predicted, my leaden stomach, heart sickness, and tears numbly submerged. Unplugged and empty, I realized being homesick was wrong and, even more, a criticism of her.

Aunt Jean, I was soon to learn, was the sort of person who was too proper to run down other people's characters herself, but relished the occasion when somebody else did it. Frank, like many adolescents, loved to make fun of others, and Aunt Jean condoned his mischief with her laughter. I don't recall Frank's teasing me when we were alone. He preferred the public arena of family dinners, where he drew the approval of his mother. One evening Frank made fun of my American pronunciations.

"Mummy," he asked, "why do Americans say stoopid instead of styoopid or noo instead of nyew?"

He said it the British way, with a strong, long u. I understood it must have been because I was stoopid. The Collins were proud Canadians from Ottawa.

"Oh, they're just lazy," she said.

I fashioned ways to stand up to Frank. Learning to walk on stilts was my first strategy. I tottered a foot above the ground on sturdy wooden stilts, holding myself erect by muscle and will, my hands grasping the handles and lifting my feet step by peg leg step. Momentum prevented falling. Once I hit my stride I could walk past the seminary where Uncle Ralph taught, and through the woods, all the way to school with the wide gait of a long-legged giraffe, much taller than Frank.

For Christmas that year I had asked for some miniature matchbox cars, a way to engage in boy activities, I suppose. When I returned to Dondi in January, Mary and I tied string to the cars and pulled them after us to school. One afternoon we took our matchbox collection over to the Childs' house, where Joy and Kathy Steed were living. We climbed the stairs to their huge attic room. I stood by the window, looking down on the outhouse, a two-seater kept sweet by sprinkling ashes from the cook stove into the hole after use. Beside it, growing in the rich earth, loomed my favorite mango tree heavy with ripening fruit. I thought I might climb the tree on the way home and pick the yellowest mango I could reach. I knew they weren't ready and I'd get cramps and diarrhea, but mangos of any hue were a temptation I couldn't fight. I gazed at the fruit dangling on the tree and asked my girlfriends, "What do you think it feels like to have a penis?"

"I don't know," they giggled in response. "Do boys feel them hanging in their underwear?" one of them asked. We decided to experiment.

"Let's see, what do we have to make pretend penises?" One girl rummaged around the room and found a large barrette. Another rolled up an embroidered handkerchief.

"Hey, I have this," I said. I felt in my pocket and brought out the lipstick-sized menthol inhaler. I shoved it into my underpants, where it poked against me like a permanent erection. The hard plastic was uncomfortable. I suspected my inhaler wasn't a good substitute for a real penis, but it gave me an inner confidence. I felt a surge of boldness. The beauty of pretending to be a boy was that Frank never had to know. I'd found my secret weapon against him.

Frank also targeted our teacher, Miss Neumann. She taught twenty missionary kids in grades one through eight. Miss Neumann, my first real teacher since first grade in America, was a tall, old woman with pure white hair. She lumbered on size twelve feet, walked with a slight stoop, and talked slowly, as if each word needed consideration. Sometimes, if she sat too long, I'd see her eyes sliding shut and her head nodding. She never raised her voice in anger at us, whether from extreme patience or inattention, I wasn't sure.

Afternoon was my favorite part of the day because Miss Neumann read to us. It was one activity we could enjoy whether we were six or twelve. Despite her thin high voice, the stories of Mrs. Piggle Wiggle and Long John Silver carried me into other worlds. Soon I was far away from the classroom, discovering treasure hidden in the dank cave. Sometimes we persuaded Miss Neumann to read all afternoon until time to go home.

But home at the Collins's, I listened with dismay to Frank making fun of Miss Neumann. He walked awkwardly into the dining room, his eyes drooping, his voice pitched artificially high. I had to admit that he captured her perfectly, but I was shocked that Aunt Jean burst out laughing. I didn't dare come to Miss Neumann's defense. She wasn't a great teacher and Frank sure had nailed her, but Aunt Jean's open delight at Miss Neumann's expense unsettled me. My mother had always told me, "If you can't say something nice, don't say it."

At the end of the school year, my mother drove up country to take Kathy and me home for the summer. With Mom at the wheel of the pickup and Frank and me in the cab with her, we were shuttling over to Lutamo to see Kathy. Mom had shifted the truck into low gear to get up the curvy hill. On the left side of the road, the woods fell down toward the river and on the right side they climbed a rise. Suddenly, a dog scrambled down the hill onto the road, causing my mother to swerve to avoid him. Just as quickly, Frank reached over and grabbed the wheel, turning it back toward the dog.

"Stop that, young man!" my mother yelled.

She snatched back the steering wheel, crammed on the brakes to avoid a collision, and laid into Frank.

"Gadsakes! Don't you ever, ever do that again! Do you understand?"

I hadn't written home about Frank's subtle taunts, but I savored the sharp tang of vengeance when Mom put him in his place.

In fairness to Frank, I was an interloper in his house, in competition with him for his mother's attention, and he was an adolescent boy. Later, when his parents sent him to school in Rhodesia, he revolted and was allowed to come back home, which he said taught him he could successfully look out for himself. A few years ago in answer to a survey I sent to missionary kids and others who grew up overseas, Frank wrote "having an earlier life abroad is an almost unalloyedly good thing, but there is the unavoidable fact that the overall scheme was service in Angola, and we were to fit in... It means that [now] I am almost single-mindedly a family man."

Every Monday, Miss Neumann would say, "Class, what do you do on Mondays?"

In unison, we pulled out our notepads to write to our parents. I wrote about our group activities, faithfully recording our swimming in the pool or at the falls, but mostly I peppered Mom and Dad with questions.

October 1954. "Dear Mommy and Daddy, How are David and Mark? Does David still roll his R's even in English? Is Mark walking yet? He's almost one! Do you think Mark will remember me at Christmas? XOXOXOXO Love, Nancy H."

February 1955. "Dear Mommy and Daddy, Did you get our valentines? How are the Dahlkamps? Are you coming up in March? Answer all my questions! Answer! XOXO Love, Nancy H."

Every week I opened Mom's carbon-copied letter sent to Kathy and me, looking for answers to my questions. She told us what guests were visiting, how many kittens Flick had, about the new boxer puppy named Peter, what services and meetings she and Dad had attended, that Aunt Marjorie had come over from Benguela. I just wanted her to answer my questions and acknowledge my handmade valentines.

Now I can appreciate my mother's need to condense letter-writing into one-size-fits-all. She carried on a vast correspondence with her extended family in America and friends in Angola and Europe. She found efficiency in typing multiple copies of the same letter. Her children, when away at school, received weekly letters, but still they were carbon-copied. As a child I wanted letters that felt more like they were from her to me, addressing questions I brought up in my weekly conversations by mail. "Answer my questions," I barked back at her. Pay attention to me, I seemed to say, and just to be sure she knew which Nancy was writing, I signed myself Nancy Henderson or Nancy H.

Early in the school year, the Collins and I went to church one Sunday, as usual, at the Institute, an Angolan boys' boarding school in the center of the mission. In the middle of a grassy expanse, the huge red brick church and tall bell tower dominated that part of Dondi. Schoolboys swinging their sickles could be seen cutting the grass most days of the week. There was that much of it. On Sundays the church bells drew people from the hospital compound across the river, from Lutamo and Means School up the hill in the other direction, from the seminary where the Collins lived, and from all the houses in the central mission. The girls at Means School, in white dresses, sang as they marched in a double line from Lutamo to the Institute. They met the Institute boys lined up in their white shirts and dark pants, and joined their lines to file together into church, white clothes dazzling in the sun and glowing in the dim light of the church. After the service the hundreds of people in the congregation spilled out onto the grass to greet each other, and I followed along, blinking in the sun.

When my eyes had adjusted, I realized I had lost the Collins. Where had they gone? I looked for anyone with white skin and I spied the Gilchrists, Aunt Lillian, the Coelhos, the Childs, Aunt Muggy and Aunt Bib, everyone but the Collins. I darted through the crowd, searching, panicking.

I've lost them, they've left me, they've gone home and they'll be mad at me... I thought.

I turned and headed across the grass toward the seminary, running in my best Sunday dress and shoes, my heart pounding with fear. I ran the path connecting the central mission to the seminary, past the seminary classrooms to the Collins house. No car to be seen. I ran into the quiet house. Empty.

I was confused. Were they still at the Institute? I ran back, wondering if they even knew I was missing, sure that if I didn't keep myself right in view, they'd forget I belonged to them now, not to my parents three hundred kilometers away in Lobito. I wiped the tears from my cheeks and was startled to feel a solid face. I was feeling more and more wraithlike and only the thump in my chest and the evident reality of my face told me I was a flesh and blood girl. I knew I had to fit myself out with a face the Collins would recognize. I assumed the mask of a grateful, good girl and thrust it desperately into the faces of the crowd hoping I wasn't truly invisible. The crowd had thinned, and I found Aunt Jean, Uncle Ralph, Frank, and Mary engrossed in talking to some friends. I stood quietly beside Mary, who turned to say hi. Aunt Jean continued talking in her forceful, no nonsense way without even looking at me.

If Mary can see me, I thought, I must not be invisible. But then how could I be so forgettable to Aunt Jean?

In March of 1955 I wrote home, "I'm so excited about seeing you and David and Mark at annual meeting in Bailundu."

Missionaries and Angolan church leaders from all our missions—Bailundu, Elende, Chilesso, Dondi, Camundongo, Chissamba, Bunjei, Lobito—gathered for fellowship, planned for the coming year, and updated vaccinations. I didn't relish the sore arm I invariably got from my booster shots, nor the brave face I had to put on in front of all the younger kids, but otherwise I loved annual meetings. They gave me a chance to reacquaint myself with all my missionary aunts and uncles and their kids, who lived all over central Angola. While the parents were ensconced in meetings, the dozens of children had free run of the mission and a chance to explore a new place. In the evenings we attended choral concerts by Angolan school children and put on skits of our own for our parents. Of course, this time I was going to see Mom and Dad for the first time since Christmas. They would see how much I'd grown and admire my new hairstyle, a perky topknot, spouting like a fountain from the top of my head. We'd all be together. I looked forward to sitting next to my father with his arm around me.

I drove with the Collins to Bailundu, about 60 kilometers north of Dondi over red dirt roads. My family had already arrived at the Welch's house when the Collins dropped me off. Tommy and Kenny Welch and my sister Kathy had come to Bailundu with the Tuckers. I appeared at the Welch's when everyone was busy greeting each other. My parents, Aunt Betty, and Uncle Max were catching up with each other after a year of separation. My little brothers, who were four and one, were sizing up Tommy and Kenny's little sisters, Susie and Patty. Tommy, Kenny, and Kathy had been hugged and welcomed by the Welches. Everyone was still milling around when I walked in.

"Hi, here I am at last," I announced to the tangle of people, with my parents in the middle. My voice barely penetrated the din.

Standing in the crowd of twelve Hendersons and Welches, my expectations about joining Mom, Dad, and the boys suddenly seemed to be pure fantasy. Annual meetings were not about family gatherings; they were about group connections. Annual meetings weren't for families who hadn't seen each other in months; they were focused on the business of running missions, allocating funds and personnel. During previous annual meetings, I looked forward to seeing my friends. This time, in my yearning to see my mother and father, I had fooled myself into thinking they were coming to see me. By the time annual meeting ended, sending us all back to our respective missions, I was in turmoil. I wanted to stay with my parents but was afraid I'd miss my ride back to Dondi. I couldn't concentrate on anything but waiting outside by the road with my bag for the Collins to come for me. When they drove up, I climbed into the car without saying good-bye to my parents and brothers. I disappeared without a word.

During the lunch break at school, my classmates and I commonly gathered in the huge eucalyptus tree across from the school, where we each ate our lunch on our own perch. Miss Neumann walked home to eat. One day, a few kids and I decided instead to find an open window in the school to crawl through. Inside the hushed building we kept our voices low. We wandered aimlessly once we got inside, but then I needed to go to the bathroom. With a surge of creativity, I carefully deposited small turds down the long hall, squatting, taking a step, squatting again, to the admiration of the other kids. I was thrilled at my daring, the way I controlled my performance, and commanded my friends' respect. But the disgusting smell drifting behind me down the hall let me know I was bad. I quickly crawled back out the window and away from the scene of my crime. Everyone else followed, and we swore ourselves to secrecy.

For a couple of days no one said anything to me and I went along as usual, but when I rode my bike out to Lutamo for my piano lesson with

Aunt Kay, Uncle Tommy pulled me aside. His bulky body loomed over me and, with a severe look and unwavering eyes, he launched into a lecture about "what I had done." He told me I should be ashamed of myself, that my mother and father would be horrified if they knew, and that he couldn't imagine what had possessed me. He went on and on. I could feel myself shriveling up even smaller than my nine-year-old, fifty-pound self.

I stared stolidly back at Uncle Tommy, holding his gaze for fear he'd think me weak or sorry. He can't make me say anything or tell me what to do, I fumed, my impassive face hiding my anger.

I didn't know why I acted the way I did. I knew I'd done wrong and I was bad, but part of me exulted in having dared to go ahead. Invisible to the adults in charge, lost from the love of my parents, my turds proved that I was real.

Aunt Jean never said anything to me about it. She probably thought I did it to spite Miss Neumann, but actually I think I had Aunt Jean in mind. In the few months since I'd left home, she had come to embody the unfeeling, dismissive, sarcastic adult world against which I felt powerless.

Looking back fifty years, I still find it hard to own up to my dirty deed. What could I have been thinking? I've gleaned some insights from others who also grew up abroad. In a survey I conducted of mostly missionary kids, the eighty respondents, to a person, loved growing up among other cultures. They gloried in knowing worlds unimaginable to their North American peers. One woman said her early years "made me a resilient and open person." Another said, "Being part of my parents' work gave me a structure of consciousness." "Positive!! My God, I learned so much," was the predominant feeling.

But going away to school at a young age was one of the most difficult parts of living abroad. My brother David remembers "very intense suicidal feelings while living with the Okumas." He was eight at the time. "I wished I was dead and worked out various plans for how to kill myself." He had had problems before going away to school—recurrent nightmares, bedwetting, and rages—but he says, "being sent away feels like the event that finally broke me. One long term effect has been a deep hatred of universities, because in my mind the purpose of losing my family, home and friends was that eventually I would go to university in the U.S." One of the Childs' daughters described her high school years in South Africa as a shocking experience that put her in a suicidal depression. Barbara, who grew up in Angola and went to school in Rhodesia with me, found that living away from her parents for long years had affected her relationship with them. Her mother especially was distant and unsympathetic to problems that Barbara had raised with her. To compensate, Barbara had learned to find other mothers in her dorm parents, the mothers of friends, and other friendly women. Well into her forties, she struggled to form a connection with her mother that she finally realized was simply impossible.

For a child like me, who believed my mother when she told me to expect adventure, but who didn't have the inner tools to absorb the shock of being on my own, excrement must have stood in for all the anger, loneliness, and betrayal I didn't know how to name or feel.

Back home in Lobito that summer, with three months stretching ahead, I lay on the couch in the living room daydreaming about becoming ten.

I'll be one decade old, I told myself. It sounded unbelievably impressive and grown-up. Ten years, one decade, a tenth of a century, I thought. I'm using all the fingers on my hands to count up the years; next year I'll have to start on my toes.

But when my birthday arrived a few weeks later, I wasn't prepared to be ten.

I should have been suspicious one day in mid-July, when Dad took Kathy and me off on a long errand out to the Machado's ice-making plant up in the hills across the bay. The errand had an artificial feeling about it. Dad hardly ever enlisted in those types of duties, nor did he take us with him if he did. And when we arrived at the plant, I couldn't figure out why we had come. But both he and Mom had insisted that we accompany him. A couple of hours later we returned home. I leapt out of the car, anxious to resume playing, but instead was greeted by an enthusiastic group of Portuguese and Angolan friends, who ran out of the living room yelling,

"Feliz aniversário! Happy Birthday!"

At that instant I knew I didn't want to be ten. I didn't want to be any older. I didn't want to pretend I knew how to take care of myself away from home. The dread of again leaving my parents overtook the thrill I'd felt about growing up. Without a word of greeting to my friends, I bolted. I ran around to the other side of the house and slid down to sit against the house, my legs sprawled out on the cool cement floor of the verandah.

"I don't want a surprise party," I muttered. "No surprises. No pretending to be happy," I grouched to myself. Mom came in search of me.

"All your friends are here and we're sitting down to have cake and ice cream. You need to come back," she said.

I stood up, followed her to the dining room, and coated my irritation and anger with a thin layer of sociability.

When the school year opened in September 1955, Kathy and I, and the other kids who had boarded with families, moved into the dorm that had served as our school the previous year. The mission had found an empty room at the seminary for our new classroom. I never thought of myself as being at "boarding school," which I envisioned as a British institution, with the living quarters and school on the same plot of ground and under the same strict management. In my mind, our dorm and school were quite separate operations. Miss Neumann had been recruited from a school in California specifically to teach. Our dorm parents, both years I lived in the dorm, were ordinary missionaries who were given the dorm as their assignment for a year. They brought their own kids with them and acted like our aunts and uncles.

The dorm accommodated sixteen kids in four bedrooms, with two more bedrooms for the dorm family. We ranged from Genevieve who was six, to Mimi who was twelve, approximately half girls and half boys. We all shared two bathrooms, one at each end of the hall. I suppose that was why we washed the red dirt out of our necks and hair only once a week. Even then, four of us were assigned to bathe together.

Uncle Robin and Aunt Fran Markham had been given the assignment of dorm parents. At last, Dondi was beginning to match my mother's promise that I'd be with my friends at home and at school. Though it might seem counterintuitive, dorm living was friendlier for me than living with a family that wasn't my own, where I'd felt I was the odd one out and rules from home were not always applicable. In the dorm, we didn't have to pretend we weren't homesick because we were all living away from home, with the same rules, routines, and expectations.

One morning, while my roommates Joye Ferguson, Kathy Steed, and I dressed for school, Pauly still lay in bed facing the wall, her back radiating loneliness out to the room. I sat at the foot of her bed and rested my hand on her legs.

"Pauly, do you want me to tell Aunt Fran you feel sick again?" I asked.

She turned to look at me through bleary eyes and nodded. Pauly frequently stayed home from school with upset stomach, fever, or cold. Because she was as old and tall as my sister, I thought she'd be braver and stronger than me. But Pauly's sicknesses made me realize how fragile she was. My slight frame didn't feel tough either, but I pushed my fears and sadness out of view so expertly that even I thought they weren't there. At school I saw Pauly's empty seat and was sure Aunt Fran was showering her with attention, bringing in aspirin and *gasosa* (soda pop). I jealously imagined Aunt Fran sitting on Pauly's bed, testing her forehead for fever, touching her! I yearned for that attention myself, but my body wouldn't cooperate. The closest I could get to it was a contact high from watching Aunt Fran minister to her baby.

The Markhams were parents to two little girls: Vicki, who was three, and Nan Jean, who was one. After school one day, Aunt Fran's laughter wafted to my room, luring me down the hall. She was changing the baby's diapers, wiping her bottom clean. I'd often changed my brother Mark's diapers and seeing Nan Jean's chubby legs made me lonely for him. I stood beside Aunt Fran, who was barely taller than me. She was young, in her thirties. She was patient with Nan Jean, even when she tried to squirm out of reach. Aunt Fran pulled her back and kissed her, and I thought if I stood close enough to Aunt Fran, some of her touch would brush on to me.

Throughout the year, Pauly and I played an elaborate game of paper dolls, with paper mothers, fathers, and children of all ages. We spent early mornings after breakfast and long afternoons after school designing clothes for our paper doll families, tracing around their bodies, and coloring in dresses, shirts, pants, shoes. We cut out each small item, leaving several tabs around it to hook onto the doll. I told Pauly, "I'm going to ask Aunt Fran if we can leave our paper dolls on the bed." I didn't want a black mark on my chart.

The Markhams ran the dorm efficiently, managing sixteen kids with incentives and charts for keeping our rooms tidy, making our beds, and bathing and washing our hair. In our rooms, everything had to be put away in drawers or in the closet.

"Kids, I want your beds made, everything off the floor before you go to school," instructed Aunt Fran.

Any clothing strewn on the floor or on our beds gave our room a black X. At the end of the month invariably the boys had more black marks than the girls, and they were required to throw us a party. In my room, Pauly, Joye, and I embraced this competition. We were determined to avoid black marks. In our view, Kathy Steed was dangerously sloppy. Her sweaters, shirts, and underwear were a jumbled mess in her drawers, and her part of the closet threatened to spill shoes and dolls out into the room whenever we opened the door. When she ignored our requests to tidy up her space, we dumped all her clothes into a heap on the floor and piled her closet mess on top.

And then we made her put it all neatly back before Aunt Fran graded the room. No one could accuse us of being irresponsible shirkers.

"Aunt Fran says it's fine to leave our paper dolls on the bed, as long as they're neat," I reported back to Pauly.

School life was a lot like dorm life, with an adult in charge of us, but not really involved in our activities. Miss Neumann and the Markhams gave us our assignments, and then expected us to carry them out, with little direction or personal attention. We worked and played, laughed and cried together, supported, teased, or meted out justice to each other, mainly without the adults. In the dorm we ate together, played large group games, and put ourselves to bed under the distant but watchful eyes of our dorm parents. At school, in eight different grades, we worked with our grade mate and grading buddies under the detached supervision of Miss Neumann.

Tommy Welch and I, grade mates in fourth, fifth, and sixth grades, worked together, reading and answering questions in our language book, calling out spelling words to each other, and figuring out math problems. I also paired with a grading buddy, older than I, who corrected my work, and I, in turn, corrected the work of my buddy, David Dahlkamp, who was younger. I don't recall Miss Neumann looking at my work, unless to check that I had written my weekly letter home to Mom and Dad.

In fifth grade, math word problems confounded me.

If Farmer Brown's 3 sons picked 6 bushels of apples in half an hour, how long did Farmer Black's 2 sons take to pick 10 bushels? A train going 65 miles an hour passes another train going in the opposite direction ... How many, which one, how long... One question after another. They made me dizzy. I grabbed my answers out of thin air. When my grading buddy returned my work to me, criss-crossed with big fat X's, I felt hopelessly dumb and alone in the world.

From my desk halfway up the steeply sloped floor of our classroom, Miss Neumann seemed tiny and far away. Math had made me so dizzy and bewildered, I thought I might faint from the altitude. I didn't know I was allowed to walk all the way down the hill to get help from her. I didn't want to draw attention to my ignorance when everyone else was working self-sufficiently. Miss Neumann sat in front of the black board, the first and second graders gathered around her on miniature chairs, teaching them to read and write. Miss Neumann was an Official Teacher, the teacher Mom and Dad had sent me to Dondi for, but she didn't teach me. I taught myself.

In sixth grade we had different dorm parents.

"Dear Mommy and Daddy, Guess what? The Welches are our dorm parents this year. They let us turn the living room into a tent by turning furniture upside-down and draping it with sheets and blankets. Love, Nancy H."

Aunt Betty and Uncle Max encouraged creativity. For a whole week, they allowed us to disrupt the living room for any normal uses. We fashioned rooms out of the maze of chairs and tables under our tent, and played house on all fours. One rainy day, we transformed our playroom into the interior of an airplane, chairs lined up, two by two, on each side of the aisle, to fly us to Paris to buy new dresses. Our stewards, the housemen, served us lunch on trays as we flew through the air. In the evenings Uncle Max sang and played the piano and the musical saw. Sitting on a chair, Uncle Max propped the saw handle down between his feet and bent the blade as he stroked the smooth edge with a violin bow, producing an ethereal melody, more haunting than a violin. If we weren't playing a group game of "sardines" or "run sheep run" outside in the dusk, we begged Uncle Max to play his saw. We lay on the living room rug, soothed by the music. On cold evenings we gathered in front of the fireplace to hear Aunt Betty read us *Twenty Thousand Leagues Under the Sea.* She toured our rooms each evening to tuck us in and wish us goodnight with a poem or silly ditty. Sometimes, in her low voice, she recited Poe's "The Raven:" "Quoth the raven, nevermore." Sometimes she recited Edna St. Vincent Millay's

"My candle burns at both ends,
It will not last the night,
But, ah, my foes, and, oh, my friends ~
It gives a lovely light!

Or she might say, "Good night, sleep tight. Don't let the bedbugs bite. But, if they do, take your shoe. And hit them till they're black and blue." We'd giggle and go to sleep.

The year the Welches tended the dorm was my happiest year in Dondi. I was eleven by then, an old hand at living away from home and more secure in my independence. I'd also known the Welches since I was two years old in Portugal.

With the Welch's encouragement, my friends and I roamed beyond the dorm, exploring distant parts of the mission on our bicycles. I'd *br-r-i-i-ng* my bell, with a flick of my thumb, as I spun by pedestrians like a hotshot demon. But the accessory that bolstered my illusion of power and speed was the stiff playing card I attached with a clothespin to the front fork of my bike. I'd speed along, the card whapping against the spokes, sounding, I was sure, exactly like a motorcycle. On one bicycle excursion, our friends whose families lived in Dondi showed us the leopard cave. We dropped down through a narrow slit into the musty darkness, barely able to see a ledge to stand on. While my eyes grew accustomed to the dim light, I huddled with the other kids, afraid of confronting the leopard, which we'd heard had recently attacked someone. A ping, a flutter, a scrape made my skin crawl. I half hoped he'd appear. Eventually I could see that the slick rocks in the cave sloped down too fast for comfort. It gave us the perfect excuse to pull ourselves out into the sunshine.

Just below leopard hill, we could look down into the river valley and see the road winding up to the backside of Means School. Beside the river were the ruins of an old mill. When Stephen Collins, Frank and Mary's brother, was home from school in Rhodesia, he used to lead us into the murky tunnel of the mill and tell us ghost stories. It was scary in the tunnel, but not as creepy as the cave up on the hill. Leopards, I knew, were real. At home, Mom had a leopard skin that she draped over a trunk on our verandah.

On Saturdays, we often rode into Bela Vista, the little one-street Portuguese town a few kilometers from Dondi. Bela Vista gave us a taste of urban bustle. The Benguela Railroad stopped there on its way from Lobito to the Congo, attracting the commotion brought by travelers and freight. Usually, we steered directly to Fadário's dry goods store, leaning our bikes against the whitewashed building. Dust from the unpaved street drifted through the open door. When I stepped in, the fishy smell of dried salt cod, stacked in flat slabs at the back of the store, mixed with the acrid, metallic scent of nails and screws in boxes on the left and the sweetness of Jordan almonds near the check-out counter. Over on the right, Fadário's sold bolts of the dark blue gingham that Angolan women bought in lengths. One length was sewn into a square-necked blouse, another length wrapped around the waist as a skirt, and a third strapped baby snugly to back. I headed straight for the chewing gum. Portuguese gum came as flat, almost translucent, pink rectangles, wrapped in paper. One piece chewed up into a tiny ball and retained its flavor only a few brief seconds. To prolong that burst of sweetness, I fed one after another into my mouth until I had a satisfyingly huge mass of gum to work on. Even so, it soon was as tasteless as a ball of wax. To add worth to my investment, I'd post the hunk of gum on my dresser overnight and chew in a new piece the next morning. I was loath to throw it out altogether.

Provisioned with picnic lunches, some Saturdays we spent all day at Kutatu Falls. Where the river tumbled into falls, at the top of the run, I sought out the cool, misty space behind a curtain of water. In the din created by water and a dozen kids, I found a place to spy on the others. Then I'd slide down the rocks and float to the wet bank, guiding myself so I didn't get sucked into the swifter current below. I climbed out by grabbing onto the branches and roots of the small bushes on the bank. Just a few feet downstream, a string of boulders across the river created chutes, and the water plunged through them. Like an intrepid mountain goat, I pranced back and forth across the boulders, from one side of the river to the other.

One night, a robber stole into our midst.

Pauly and I were lying together in my bed, whispering so we wouldn't disturb Joye and Kathy. It was March of 1957; I was in sixth grade. I had awakened Pauly to accompany me down the long hall to the bathroom, as we often did (the same hall where I had laid down my turds in anger two years earlier). We were talking before falling back to sleep, when we were startled by an anguished voice, a strangled bleating that I knew right away was Uncle Max, yelling "Help, help."

We heard feet pounding down the hall and a door banging shut, and then silence. We lay in bed, not daring to stir, until we heard the older girls in the hall talking to Aunt Betty. We crept to our door and joined the swarm of dorm kids who had been awakened by Uncle Max. Aunt Betty held a kerosene lamp in one hand and hugged her small daughter, Patty, with her other arm. We huddled around her, pressing close against her, scared of what we might learn. Patty clutched her mother's nightie, pulling it crooked.

"What happened?" we all asked. I knew it had to be something bad.

"Well, kids," Aunt Betty explained, "a man came into the bedroom, perhaps thinking it was a study where money might be kept... because we have a desk in there."

Somehow I was reassured that he was after money, not people. But Aunt Betty continued, "Patty had just climbed into our bed. When she sat up to see who the man was, he startled, maybe because he didn't expect to see people in there, and began thrashing Uncle Max over the head with a stick."

We inspected their bedroom, the scene of the crime. In the dim light of the lamp we could see that chunks of bark from the stick had flown all over the bed and the room.

"Oh! that's when Uncle Max started yelling," Pauly said.

The robber then dropped the stick and dashed out of the dorm, with Uncle Max close behind.

Aunt Betty led us to the kitchen to calm us with hot cocoa. Carefully laid out on the counters were all the kitchen knives. I looked at Pauly and she looked at me. The hair on my arms and legs stood on end.

"Pauly, when we were going to the bathroom," I said, "that robber must have been right across the hall in the kitchen, pulling out all those knives. He could have seen us."

We put our arms around each other and squeezed tight.

Kees van der Graaf told us, "I saw the robber in our room, rummaging in the drawers, but I just lay as still and quiet as could be."

"Yeah, and he was in my room, too, at the end of my bed," said little Patty, "and he was waving a white handkerchief at me."

After a while Uncle Max and the housemen came back in. They hadn't caught the robber, but they had found piles of loot all around the dorm: sacks of clothing, toys from the box in our playroom, cameras (but not my little Brownie camera), keys and watches, pots and pans. More and more clearly, I realized that while Pauly and I were awake, going to the bathroom and talking, the robber was creeping around the dorm collecting all that stuff.

After we told our stories, where we were, what we saw, what we did, what we knew and didn't know, and after we gleaned every possible detail of the robbery, the knives, the bark, the stashes under the trees, Uncle Max took us into the living room where he sat down at the piano and played "The Parade of the Toy Soldiers" from the Nutcracker story.

The Nutcracker ordered the toy soldiers to attack the mice, but the mice fought back, decimating the soldiers. The Nutcracker leapt into the fray only to be attacked by the huge Mouse King. The young girl Marie hurled her shoe at the Mouse King, distracting him and giving the Nutcracker the time to plunge his sword into the Mouse King's heart. And the interloper fell over dead.

Uncle Max played "The Parade of the Toy Soldiers" over and over until we believed that the invader was gone, until we were ready to return to bed. Together Uncle Max and Aunt Betty lit a kerosene lamp in each of our rooms and turned it down low enough for us to sleep but high enough to ward off robbers.

Uncle Max's tune replayed in my head, chasing away sleep. I envied Marie's brave rescue. I wished that by being brave and good, I could reclaim my nine-year-old, best-birthday-ever dreams of independence and adventure. But doubt crept into me like that robber. I suspected that, in real life, little girls were not rescued from the enemies besieging them, even a girl strong enough to leave home, clever enough to defend herself against Frank, and brave enough to demonstrate she wouldn't take any more of it. Even a girl that would leave a trail of her real self in the world.

Over the following weeks, the missionary community learned who the robber had been. He went by the unusual name of George Wilson, an English name from his Nigerian father. George had been imprisoned for petty crimes and had escaped from prison several times. Before the end of the school year, some villagers near Dondi spotted him and, much to my relief, captured him. At around the same time, I remember hearing talk among the missionaries about a man named Holden Roberto who was a leader of UPA, one of the emerging nationalist movements. Holden was another unusual name for Angola. The man had been named for a British Baptist missionary. Picking up on fear of violence in the voices of the missionaries, and imperfectly understanding politics, I confused Holden Roberto with George Wilson. They were both, in my mind, robbers of innocence.

Chapter 5 — Guests in My Home

Ndonga wema, Mukungulu yu, (Muele wa enda; ovilinga via siala.)
A pessoa passa, mas a memória dos seus feitos fica. O rio seca,
mas o seu leito fica.
A person leaves, but the memory of his deeds stays.
The river dries, but its bed stays.

Umbundu proverb

"Uncle Francis, kneel down," I demanded. Francisco Figueiras dutifully crouched down and I took a flying leap onto his back. He was somewhat disconcerted by my behavior, atypical of little Portuguese girls. He called me a tomboy. He was newly emigrated from Portugal, a bachelor, around thirty years old, and lonely for the companionship of the nieces and nephews he'd left behind. The year I was eight Uncle Francis came to Sunday supper every week. He was first attracted to our house when Dad established the Portuguese-language church in our living room. Soon Uncle Francis lingered after church to play with Kathy and me and practice his English with us.

He brought his talent for art to our afternoons together. He was an accomplished watercolorist. In the portrait of Kathy and me he painted, we sat with our arms around each other, wearing red dresses with lacy yokes. Big blue bows perched like butterflies on my blonde head and at the ends of Kathy's braids. He titled it "Two Little Princesses." I was his tomboy princess.

Under Uncle Francis's tutelage, Kathy and I published *Tic-Tac*, a little magazine of stories, poems, silly puzzles and drawings, which we sent off to our friends in the up country missions of Dondi, Chissamba, and Camundongo. Kathy was the sub-director under Uncle Francis, and I was the secretary. He typed our poems and stories on tissue-thin pink, gold, and blue paper then added his delicate ink drawings to each copy. *Tic-Tac* was a veritable rainbow springing out of the envelope. It was named after the donkey whose adventures Uncle Francis wrote about each month.

After working with us on our writing all Sunday afternoon, Uncle Francis stayed for supper buffet. I pronounced it BOO-fay, imagining that to be the correct French accent. Sunday afternoon and evening were our cook and house servants' time off, when they could be home with their families and we were on our own. A half-day or a day off a week was typical for household help in those times. Until they married, Tomás and Cipriano lived in a room between the kitchen and the garage. In the slack time between lunch and dinner, they would sometimes take a couple hours off to ride bikes into town, a privilege my mother told me was not often accorded to the servants of our neighbors. Though my parents were liberal with their servants and treated them with respect, when I, as an adult, started thinking about hiring a house cleaner I had a great deal of difficulty imagining myself taking on the role of authority. In the America of equal rights, convenience foods, washing machines, and vacuum cleaners, I had to convince myself that hiring a cleaner was OK. But in Angola, not to have servants would have been remarkable. Wealthy and not so wealthy whites were expected to give employment to the Angolans, and running a large household without help, when all food had to be prepared from scratch and clothes had to be washed by hand would have been hard. In the end, I realized the cleaner and I could have a straightforward exchange of money for service without the paternalism that pervaded the transaction in Angola.

Before our cook Tomás left on Sundays, he usually put a pot of brown beans on the cook stove for us, and we'd stop at the bakery to buy a loaf of melt-in-your-mouth white bread. I liked the chewy thick-crusted everyday Portuguese bread, but for Sunday buffet I craved white bread. I could eat a whole loaf myself. Mom made coleslaw and a salad of fruits in season: papaya, banana, mango, guava, and orange. We loaded up our plates and carried them into the living room to eat, balancing them on our laps.

Later, Uncle Francis was surprised to find that we ate at the table for most meals. He thought Americans always ate buffet on their laps.

Five issues of *Tic-Tac* and dozens of Sunday buffets later, Uncle Francis got homesick and decided to move back to Portugal, to his home in the Algarve, where he taught German and English in the high school. After he left, I missed him terribly. In the last issue of *Tic-Tac* he wrote a farewell to all the subscribers. "Because my dear little friends Kathleen and Nancy Henderson and I have been together so often, I am awfully sad to part from them now, and for a long, long time I will be missing them. Lots of love from your Uncle Francis."

The day his ship sailed for Portugal, we didn't see him off at the docks. Instead, Kathy and I stood on the beach in front of our house, watching the ship make its way down the bay. As it passed our house, we swam out as far as we dared. We spotted Uncle Francis on the deck leaning on the rail. "Uncle Francis! Good-bye!" we yelled. He heard us and waved until we could see him no longer.

Uncle Francis left Angola after only a couple of years, but lingered in my affections, and those of our whole family, ever after. My parents had bought several of his watercolors. He painted Lobito scenes of grizzled men, young mothers with babies, and the Catholic church up the avenue that still hang in our houses. Until his recent death, we corresponded with him and visited him whenever we were in Portugal.

Uncle Francis was typical of the guests streaming through our house. Rarely did our family sit around the dining table alone. A year after arriving in Angola in 1948, my parents accepted the mission's assignment to work on the coast. Placing full-time missionaries in a city was a new venture for the mission that until then only had rural stations. We moved into the large house on the bay originally established as a hostel for missionaries in transit. Bundled into my parents' new job was a procession of guests. I became so used to the bustle of people in the house that, when our family was by itself, I felt unsettled. I think my mother, who even today abhors inactivity, felt the same. She invited friends over for tea or dinner whenever we didn't have houseguests.

Most of our guests at the Casa Missionária came on ships from across the Atlantic and stayed with us for days and sometimes even weeks. Often I didn't know them because they were Baptist, Brethren, or Swiss missionaries, not from my parents' Congregational mission. My father met the guests at the docks, ushered them through preliminary customs procedures, and brought them home to my mother's care. I recognized that weary, long-time-at-sea droop, the shaggy needs-a-haircut look, and the rumpled clothes of a returning missionary. But soon they'd relax with tea on the upper verandah refreshed by bath and nap. My mother choreographed the dance of laundry from Mãe who washed and ironed to Cipriano who made the beds and cleaned. She decided who would sleep in the large front bedroom looking out on the bay and who would get the smaller back room in a sheltered corner overlooking the driveway. Usually she assigned the raft of beds on the shuttered end of the upper verandah to the children of the families but, if we were bursting with guests, she gave them to single women.

Single missionary men were rare and rarely stayed single long. Single women were plentiful. The Women's Missionary Society, associated with the Canadian board, actively recruited women. Perhaps lack of other opportunities for adventurous women may have explained the imbalance between single men and women. In any case, single women were indulgent with missionary children. I was very curious about Aunt Mary, a newly arrived missionary who stayed with us. I knew she had worked in China, an impossibly exotic place, before coming to Angola. I hung around her up on the verandah while she regaled us with stories about being arrested by the triumphant Communists.

"The Communists couldn't figure out what my lipstick was," Aunt Mary said. "They thought the tubes might contain contraband and they picked each one apart, leaving a red mess!" She laughed as she described the scene, as if it were the funniest thing she'd ever witnessed. She taught me her version of a Chinese greeting and response, which I repeated with a worldly swagger to my friends.

"Ha boo how. Ting how."

Aunt Muggy and Aunt Bib (whom we children usually called *Uncle* Bib when they weren't around) lived together in Dondi. Aunt Muggy was a small redhead. She painted watercolors of mothers and children in her spare time. Aunt Bib was tall with cropped hair. They both worked at the girls' school in Lutamo. Although I had never heard of lesbians, I identified Muggy and Bib as a couple, taking vacations and furloughs together. At Halloween, when I went to school in Dondi, the dorm kids, sixteen of us, stopped by their house on our rounds. "Trick or treat!" we yelled. They came to the door and invited us in for a drink. We sat on the floor and available chairs enjoying the juice. They stood close to each other, appreciating our costumes, "Tommy, you're some cowboy! Would you look at that ballerina and who is the ghost?" Properly feted, we trooped outside and they waved goodbye from the porch.

One year, single women were just a few among the 200 signatures I counted in the guest book. For me, our guests were interested and engaging adults with the time to converse. From their constant presence, I learned that the world was full of funny, friendly, and occasionally sour and disagreeable people. I learned flexibility and openness. I admire my mother for persisting at the task of preparing three meals a day for up to fifteen people at a time. She never set her guests loose on the kitchen. Aside from the problem of tripping over each other because of sheer numbers, producing a meal from scratch without the luxury of frozen or packaged foods was complicated, even with a full time cook and part time kitchen assistant. My mother marshaled our meals, tabulating the number to feed each day, consulting with Tomás on menus, running to the market downtown for cabbage, carrots and kale, live chickens, and huge stalks of bananas. Fish was on the menu almost daily. Tomás, hearing the fishermen calling *garopa, garopa*, would hustle across the street to the beach and hail the passing fishing boat on its way to market. The boats looked like Egyptian dhows, but had only one tall wooden mast, one huge triangular sail, and three or four fishermen who rowed when the breeze died down.

My father was responsible for rescuing guests' baggage from Customs. The boxes and trunks could be stuck in Customs for long periods, unless Dad and the guest negotiated, bargained, and finally wrested the goods from Portuguese Customs control. Every day for weeks they went down to the docks to fill out another form or talk to another official. Every day they explained that these trunks contained clothing and necessary items to help the family survive through the next five years. Every day they explained that the typewriter or pump organ was to be used in a school or church, until at last everything was released. The Customs officials, as members of the Portuguese state bureaucracy, were suspicious of Protestant missionaries and their intentions. The Fifties were a period of authoritarian Portuguese government allied with an ultra conservative Catholic church. Neither group trusted American Protestants, who were considered to espouse dangerous democratic ideas. The Customs officers spent long hours deciding whether the typewriter should be allowed in the country. The wearying struggle seemed to me simply part of my father's life, imposed, I thought, by the Pope, who didn't want Protestants to have typewriters, or by the dictator Salazar off in Portugal who appeared to be mad at us.

Fighting with Customs wore Dad out. He'd rather have spent his time working on church activities. But I liked having the guests around, especially if they had kids. After morning lessons in second and third grade, I was free to play on the beach or in my playhouse with guest children. We played hopscotch, rode bikes, jumped on the beds out on the verandah (even though Mom didn't want us to), dressed our cat Fluffy in baby clothes and pushed him around the block in a doll buggy. When they left, another family would take their place.

My parents weren't occupied solely with our guests. Mom organized women's sewing, prayer, and literacy groups. She taught school to my sister and me and Sunday school at church. She took care of my little brothers. Dad preached and traveled to other villages and towns. He managed the money for all the churches, schools, and clinics on the coast. They were off day and night working, worshipping, and discussing. I resented my parents leaving after supper for a meeting or church service and wished they were downstairs talking or reading while I slept upstairs. But our guests were comforting presences in the house.

At times our guests weren't missionaries at all. Strangers who didn't fit easily into a category were directed to the Casa Missionária, where everyone in town knew that an odd assortment of people gathered. When I was eight, Hannig and Jentsch buzzed into town on a motorcycle all the way from Austria. They had traveled across the Sahara desert and down Africa till they landed at our house. They stayed with us for weeks while they waited for a visa to go to South West Africa. Hannig and Jentsch fascinated me. Only Jentsch could speak English, and that with a heavy accent. Hannig stood by, not saying anything. Most astonishing to me was the hook that sprung out of the end of Jentsch's right arm. He attached the hook to his arm with a leather strap and wires ran up under his shirt to his biceps. The wires mysteriously helped him operate his hook. With a look of concentration, he willed the hook to open, grasped the tool he was about to use on his motorcycle, and closed the hook on it.

While they awaited their papers, Jentsch tinkered with the motorcycle engine, taking it apart, cleaning it, and revving it. Hannig and I stood by watching, not saying anything. A low-slung sidecar was attached to the motorcycle. They let all the kids climb on the motorcycle or sit in the sidecar. I daydreamed about riding across the hot Sahara desert, climbing giant sand dunes. Despite the hook, Jentsch did most of the driving while Hannig sat in the sidecar. Sometimes I wondered why Hannig had come along. He couldn't speak or fix the motorcycle, even though he had two good hands, and he didn't drive. Jentsch was the one I talked to about their trip and about life, but really Hannig's curly blonde hair and crinkly eyes made me want to talk to him. He was silent and shy, all the more tantalizing to a smitten but bashful little girl.

One of the strangers who showed up on our doorstep when I was ten was an ivory carver from northern Angola. As an African in colonial times, he couldn't stay in the whites-only European hotel, and as a Bakongo, he spoke a different language from the Ovimbundu of central Angola. He stayed with us for about a month, waiting for his travel documents, and while he was our guest, he tried to sell his ivory pieces to our other guests. He displayed them in our dining room, along the deep windowsill looking out to the bay. From my place at the table, I'd stare at the long procession of elephants carved out of one gracefully arched tusk, with babies at the tapered end and trumpeting adults at the thick end. He had carved each elephant in delicate detail, the hairy ends of the tail, the flaring nostrils of the trunk, thick toes on chunky feet, flapping ears. Even frozen in ivory, they looked alive, as though they might step out of the procession and wander around the sill. After the meal, I'd run my fingers along the silky ivory, aware of how rare and precious it was.

I wanted Mom to buy the elephants, but she told me, "They are too expensive for a missionary's salary."

"Well, then, how about one of these heads?" I asked.

They were almost as big as my head, busts of men and women held proudly on long necks, heads with high foreheads, wide noses, and wide-eyed stares, heads with hair sculptured at odd angles. The hairdos reminded me of women in the Vamuila area of southern Angola who mixed red clay with cow dung and plastered it in their hair to hold it in place. I tried to imagine swathing my hair in such a mixture. What a smelly mess it would be when I went swimming.

"No," Mom said. "You can choose between the smaller birds or crocodiles."

We already had some birds carved out of cows' horns, gray-brown not creamy white like the ivory birds. I chose the crocodile. He snarled at me, whipping his tail from side to side, baring his sharp teeth, like the real crocodile kept in a pit in Catumbela.

We often stopped in Catumbela, a tiny village a few kilometers down the coast south of Lobito. The crocodile was just one of the attractions in the village, which had all the elements of a sideshow at the fair, full of freaks and wonders. Catumbela was the headquarters of the sugar cane company. On the way into town, we'd stop at a sugar cane field, where we'd cut a juicy stick of cane to chew on as we toured the town. Mom would strip off the tough bark to reveal its tender fibers, saturated in sweetness, and would hand it to me to suck and gnaw. Cane juice dribbled down my chin and my fingers stuck together. Across the street from the fields on a little hill perched the few stores in town, including the shoemaker. The shoemaker was a dwarf, even shorter than me. We always stopped there to buy shoelaces. I'd stare at the dwarf's large head, stubby arms and legs, and the way he waddled when he walked, transfixed by his deformity and finally relieved when I saw my own normally proportioned body reflected in the glass. On the way out of town, we would stop to see the crocodile. He lived in a deep concrete pit partially filled with dirty water. For a fee, the attendant would poke the quiet animal with a long pole, rousing him to snarl and growl and thrash around. I leaned over the railing into the pit to watch him in action, but I was always afraid the pole would poke him too hard and go right through his head.

Back at home, I told Mom I wanted the ivory crocodile, a perfect rendition of the feisty animal in the pit. After a while the ivory carver packed up his elephants and heads and moved on, leaving a windowsill full of nothing but the little crocodile.

The ivory carver and Hannig and Jentsch added spice to our guest list, but my favorite guests were our friends from up country. Sometimes they were on their way to or from furlough. Other times they came to vacation at the beach, attracted to our salty bay, lined with palms, and our sand dollars, so numerous that I never bothered to collect them. I skipped them across the water, jump, jump, and jump until they sank to the sandy bottom. Our up-country friends came for our wide beach, perfect for building sand castles and towns, and the bustle of our port city.

Growing up on the coast, an American girl on the edge of Africa, instilled in me a desire to look out, to see not only open space, but to look toward other continents. Later, as an adult, after nine years of living in the American Midwest, I needed to escape. I felt claustrophobic in the interior of the country, despite the huge open skies of the prairie. I needed to stand on the eastern edge of America and know I was looking toward Africa. I moved to North Carolina.

Among our guests, I always looked forward to the Gilchrists' annual visit. Uncle Sid would burst out of their little red jeep full of energy and laughter. He was a doctor and had delivered both my brothers at his house in Dondi. Aunt Frankie would step out elegantly, her long hair gathered up on her head, beautiful even after traveling three hundred dusty kilometers on dirt roads in an open jeep from Dondi. One night I dreamed that Mom and Dad died and the Gilchrists adopted me as a member of their tribe of nine kids. Their children were grown and living in Canada or buried in the little missionary cemetery in Dondi, the source, I imagined, of Aunt Frankie's sad smile. At the time, I felt guilty for, in essence, killing off my parents and leaping at the chance to join the Gilchrists. The dream occurred during the period when my sister and I had left home for school in Dondi. I suspect the dream reflected not hatred of my parents so much as an unconscious grappling with our changed relationship. Away at school for months at a time and living with another family, I *had* lost my parents.

The Gilchrists usually stayed a couple of days on their way to a camping vacation in Jomba, a huge tract of land on the barren hills across the bay. The beautiful beach, spilling like a white lacy fringe from the shoulders of the hills, had natural waves and gorgeous swelling breakers, because it faced the ocean at the mouth of the bay. The beach was wide and they pitched their big canvas tent snug against the limestone cliff, safe from the crashing waves.

Sometimes the Gilchrists invited us to spend the day with them in Jomba and sometimes, even when the Gilchrists weren't there, Mom arranged for us to visit. We drove from the flat paved streets of the city up into the twisty-turny dirt roads of the hills, past the cement factory across the bay from our house, out toward the lighthouse that guided ships into the bay. After the hot drive, we leapt out of the car like frogs out of a frying pan, racing down to the water to cool off. The waves at Jomba kept rolling in and sucking out, crashing in and drawing out, without cease. Jomba offered up the same sense of the infinite and mystical I had when I looked up at the Southern Cross in the night sky. The restless energy of the waves was so like the energy of my house, endlessly filling with guests and emptying and filling again.

Our guests energized me. For lack of a conventional family centered on mom, dad, and kids, I embraced the guests. I didn't know that our family was unusual, except that we were American and our neighbors were Portuguese, Umbundu, or English. But our guests exhausted my mother. At the age of thirty-six, with two pre-school boys, two daughters about eleven and twelve, and a husband afflicted with stomach ulcers, she asked the mission to lighten her load. After seven years of planning and serving meals, making and stripping beds, presenting her best cheerful face, she arranged for the vacationers to stay in a rented apartment down by the Radio Club. I helped her move some of our extra furniture, linens, and dishes into the apartment. From then on, only people who were in transit stayed at our house. I wonder if waiting on her peers, the vacationing missionaries, didn't irk her in the same way as her sister's annoying habit of getting out of dishwashing when they were girls. It must have been irritating to cater to their colleagues since my parents made time for few vacations when I was growing up. I knew Mom was truly tired because this was the first time I'd ever heard her say no. She took earnestly and energetically Christ's admonition to feed, clothe, and take in the stranger knocking at the door. But, I wished my mother would keep our vacationing friends and put the strangers in the apartment.

I'm not sure when Pauly Ferguson and I decided that we were best friends, since we lived hundreds of kilometers apart and met only at Annual Meeting and occasional trips up country until we both went to school in Dondi when I was nine and she was ten. We erased the distance between us by writing to each other several times a week, keeping each other posted on family news and stories about our animals, writing to maintain our connection, sending out multiple X's and O's. And so, when the Fergusons left Angola for good when I was thirteen, Pauly and her sister Mimi, who was Kathy's best friend, stayed in Lobito with us for several weeks before boarding the ship for Canada with their family.

We were saying good-bye, not knowing when we'd see each other again. I didn't know how to let her go. Talking to her about leaving would have made it too real, too imminent. Better to swim or walk the beach. Take a trip to Jomba. Admire the life-size cloth dolls she had made, each with a distinct face. Pauly had skillfully stitched the muslin pieces together, stuffed them, and dressed them in real baby clothes. She brought me a toddler-sized doll as a goodbye present that I still have stored away in an attic trunk, with dark brown curly hair of yarn, a small nose, and a sweet embroidered mouth. In America the year before, I had noticed that girls in seventh grade didn't play dolls any more. I had felt shy about admitting I liked them. But back in Angola, I was free to play with dolls. Pauly didn't feel self-conscious about dolls either. We'd sit on the upper verandah with our babies in our laps, happy to be best friends together. Still, sometimes I did wonder if I was too old for dolls. My budding breasts and wispy hair under my arms drew me toward the promise of the grown up world but dragged me away from my childhood. The more I tried not to think about Pauly boarding the ship and steaming away to Canada, the emptier I felt.

Pauly and I had been best friends through the tough times away at school in Dondi. I knew how she felt when homesickness seized her, but I didn't know how to console her. Now I didn't know how to console myself, except through her gift of the doll. She had given me part of herself, but a part I thought I should be setting aside, because in a few months I'd be going off to high school in Rhodesia. Pauly's doll reminded me of everything we had and everything I was losing. In Rhodesia I'd be a guest again, a guest in a new country, a new school, and a new dorm, a temporary resident, uprooted from home.

The day she left, we ate a lunch of *bife e batatas fritas* (beef steak and fried potatoes) with her family at the Hotel Terminus. Eating at the hotel or eating out at all was a rare treat. Normally I loved *bifes*, but that day my throat was too thick to swallow. After lunch I snapped photographs of the whole Ferguson family. Pauly stood stiffly, giving me a tentative smile. The humidity had curled her auburn bangs into wisps around her freckled face and her ponytail hung in long rings down her back. I wondered what her life in Canada would be like. How could she bear to leave her home in Angola? Too soon, they had to depart. We drove over to the docks and found their ship. They climbed the gangplank to the bottom deck and leaned over the railing, five of them in a row. From the dock, I leaned back to gather every detail of Pauly's face, but she looked so faraway. We waved good-bye to them as the ship pulled away from the dock, then dashed home to wave white towels from our upper verandah. The ship gathered speed for the long journey and left its waves lapping on the beach.

At the last ripple, I knew she was gone forever. I ran sobbing into my parents' room and threw myself on their bed.

"How am I going to live without Pauly?" I asked my mother. I already missed her so much.

Mom stroked my hair and patted my back until my tears ran out and I lay exhausted. A headache stabbed my temples and I snuffled my nose. When I went back to my room, I found Pauly's hand-sewn doll on my bed. I hugged the doll tightly, squeezing every whiff of Pauly from it.

In the doll's embrace I remembered one Jomba day, a couple of weeks earlier when Mimi, Pauly, Kathy and I had ridden the swells out beyond the breakers. The others had gradually made their way back to shore, leaving me alone on the restless ocean. I searched the blue sky for birds; I looked for signs of ships rounding the sand spit into the bay; I turned face down into the roiling water and remembered the sailor who had been sent to his watery grave. I shivered. Everyone on shore looked like tiny plastic dolls. Suddenly impatient to reach the beach, I pulled hard with my arms and kicked my legs.

As my legs churned, they hit something solid. It couldn't be the bottom, I was sure. Could it be a huge fish or, my scalp crawled at the thought, even a shark? My heart pounded and my legs weakened.

Get out of here, quick, swim to shore, my brain told me, but my body was paralyzed. Something large and dark nudged me from below. Still I was immobilized. I was nudged again, almost buoyed up, and when the animal arched out of the water, I recognized through my terror that the shark was a dolphin. Dizzy and shaken, I sprawled into a float, as the dolphin swished around me, then swam away. As I calmed down, I wondered how the dolphin had known I needed his touch at that moment. The nudge, unforced and unbidden, tangibly connected me to another living being in a rare and serendipitous encounter.

When I gathered strength, I swam in to shore, awed by my brush with the dolphin.

The guests in our house were the perfect frame for our family, holding us together. When my sister and I went to school in Rhodesia, my parents and brothers moved from the coast to a remote inland mission. There, where family time was more plentiful, where guests rarely ventured, the family began drifting apart.

Our family newly arrived in Angola in 1948. I was three, Kathy was four

Dad clowning with a friend

Canata kids at the beach by our house

Tomás, our cook, on the left and
Cipriano, our houseman, on the
right, with brothers David and
Mark

Mãe Florença, our laundry lady, on the right, and an assistant

Looking toward the post office (Correios) and the docks in Lobito

Aerial photo of Lobito with "the end of the spit"
at the lower left, the docks at the upper right,
and saltpans and Canata at the upper left

Our house, as it looked from the bay

Taken from our verandah, with a papaya tree in the foreground, a fishing boat coming in with its catch, and the cement factory on the hills across the bay

The church and school in Canata

Splashing in Lobito Bay soon after our move there in 1949

At age seven with our cat Fluffy

The cross-Africa train we took to Dondi and Rhodesia

The Austrian motorcyclists, Hannig (left) and Jensch (right), with (from front to back) Jereminha, David, Nancy Tucker, Kathy, and me steering

My first year at school in Dondi (age nine), with Miss Neumann standing in the back. I am holding my brother Mark

Pounding corn

An onjango (community meetinghouse)

A baobab tree

Women hoeing their field

Pounding corn on the Dondi rocks

Poem: Chicucuma

Beware little boy
Chicucuma will get you
Nasty boogeyman

Scary police state
Repressive Catholic Church
Not one person safe

Chapter 6 — Chicucuma

Cimbungu o kuatela voku sikama.
A hiena apanha a presa no tempo de serão. Cuidado quando descuidado!
O inimigo fila quando menos se espera.
The hyena captures his prey at night. Beware of being careless!
The enemy pounces when you least expect him.

Umbundu proverb

In my years in Lobito, we lived our lives on the verandahs, open and secure. To get from my bedroom to my parent's room next door, I walked in my nightie along the verandah facing the road and the beach just beyond, as unaware of passing cars or people as if it were an enclosed hall. Open-air stairs, sheltered by the foliage of a bougainvillea vine, connected the two verandahs. My walk-in dollhouse blocked off a whole corner of the upper verandah, and later I studied the Calvert correspondence course at a table on the opposite corner. If we had more company than usual in the dining room, we kids happily ate out on the verandah. At 4 o'clock in the afternoon, I helped Mom or Tomás prepare a pot of hot black tea, a small pitcher of milk, sugar, and a pot of hot water to make cambric tea for the children. We carried the heavy tray upstairs to the verandah overlooking the bay and watched ships steam by our house, while we sipped our tea and crunched into freshly baked sugar cookies.

Beyond the house, I was free to explore the city by myself or with my sister and brothers, starting with the beach fifty feet from our house. As we got older, we occasionally carried a picnic to the end of the narrow sand spit on which the city was built, to the point where the ocean met the bay.

"Pay attention to the drop-off," Mom admonished us. "Stay close to shore!"

She didn't need to say more. At the end of the spit, a few feet into the water the beach plunged and, if I stood on the edge of the drop-off, cold water from the deep shivered against my legs, unlike in front of our house where the sand subsided gradually into deeper and deeper water. Still, at the spit I knew if I stayed within the bounds I'd be safe.

Sometimes my sister and I ventured downtown. The first commercial area began with the Bar Restaurant, painted minty-green with shaded verandahs, the only place in town where Mom allowed us to buy ice cream.

"No, you may not have a cone," she'd say, when the ice cream vendor came by our house, pulling his cart behind his bicycle and ringing his bell.

"It's not sanitary. They don't boil their milk and water and we don't know what kind of germs are breeding in there." She was confident that the Bar Restaurant ice cream was safe. I licked my dripping cone as fast as possible, and I never got dysentery.

Up a block or so, the movie theatre on rare occasions showed a children's film. The Portuguese government, in conjunction with the Catholic Church, rated movies by age. Even as innocent a movie as *Snow White and the Seven Dwarves* was considered dangerous to those under twelve. I was permitted to see the Cantinflas movies that came to town. Cantinflas was a goofy Mexican comic whom I adored. He was master of the incoherent, mixing up words and inverting phrases. Even dubbed in Portuguese, he drove me crazy. Protected by the government and the church, I sank into the plush, velvet seats of the theater. The heavy maroon drapes and a shimmery, transparent curtain were drawn open, and Cantinflas stumbled to life.

Beside the theater, at the post office, mail fluttered in and out. Letters from my friends up country and our distant aunts, cousins, and grandmother in America arrived at our post office box, C.P. 109, Lobito, Angola, Portuguese West Africa. Behind the glass front, letters, the *Christian Science Monitor*, and *Time* magazine were stuffed into the narrow slot. Letters connected us to everyone we knew in those days before telephones were freely available. And when I went away to school at age nine, letters tied me to my parents for months at a time.

Letters were the vehicles that carried my mother's love and kept me apprised of the daily activities at home. They were essential to our communication, but carried within them an intrinsic difficulty: they were one-sided. In a telephone conversation, the parties can respond immediately and convey emotion through tone of voice and inflections, even without seeing each other. Letters are composed, not spontaneous, dialogues. They are capable of carrying emotion, but by their nature cannot elicit a fast reaction. For a child away from home, experiencing homesickness and feelings of isolation from the family, letters could not substitute for the instant comfort of a mother's hug. In those circumstances, my emotional development was largely solitary and internal; it took place away from the warm arms and encouraging voices of my parents.

Despite their inherent shortcomings, letters arrived reliably at the post office and we depended on them to hear news and keep tabs on friends and family.

At the train station across from the post office, trains shuttled commuting workers to and from the nearby towns. The arriving up-country train, the one we rode from Dondi, puffed in around noon, disgorging passengers, freight, and, once a week, a bushel basket of fresh vegetables for Tomás to cook. In late afternoon the train departed, a shower of cinders pouring out of its chimney, for a journey across Angola to the Congo. My parents met someone at the train almost every day, it seemed. If my sister and I weren't leaving or arriving, we knew someone else who was, someone who brought us news from up country.

"Do you want to come with me?" my mother would often ask. "I'm going to meet Aunt Lillian at the train." Or any of a number of aunts and uncles. Aunt Lillian was my missionary aunt, not my blood aunt, but we bonded with each other in a huggy, jokey way that was impossible with our faraway relatives. She threw her fat, jiggly arms around me and smothered me in her soft chest. I helped carry her bags to the car for the short trip home.

In that part of downtown, closest to our house, I was right at home. I could negotiate the walk or short bus trip from home, feeling perfectly at ease with the language, perfectly secure from personal harm, perfectly competent.

I didn't venture to the commercial area on the far side of downtown without my mother. Mom made me wear shoes when I went to the large market with her. That and the smells made me think twice about going along. Humidity and the equatorial sun did their work on the foods for sale. In the stalls on either side of the center corridor, Mom picked through the rotting cabbages for one she could put in her string bag. We avoided the fish stalls since Tomás bought our fish off the boats as they passed our house, but the acrid stench of chicken and pig waste hung heavy in the air. Live chickens, their legs tied together, flopped on the ground and pigs were tied on a short leash for our inspection. After the market we often stopped in at Casa Holandesa, where Mom stocked up on cases of Dutch powdered milk, and at Casa Inglesa for Bovril, an English beef tea. Creamy milk, robust Bovril, nutritious and comforting.

In the heart of downtown, though, the police station gave me my first intimation that life was dangerous. From it emanated moans, wails, and the steady whap of a beating being administered. I held my breath until the sounds of distress and violence faded. I didn't fear for my own physical safety.

My world was wealthy and protected. And white. But in every interaction between black Angolans and white Portuguese danger skulked.

I came to realize that the beatings were not always for criminals. Just as likely, they were brought on by political transgressions. No doubt when I was young I overheard conversations alluding to such matters between my parents and other adults, although I don't remember them specifically. The authoritarian atmosphere of the dictatorship in itself was enough to wordlessly convey threat and coercion. The weekly ritual of my father signing our servants' work permits may have been the first overtly political lesson I observed. At the end of each week, Dad methodically dated and signed the permits, attesting to the fact that Tomás, Cipriano, and Mãe were gainfully employed. Mãe would have strapped Jereminha on her back and set her basket on the ground ready to be hoisted to her head. Tomás and Cipriano would hold their hats in hand, petitioners waiting to collect permits that granted them the right to be in the white part of town. Signing day turned them subservient. Any other time of the week, they were adults going about their business, sometimes serious, sometimes playful.

Cipriano lived with us, in a room by the kitchen, until he married. Besides cleaning and making beds, Cipriano carried food from the detached kitchen across the verandah to the dining room. One day a heavy tray slipped from his hands, crashed to the floor, and he burst into tears of shame. My mother helped him clean it up and tried to console him, but for a long time he thought he had failed us. Tomás, who traveled by bicycle to his family in the African section of town, was more relaxed. He found humor in almost any situation, a good trait for someone who had to cook three meals a day for a houseful of guests. Mãe was the sole wage earner in her family of three sons, including Jereminha, who was a toddler and accompanied her to work each day until he started school. From our house, she walked to the station and caught the train to the sugar cane town of Catumbela where she lived, a twenty-five minute ride south. At seven, I already connected the solemnity of the permit-signing ritual with dread that they might be caught without the right papers when they ventured from the protection of our house. To be picked up and beaten by the police was a real fear. Around town, I had seen men and women with bloodied heads and swollen eyes, the result, my parents told me, of such beatings. I easily imagined Cipriano locked in jail or Mãe flung to the ground, Jereminha screaming and clinging to his frightened mother.

Lobito was divided into the black *sanzala* on the barren salt flats and the white city on the sand spit, with its spacious houses on shaded lots by the water. From an early age, I understood how separate these parts were, even though my parents invited Africans into our home without apology to our white neighbors. Benches and restrooms weren't labeled by racial group, as in apartheid South Africa and the American South, but geographically and economically, the African and Portuguese parts of town were segregated. Our comfortable house in the white city, halfway down the tree-lined avenue between downtown and the end of the spit, contrasted with the puny one-room houses of stick and mud in the *sanzala*. On our frequent trips to the *sanzala*, we drove up the paved avenue bordered by shady sidewalks, past the railroad station, the colonnaded post office, the docks, movie theater, police station, and market. We passed more Portuguese houses and apartments, painted in mint, terra cotta, lemon, and finally drove over a bridge into the desolate *sanzala*. We skirted the open garbage pits and passed an occasional water pump that served thousands. We drove past the row of outhouses, perched precariously on stilts out over the tidal flats. One day they collapsed and were never replaced. Usually our destination was the *Igreja Evangélica de Canata*. To my young eyes, the enormous lime-washed church and school rising white, a veritable Taj Mahal, out of the salt flats, looked like the one building in the *sanzala* that could survive a disaster.

Sometimes I rode along with my mother to the *sanzala* when she brought a present to the family of a new baby or comforted a sick person. When I was eight, I went with her to grieve with a family that had lost an infant to diarrhea. We parked the car where we could, among the stick houses that sprouted haphazardly from the sand, and walked. Because the houses were so tiny, most living was done outside. The local tailor had set up his pedal sewing machine outside his house. Clean clothes had been washed and spread out to dry on the sandy dirt. A mother squatted in her outdoor kitchen and stoked the fire under a blackened pot full of *eputa*, thick corn meal mush. No one was outside at the grieving family's house. Mom knocked on the door and identified herself. They didn't know we were coming because neither they nor we had a telephone.

"É Dona Ki. Queremos offrir as nosas condolências. It's Ki. We wanted to offer our sympathy," she said in Portuguese.

The dead infant's mother and father came to the door and clapped their greeting. "Kalunga, kalunga. Welcome, welcome." Two little boys looked at us from behind their mother's legs.

And Mom slipped into Umbundu in response, "Ku ku, ku ku. Thank you, thank you."

I listened with half a mind to their conversation. With the door and wooden shutter on the window closed and no electric illumination, sunlight filtered in through the chinks in the mud and sticks. We sat in gloom on a low, backless bench. The room contained only a small hand-hewn wooden table, a couple of low stools, and a shelf that held a cooking pot and a few enamel plates and mugs. No eating utensils were necessary. *Eputa* was eaten by hand, chunks of plain corn meal mush scooped up barehanded, only rarely seasoned with fish or chicken sauce. From the sitting room I could see into a tiny bedroom, with plain straw mats on the floor for sleeping.

I was struck by how unfair life was. I wished I understood why we ourselves had a big, substantial house of cement and stucco with large, high-ceilinged rooms full of furniture. And why we had iron beds with real mattresses, sheets, and mosquito nets. And why we had electricity, cold running water, bathtubs, and toilets. And why we had all the food we wanted. And why my little brothers were healthy and not in danger of dying from diarrhea. And why we lived on a beautiful beach. And why the dead baby's family had so little.

Several years later, in 1958 when I was thirteen, I accompanied my sister Kathy, little brother David, and Mãe's son Jereminha on an outing to the Radio Club swimming pool a few blocks down the beach from our house. The boys were seven years old.

"Mommy, we'll be back for lunch," I called out, as Kathy and I set out for the beach.

David and Jereminha, barefoot and in shorts, had already scurried ahead. From behind, all skinny arms and legs, they could have been twins. We sauntered down the beach, collecting sand dollars and skipping them on the bay.

At the Radio Club, the steep concrete steps led up to the pool built into a slight hill sloping down to the beach. David and Jereminha flung down their towels and unhesitatingly jumped into the cool water. David, who had been taking swimming lessons at the club, swam to the middle of the pool and called to Jereminha to join him.

"Vem cá, pá. Come on, buddy!"

But Jereminha was less confident of his swimming and stayed near the edge. I plunged off the diving board, touched the bottom with my feet, and pushed myself to the surface. As I burst up for air, I heard a Portuguese man yelling from the side. He bent over, his arm raised to strike, and I realized, with stomach-wrenching fright, that he was going to hit Jereminha. With one arm, Jereminha clung to the side of the pool and, with the other, he tried to protect his head. While Kathy, David and I watched, paralyzed, the man yanked Jereminha out of the pool and flung him onto the concrete deck. His yells and Jereminha's shrieks echoed off the walls.

"How dare you swim in this pool? Who said you could? What makes you think *um preto* (a black) can use this pool?"

He walloped Jereminha for what seemed liked ages, and then ordered the little boy off Radio Club property. We gathered our towels in silence and shepherded the weeping Jereminha and terrified David home.

"Daddy," we shouted into his office, "a man at the Radio Club beat up Jereminha for swimming in the pool."

Dad came out to the verandah to hear the story. He gravely inspected Jereminha and asked a few questions before he strode over to his motorbike with the grimmest face I'd ever seen him wear. Dad never got angry. I never heard him make intemperate remarks or lose control. But the way he pulled the motorbike off its kickstand, fired it up, and zoomed out of our driveway, I knew he was mad. I didn't know where he was going, but his decisiveness reassured me, because the man's shouts and Jereminha's screams still reverberated in my head.

When Dad returned home, he told us that he had gone down to complain to the Portuguese *chefe do posto*, the chief administrator.

"They told me he was out, but I could see him sitting in his office. His door was ajar, so I walked back and told him what had happened to Jereminha. He agreed that the man had been in the wrong and that, most assuredly, Jereminha was allowed to swim in the pool."

But of course, Jereminha never returned to the pool and I couldn't swim there myself without feeling guilt, which turned into rage when no action was taken against the Radio Club man. A private assurance between the *chefe* and Dad couldn't convince me that the same sort of brutality wouldn't happen again. And though Dad had acted as aggressively as he could, he knew it wasn't enough.

Dad had been a member of the Fellowship of Reconciliation since his college days in Tacoma, and believed deeply in its pacifist tenets. During World War II, he had worked with the American Friends Service Committee when, two months after the bombing of Pearl Harbor, on February 19, 1942, President Roosevelt issued Executive Order #9066 commanding the internment of all Japanese Americans who lived along the Pacific coast. In April, the first of Seattle and Tacoma's Japanese community, two-thirds of whom were American citizens, were given less than a week to register with the government, pack, and sell or rent their homes, farms, and businesses.

My father's role was to support the evacuees and witness their relocation. In a sense, his job in Lobito was similar. It often called on him to run interference with Portuguese administrators on behalf of Angolans, and was a constant challenge to and confirmation of his beliefs.

In fact, political tensions had ratcheted up several notches while we had been in America in 1957. That was the year PIDE, the Portuguese secret police, arrived in Angola. The presence of PIDE seemed to give the Radio Club man permission to be brutal. Ghana, which in 1957 became the first colony in Africa to gain independence, sent a ripple of nervousness thousands of kilometers south to Angola. In the minds of the authorities, the smallest action or casual talk by an African translated into treachery and political intrigue. We returned to Lobito in the summer of 1958 when I was thirteen, the summer of the Radio Club pool incident, to news that gave me a jolt.

"Where's Senhor Isaias?" I asked Dad. He had been Dad's Angolan secretary and, as long as I could remember, had been part of our household.

"He's been arrested," Dad told me, "and sent up country."

I didn't dare ask why. Even a private conversation with my father in our house seemed risky, as though my curiosity might bring in the authorities to investigate me. Later I realized that being a white American girl would have protected me from personal scrutiny, but as an adolescent, I was afraid to push, afraid to be caught out. My anxiety made me all the more sympathetic with the Angolans, whose condition of near independence mirrored my near adulthood. We both were still under the control of paternal, and, in their case, brutal, authorities, but we were experimenting with voicing, or at least thinking, our own opinions.

Before we left for furlough, Senhor Isaias had lived in the *sanzala* with his young family, and every day he arrived on his motorbike to work with Dad. His office was set up on the side verandah, right outside Dad's office, so they could talk to each other through the window. He spoke excellent Portuguese, had passed the government high school exam, and could type. While I worked on my Calvert course in second and third grades in Mom's office, I heard the tap-tap of Senhor Isaias' typewriter through the window. If I ran around the verandah, he was there writing or running the recalcitrant mimeograph machine, hand-feeding one sheet of paper at a time. Every day he ate lunch with us.

But when we returned from America he was gone, sent to jail. His crimes, I learned much later, were that he was educated and Protestant. To satisfy his curiosity about the world outside Angola, he and some friends had formed a secret cultural association. They pooled their knowledge and discussed world events. While we were on furlough, a ship arrived in port from Liberia, at that time the only independent African country. Among its passengers were Liberian government officials on a junket down the coast of Africa. Senhor Isaias clandestinely invited them to speak to his group, but an informant tipped the authorities. How perilous, I thought, how sneaky. How could he know for sure who was friend and who was enemy? In a police state, you never knew whom to trust and whom to avoid.

Showing an interest in politics and the world outside Angola had always been dangerous. It could bring the unwanted attention of the authorities. We were no exceptions. Our *Time* magazine began arriving with pages torn out. "Government censors are trying to 'protect' themselves and us from who knows what," Mom explained. It drove Mom crazy wondering what had been cut out and later, when I was in school in Rhodesia, she once wrote asking me to find a particular issue and pass along to her the gist of the article.

But to me the "protection" felt more like an insidious threat, a message from the authorities that they were spying on me and I'd better watch out. Being American felt almost as perilous as being Angolan, as though I already knew more than I should about the world and I'd better not think, talk, or even read about it.

The oppressive atmosphere impelled me, a child with an emerging political consciousness, to divide the world into black and white, love and hate. Loyalty to black Angolans came to mean hatred of white Portuguese. But, in fact, I was dancing between complex alliances of race, nationality, gender, and religion. I constantly had to shift and shuffle my loyalties. I unconsciously drank in the prevailing patriarchal Portuguese culture. Not knowing why, I cringed in embarrassment over any public acts of my mother. When she spoke Portuguese or Umbundu in a group, it took all my will to keep from clamping my hands over my ears, to shut out her ungainly accent and her weak woman's voice. Though the Angolans and Portuguese we knew were never anything but polite, I felt safer when my father was the focus of attention.

My white skin protected me, while my American citizenship imperiled me. In the fifties, thirty years after a professor at the University of Wisconsin, Edward A. Ross, presented his 1925 *Report on Employment of Native Labor in Portuguese Africa* to the Temporary Slavery Commission of the League of Nations, the Portuguese government still resented Americans. Ross had pointed out how similar the system of contract labor was to slavery. The Portuguese used contract labor in Angola to supply workers to the ports, the sugar cane fields, the diamond mines, and the coffee plantations. Portugal was furious with the United States over the allegations in the report, and by extension with any Americans who lived in Angola.

The Angolans' black skins and erupting sense of freedom drew the suspicion and oppression of the Portuguese, who didn't want to lose their colony. The government and the Catholic Church feared the Protestant community, made up of missionaries, Angolans, and Portuguese. One source of their fear was the close connection between the emerging nationalist groups and Protestant missions. Most of the leaders of the groups had been educated at mission schools. But if I hated the Portuguese, how was I to reconcile that hate with my close ties to our Portuguese friends? Following my parents' example, I tried to forgive them their skin color, nationality, and the actions of their government, but it was an uneasy truce. Would they show themselves capable of acting like the Radio Club man? Still, I loved them because they were friendly, quirky people. And they were Protestants.

Consider the Figueiredos. Tall, gaunt Dona Ema Figueiredo, kind, generous, a wonderful cook of cod-potato pastries, but always complaining of ill health. "Ai, meu fígado. Oh, my liver," she'd say, holding her side. Her husband, Senhor Figueiredo, limped and used a cane, the result of polio when he was a boy. He was an accountant at a large import company and a vigorous hymn-singer at Sunday services. Their glamorous daughter Josinda, my sister's age, with her mother's high cheekbones and hair swinging to her shoulders, often played badminton with us.

They dwelt on the "correct" side of a divide as daunting as the black-white split, that is, the Protestant-Catholic divide. In my rudimentary understanding of the differences between Catholics and Protestants, I interpreted the 23rd Psalm to mean that "surely goodness and mercy shall follow Protestants all the rest of their lives, and they shall dwell in the house of the Lord forever." In Angola, religion inevitably mixed with politics, because Catholicism was the state religion. The Catholic Church supported the authoritarian government, which in turn acknowledged the sovereignty of the Pope. Salazar, the Portuguese dictator, and the Pope coexisted in my mind as malevolent twins who had the power to affect all our lives directly.

Compared to Protestantism, Catholicism seemed, from my young perspective, a secret, mysterious, superstitious religion, a good match for the secret, oppressive government. Both government and church embodied what Saint Benedict in the sixth century called "wicked zeal," a fanaticism and absolutism that oppresses.

Once I heard Dad talking about confession in positive tones. "Catholics are required to confess their sins," he said. "We all sin and I think it's rather useful to confess our sins to a priest." Had he gone over to the enemy, I wondered. I couldn't get past the vision of speaking to someone sitting in a dark closet, nor the idea that after chanting a bunch of "Hail Mary's" to the beads on their rosaries, Catholics were suddenly absolved, off the hook. Mumbling to the rosary for forgiveness seemed like hocus-pocus. What did it have to do with faith? I couldn't reconcile that absolution with my belief that treating people well was the way to God's heart.

When I was about thirteen, my mother was talking to me about a family with several children who lived up the street. The mother was pregnant again. "You know, she's having some difficulty. If she continues the pregnancy, she'll probably die. But, if the doctors try to save her, the baby will die. If the situation boils down to saving one or the other, Catholic doctors will allow the mother to die."

It didn't make sense to me. What about her other children and her husband and everyone who loved her? And what about the baby? Who would take care of it? I wanted to protest. The people already here should have first claims. In my own adolescent absolutist way, I thought Catholics were barbarians. Was this some sort of religious martyrdom? I remembered visiting Rome a year earlier, on our way back to Angola after furlough. I'd seen saints' relics stashed behind murky glass in niches along the aisles of cathedrals. Would this mother be cut into little pieces and preserved? It seemed as savage as the beatings dispensed at the police station.

In recent years, on writing retreats at a Benedictine monastery, I've discovered with relief that my childhood antagonism toward Catholics was time and place specific, tied to particularly authoritarian phases in the Catholic Church and the Portuguese state. I've had to adjust my teenage judgments in light of the monastic community's openhearted acceptance of visitors of all faiths or even no faiths. I have never been asked what my beliefs are, never been either compelled to or discouraged from attending vespers and compline, and have always been welcomed back the next year. That openness, and the playfulness of Sister Miriam, who in her 80's still rides her bike and swims in the Pecos River, and Sister Jeralyn's vast knowledge of nearby hiking trails, have humanized the Catholic church in my eyes, and changed my earlier limited perspective. Thomas Merton, the Trappist monk, says in his autobiography, *The Seven Storey Mountain*, real reverence is derived from peacefulness and simplicity and repetition, the repetition not only of the rituals of chants, prayers, and hymns, but of everyday routines and ordinary tasks. Including, perhaps, swimming and hiking. I am troubled by Merton's insistence that Catholicism is the One True Faith, the only way to live, which dangerously parallels the Muslim assertion that Islam is the One True Faith. Such centuries old events as the Crusades and the Inquisition, and, more recently, 9/11 have proven the frightening power of that belief. I do believe the young Merton's argument, before his conversion to Catholicism, that "every religion was good; they all led to God, only in different ways, and every man should go according to his own conscience, and settle things according to his own private way of looking at things."

In Angola, in that long ago time and place, where Portuguese Catholics were top dog, I understood that the white Figueiredos, as Protestants, trod almost as precarious a path as black Senhor Isaias, Dad's imprisoned secretary.

By the time I was in high school, I realized that the government had further reason to be suspicious of the Protestant missions. Protestants fostered the democratic ideals of free speech and participation in government considered dangerous to the health of the dictatorship. The business of the Protestant Church was conducted openly, with discussions and votes. The catechists, deacons, deaconesses, and pastors, the teachers in the mission schools, the nurses in the mission hospitals and clinics, all had a say in decisions. Whether by happenstance or on purpose, my parents' church had tapped into a deep Ovimbundu custom. In traditional villages, the *onjango*, or elders' discussion group, met in a building dedicated to that use. If a dispute arose that couldn't be resolved within the family, the village chief summoned the elders to examine the dispute from all sides and propose a solution. Perhaps because of the *onjango* tradition, the way Protestant churches went about their business seemed familiar to the Ovimbundu, but dangerous to the closed Portuguese government.

The *onjango* building I recall most vividly was at Dondi Hospital. I was curious about it because it seemed oddly out of place at the hospital. It wasn't of European design, a brick hospital wing, a lab furnished with microscopes, or an operating room with mirrors. It didn't tend to abandoned babies as the orphanage did, nor to illness and deformity as did the leper colony. Set adjacent to the main courtyard of the hospital, its circular structure set it apart from traditionally square Ovimbundu houses. Thirty feet in diameter, it had upright log walls, several open doorways, and a steep, high, thatched roof. Inside the dim unlit interior, benches lined the perimeter so that the dispute settlers faced each other in one continuous circle.

I can see now that the *onjango* embodied the spirit not only of traditional conflict resolution, but of the missionary enterprise, as I knew it. A place to petition for mercy and justice, a sanctuary or shelter, a safe place to smooth out the tensions of the world, the *onjango* was a metaphor for the hospital as a place of healing. Through the *onjango,* rifts in the community were repaired, wounds mended.

I was standing on the sidewalk in Lobito one day—I must have been about ten—when I heard a Portuguese mother up the block talking to her little son.

"If you don't behave, *Chicucuma* will get you," she said.

I shuddered with fear momentarily. *Chicucuma* is the Angolan bogeyman, and although my parents had never threatened me with him, my imagination had filled in the dreadful details. But then I realized that she was pointing to the beggar with elephantiasis who had just been to our house. He did look like a monster, tall, big-boned, and deformed, dressed in tattered clothes, but I was familiar enough with him to know that within his hideous body, he was a decent man. His pants legs were slit to accommodate his thick, diseased feet, too grotesque and misshapen for shoes. His feet reminded me of the wastebasket in my father's office, fashioned from a real elephant's foot. The man appeared irregularly in our yard, clapping to make his presence known and rasping, "Minha senhora, Ma'am," to my mother. Mom walked up to him and greeted him, but I kept my distance. He offered to sell her potatoes from the sisal gunnysack slung over his shoulder. She bought a few and then she asked Tomás to make him a huge sandwich in a Portuguese bun and pulled a banana for him off the stalk hanging on the tree in our yard. She sent me off on a quest.

"Nancy, go choose a couple of tin cans for him."

She saved emptied cans under the house for such occasions.

"Nothing ever is wasted here," she told me once. "Everything can be put to some use. Cans can be used for cooking or carrying water or storing food..."

Occasionally, she gave him a shirt from our missionary barrel of surplus clothes.

"Beware of *Chicucuma!*" said the Portuguese mother.

The little neighbor boy cowered behind her, peering furtively at the African man. I can see how the African, the black man, *o preto* could be transformed into a monster, a threat, a brute, and so, how easily the boy, once grown, could become the Radio Club man. The mix of superstition, fear, and oppression caused us all to steal looks behind our backs. The swirl of apprehension and suspicion brushed us all with a streak of paranoia.

In 1975, after fourteen years of colonial war, a socialist revolution in Portugal overthrew the dictatorship and loosened the ties between church and state. The Portuguese people, weary of the grueling war, suddenly granted Angola its independence. The Angolans, unschooled in running a country, and divided along ethnic and tribal lines, became a pawn of the Cold War. The Soviet Union supported MPLA, the ruling party, while the United States and South Africa supported UNITA. Weapons flowed to both sides, sparking a bloody civil war. Even after the breakup of the Soviet Union in 1989 and an attempt at elections in Angola in 1992, the civil war continued for another decade. At last, it sputtered to an end in 2002 when Jonas Savimbi, the UNITA leader, was killed. A huge percentage of the two generations who grew up during the forty years of war are illiterate and untrained in anything but soldiering. With its history of colonial repression and war, Angola is still a dangerous place, full of landmines and ignorance. And its government, corrupted by easy oil and diamond money, has not yet begun to spread the wealth to the common people.

My life in white colonial Angola was a fleeting period of safety in the midst of a system fast coming apart.

Poem: Explorer

I am Explorer
Curious about America
Open to the universe
Surprise

I am Explorer
Crazy about baby dolls
Eager to dance to Elvis
But shy

I am Explorer
I see through new eyes
I pledge allegiance
With pride

I am Explorer
Launching back to Africa
International citizenship
In hand

Chapter 7 — Sharp Eyes

Nda wa kupuka vanja oku loko; nda ka va kumuile o yolako!
Se cair, olhe para os lados; se ninguém te vir, ri-se!
If you fall, look around; if no one saw you, laugh at yourself!
                                        Umbundu proverb

When I was eleven, my appetite ballooned. "Pass the potatoes, please," I'd say, helping myself to seconds at every meal. For the first time my body turned chubby, apparently mobilizing resources for my impending foray into adolescence. By the next summer, I had grown a couple of inches and had noticed hair in new places. When our family went on furlough that year, I was presented with an additional conundrum: how to make intellectual sense of America, my birth home. It was a year that opened me to the universe in ways I never expected.

We moved to Hartford, Connecticut for my father to pursue a master's degree in anthropology at the Hartford Seminary Foundation. He had first been attracted to the mission field because it promised him a chance to learn about new cultures while living out his religious beliefs. Now he would add academic understanding to his practical experience.

We rented a small, second floor apartment in the seminary compound, a compact campus of Tudor apartments and classrooms crossed by diagonal walkways and dotted with shade trees. I had last seen America in 1952, as I turned seven. Now at twelve, I was to enter seventh grade at Noah Webster School. While the rest of the family went to school, my mother tended to Mark and our own household, a welcomed change for her after years of managing the hostel in Lobito.

As I climbed up the hill from Hartford Seminary and rounded the corner for the first time in the fall of 1957, the three-story Noah Webster School sprang up, large and impressive. The name caught my eye immediately.

"Who was Noah Webster, Mommy?" I asked. Though I thought of myself as sophisticated about the world, my mother was still my "Mommy."

She told me he had compiled a dictionary back at the beginning of the 1800's.

"Oh, wow, you mean the Webster's dictionary, the one we have?"

I shivered; goose bumps prickled down my arms. This school, even its name, clearly reflected what I'd already noticed about America: it was big, important, and bustling. When the bell rang at the beginning of the day and between classes, hundreds of students in seventh and eighth grades swarmed the school as we moved from room to room, changing teachers every period. My schoolmates were noisy, swaggering through the halls, confidently taking up space, while I scuttled close to the wall, trying for anonymity despite what felt like a garish iridescence radiating "stranger, stranger, stranger" from my every feature.

The school introduced me to a range of new subjects. In home economics I learned to make a wool skirt without a pattern. In English my teacher tried to impose patterns, illustrating the mystery of diagramming with slants and horizontal lines, and creating confusion out of ordinary sentences. And I was studying science for the first time in my life.

1957 was a pivotal year for America, as it was in a different way for me. What began as cooperative American and Russian plans to launch artificial satellites, during the International Geophysical Year, quickly turned into Cold War competition. The United States, out-smarted by the Soviet Union's aggressive launch of *Sputnik I* in October, seized on science as a way to compete. Newspaper articles lamented the sad state of American science education and in turn my school let us know that grasping science concepts was important in order to be an educated person. Even more, understanding science had entered the realm of patriotic duty. In November, we read about *Sputnik II* soaring into space with a dog named Laika. He was a perky dog, with dark ears, eyes, and nose and a white streak down his snout. But he was a Russian dog. Suddenly the stakes rose higher. Finally, in January 1958, the United States launched our first satellite, *Explorer I* and, in March, *Vanguard I*. One late winter day Mr. Tefft, my science teacher, looked around at the class and asked, "How has the United States responded to Russia's launching of Sputnik?"

I lowered my eyes, afraid he'd call on me and I'd have to speak out loud in front of everyone. I felt fairly safe in my back seat, but since I was in the middle of the row, I wouldn't lookup in case he'd catch my eye. He had positioned the seats so we had to look toward him and the board. The windows behind me remained tantalizingly close but out of view. Muffled shouts of kids on the playground and the weak winter sun glancing off my desk tempted me to twist in my seat for a look. Instead, I glanced at Mr. Tefft who was fingering his red bow tie.

"That's right," he replied to someone's answer, "we launched the satellite *Explorer*. Actually, the *Sputniks* and *Explorer* were launched as part of the International Geophysical Year. Who can tell me what geophysical means?"

My ears perked up at the word international. While the class discussed the atmosphere and oceans and volcanoes, I drifted back to my airplane trip to America. We had boarded a plane at the little Lobito airport for a short hop to Luanda where a Sabena flight would carry us to Rome and Lisbon. In Lobito, the plane had risen through the heat waves shimmering off the salt flats below. Flamingos, unperturbed by the roar of the engine, stood in the shallow flats, placid dots of pink on a sheet of blue. The airplane droned up through the atmosphere, lost in the clouds at first but then rising into the crisp blue. I looked down on the billowy clouds, half tempted to leap into those gigantic piles of pillow stuffing. I was flying in my first airplane. The trip that used to take weeks by ship was cut to hours. The chasm dividing life in Angola and life in America was no longer measured in ship-days, but gauged by the dizzying height above the earth. Sitting in Mr. Tefft's classroom, I imagined I was *Explorer*, traveling the universe in search of new knowledge and new lands.

The school personnel apparently thought Angola so exotic that my parents were told at the beginning of the year to expect little from me academically, a caution my mother revealed to me when I was an adult. Even uninformed of their low expectations, I was well aware of my warty defects and outsider status. In science I felt plain ignorant. When Mr. Tefft asked, on a test, what compressed gas was, I answered, "It's gas that's compressed."

I didn't understand how to explain scientific phenomena. My first grades in science were D's.

"Nancy," he wrote on my test, "you must explain with different words. Come see me about this."

He expected us to work hard and he didn't accept sloppy logic.

Mr. Tefft, though demanding, attended to his students in ways I'd never experienced with Miss Neumann. For instance, he walked around the room and called on us by name. One day I sat in class simultaneously wishing to be anonymous and hoping that he would notice me. I was particularly proud of my outfit that day, the way I had combined various shades of green in my skirt, blouse, sweater, and scarf for, I liked to think, a sophisticated effect. I wasn't sure I wanted him to notice me, however, because all my clothes were from thrift shops and discount stores. Maybe it's obvious they don't go together, I thought. Maybe they look stupid. Maybe I'm becoming like American girls, worried only about my clothes and appearance.

Mr. Tefft walked toward me down the aisle. Don't come too close, I pleaded silently.

But Mr. Tefft stood next to me and, in front of the whole class, complimented me on my green outfit.

My heart thudded in my ears, as I smiled bashfully at the textbook on my desk.

By the second marking period I made an A.

I learned from Mr. Tefft, but felt closest to Mr. Donohue, my homeroom and social studies teacher. He was a bear of a man, barrel-chested, with a fuzzy buzz-cut, and he usually wore a plaid cardigan. He wasn't funny, flashy, or charismatic. He was a quiet man, who looked at me as if I might have something interesting to say, but he didn't probe. He listened and waited for me to approach him. Through the cold winter months in Hartford, I brought him pieces of my life, revealing myself little by little: stamps from Angola and Portugal, a carved bird, a picture of my house in Lobito. I arrived extra early at school before the rest of my homeroom, so I could catch him alone.

"Mr. Donohue, I brought a grass mat for you to see." I carried it over to his desk by the window. Kids were running around on the chilly playground while I basked in Mr. Donohue's attention. "The pattern is woven from different colored grasses; see the blond, red and dark brown?"

He picked up the mat to examine it closely, nodding and smiling. "Beautiful, it's very beautiful," he said.

First thing in the morning we gathered in Mr. Donohue's room for the pledge of allegiance and announcements. With my hand on my heart, I stood stiff and attentive, reciting my pledge to the flag and to the nation for which it stood. I could feel my heart beating, beating, churning up a well of emotions, as I looked at the red, white, and blue stars and stripes hanging by the blackboard. I felt proud to be from a country that declared liberty and justice for all. I was proud to be where people could say what they wanted, go where and when they wanted, in contrast to Angola where newspapers only published news sanctioned by the government. Talking openly about politics ensured arrest and prison. The comings and goings of Angolans were strictly monitored. I'd never felt such a surge of pride as was rising in my heart for America, my country of citizenship. America truly was the country I wanted to belong to... until I remembered how alien I felt in America. With relief, I thought instead about Angola, my home, the country I loved, about Lobito and Dondi, my friends, aunts, and uncles, Tomás, Mãe... Then I would remember the shouts and moans coming from the police station we had to pass every time we went downtown. Every day, as I pledged allegiance, I had to choose between loyalty to America and Angola.

World geography helped me straddle the divide. I felt cocky showing my knowledge of the world. Right away I noticed, when we got to the chapter on Portugal, that the spellings of some of the towns were incorrect. For instance, the textbook spelled the northern city of Porto with an O in front. Oporto. "That's not how it's spelled," I mumbled.

When I identified Porto on a test, I didn't put the O in front. I spelled it the correct way, the way I personally knew they spelled it in Portugal. Mr. Donahue marked me down. I thought he at least would be educated about the world. Even so, I tempered my disappointment because maybe he just didn't know any better.

My sense of self-righteousness and superiority over my American schoolmates spilled out during our study of the capitals of the world. Now I knew they'd have to pay attention to the wider world, and of course my special place in it. If I'd dared, I would have said, "Look, you guys, there really are countries out there other than the United States, and I live in one of them."

Nobody had heard of Angola. They called Africa a country instead of a continent, but I could have told them Angola itself was fourteen times the size of Texas. That's how Mom and Dad described it when they spoke to church groups. I could have told them that Angola had eight major language and ethnic groups, not counting Portuguese. But I didn't tell them anything. I let them dangle in their ignorance. They didn't deserve to know. Still, sometimes I pretended I didn't know Portuguese. The uncultured fishermen and peasants who immigrated to New England spoke Portuguese. French was the language sophisticated people of the world wanted to learn.

Making friends challenged me even more than learning how to please my teachers. In our little apartment, I played with dolls and often browsed the baby section of the nearby Woolworth's to buy clothes for them. But my friends plainly had boys on their minds. I was surprised then, one day, when a new friend invited me and several other girls to go shopping for baby dolls. As her mother drove us to the department store, I day-dreamed about the variety of dolls this huge American store would have, especially the baby dolls: newborn babies, older babies, babies with eyes that opened and closed, dolls that drank water and wet their diapers. But instead of heading to the toy floor, the group went to the girls' nightclothes department. I followed along, confused.

"OK, here are the nighties and long pajamas, now where are the baby dolls?" one of the girls asked. I tried to figure out the connection between pajamas and baby dolls.

"Baby Dolls, they're over there," someone said.

They all swarmed over to a table neatly piled with clothes in pastel colors and held up shortie pajamas to check the fit.

I'm so dumb. *Baby dolls. Babies, dolls*, I turned the words over in my mind. Had I missed a clue that baby dolls were really pajamas?

I thought back to my conversation in the car on the way to the store, hoping I hadn't shown how ignorant or foreign I was. No one was looking strangely at me, so I joined my friends at the baby doll table and picked out a set to buy. On the way home, I sat squished in the back seat of the station wagon, hugging my baby dolls to my chest. The chatter of my new friends barely penetrated, as I mulled over the weird misunderstanding.

That year in America, I rode an emotional see saw of exhilaration and dejection, catapulting off the seat with joy when I fit in, thudding to the ground with bone-jarring suddenness when I realized I would never understand. I was proud to be an American and I wanted to fit seamlessly into Hartford and Noah Webster School. I wanted to attend the school dances and be invited by a boy to dance to Elvis's music. At school, I worked hard diagramming sentences, memorizing the capitals of the world, and learning how to sew a straight seam so I could make good grades. But an event like the baby doll shopping trip reminded me that I wasn't an American. I didn't even understand their language. So, I'd heap scorn on the frivolous American kids, never aloud to them, but to my parents in the safety of our apartment. Americans were shallow, interested only in clothes and "stuff." What did they know about the world? Nothing! My father and mother listened and nodded. "But aren't you being a little harsh with your friends?" my mother asked. "They're all nice kids. What about Carol? You like playing with her."

A few years ago, I came across something my father had written in Hartford, in which he mentioned how contemptuous I'd been about Americans at that time. I never had a chance to ask him what he really thought about my attitude, but the tone of the passage indicated a mix of amusement at my vehemence, concern about my arrogance, and pride at my critique of American society.

Within the Hartford Seminary community, I glided along. The Seminary included several missionary families that worked in countries all around the world. For school reports, I frequently borrowed volumes of the

Encyclopedia Britannica from the family from Pakistan. Their daughter was a little younger than me, so she didn't become a close friend, but I never felt odd with her or her family. I came and went from their apartment as if I belonged. I also used my extensive baby-tending skills to baby-sit for the family across the street, skills I'd cultivated through caring for my brother Mark and numerous African babies. At twelve, I was confident that I could manage the family's three children, who were under the age of four. "There's supper ready on the stove," the mother would say, as she and her husband walked out, "and here's the baby's bottle. Just heat it up when he's ready for it. Try to get them bathed and in bed by 7:30. We'll see you about 10 o'clock." The three-year-old girl sat up at the table and ate. I had more of a struggle simultaneously keeping the toddler happy and tending to the two month old, who didn't understand the word wait. Supper accomplished, though, we could sit on the couch, with the little girl on one side, the toddler on the other, the baby on my lap sucking his bottle, and read *The Little Engine That Could* and *The Little Red Hen*. The baby would nod off, and, with him in bed, I could bathe the older kids and put them to bed. Only when I was alone with the television on, feeling spooked at every creak of the old house, did I wish the parents would come quickly home.

Television was the perfect way to observe America at a distance. My brothers, sister, and I sat in our living room, watching images locked in the little box, two paces from the American life around us. Television portrayed a romantic America, where the good guys always beat the bad. Twenty Mule Team Borax brought us "Wagon Train." At every commercial break a tiny team of mules ran across the kitchen floor and entered a box of borax. Zorro, with his mask and sword, swashbuckled across the screen, saving the townsfolk from the evil commandant and leaving his mark of Z. Paladin, a loner dressed in black, flipped out his calling card with "Have Gun, Will Travel," and offered his services for the forces of good. These westerns were endlessly entertaining but made me suspect that America was a lightweight fantasyland. Full Saturdays spent sitting in a darkened room in front of the television didn't help me make sense of the real America I encountered at school. Nor do I remember hearing about the school integration crises in the fall of 1957.

It's odd that I have no memory of the civil emergency prompted by the integration of Central High School in Little Rock, Arkansas. It must have been all over the television news that fall. I do remember that one of the first sensations I had when we arrived in America was fear, fear of murderers and kidnappers, fear of vicious attacks, prompted by the endless tales of crime in the newspapers. Such crimes, even if they occurred, weren't reported in the media in Angola. Perhaps the images of armed troops and open hatred directed at the black students scared them out of my memory. Perhaps I couldn't reconcile them with my pride in American democracy.

While I juggled images of America, real and fantastic, with images of Angola to figure out my place in the world, I realized I was more a world citizen than an American. I had a vague understanding that I could integrate my African and American lives, to hang onto the aspects of each I valued, and find my way in the space between.

I was stepping out physically as well, marching into the adult world with swelling breasts, underarm and pubic hair, and a final growth spurt. Of course, the bra I soon started wearing was hidden from view. Only I could feel it hugging my chest, cradling my miniature breasts. My bra was hidden from everyone's view that is, except in physical education.

The first day I wore it to school I was self-conscious, sure everyone could tell something was different about me. I changed into my P.E. uniform and joined the class climbing the ropes, leaping over the horse, and tumbling on the mats. Then the period was almost up, and we had a few minutes to shower and dress. I had never gone to school with bells marking out the time, bells ringing away the moments before we were late to the next class. The constant measuring of time made me nervous, so nervous that I dashed into the changing room, tore off my gym clothes, and ran into the shower before I realized I was still wearing my new bra. There I stood, naked except for my bra, as the water washed over my body. Conversation in the shower ceased. I froze. I couldn't look up, but a glance at the dozen still feet pointed at me told me all I needed to know.

At school dances, I remembered what my missionary aunt in Dondi had jokingly told me, as I was saying good-bye, "Don't fall in love with Elvis Presley when you go to America." I didn't know much about Elvis, had never seen him in a movie or on television. But plainly his songs—like "I Want You, I Need You, I Love You" and its first line "Hold me close, hold me tight"—did have something to do with love and sex and boys. Kathy and I stood on the sidelines, watching couples pair up to dance, twisting and shaking and rocking and rolling. I don't know what I would have done if a boy had asked me to dance. I might have bolted, as I did in school one day. We were changing classes and my next class was upstairs. As the crowd flowed up the stairs, I became aware of a boy following me too closely. He seemed to want to talk to me, but I couldn't think of a thing to say to him. My brain had deserted me. Before he could get any closer or talk to me, I found a hole in the crowd and zoomed away from him. With my heart pounding, I ran into my classroom, relieved at my escape. At the dances, also, I felt too awkward to join in, but I did want to learn the ways of Americans. I wanted to say, "Let me watch you, but don't get too close!" Although I still have a strong streak of reserve and have never totally lost my awkwardness in social situations, happily life has given me plenty of chances to learn how to accept strangers, relax, and laugh at myself.

At the end of the spring dance season, my first period arrived as a much anticipated but mysterious guest. My mother had explained the mechanics of menstruation, its monthly regularity and its connection with eggs and babies. I imagined it would be life changing. I knew that my period, more than a bra, would usher me to the threshold of adulthood. But I didn't know what my body would actually do. My period arrived quietly just before school was out for the summer. I went into the toilet one evening and was surprised to see rusty stains on my underpants. I called Mom, and she matter-of-factly announced that I was menstruating. She outfitted me with a belt and sanitary napkin, showing me how to adjust the belt and attach the napkin to it.

The elastic belt tugged at my hips and held the pad snug against me. I couldn't ignore the sensation of sitting on a thick pad any more than I had been able to ignore the squeeze of my first bra. I was *Explorer*, sitting on my launching pad, ready to soar into orbit. I was a hybrid American-African rocket, revving my engines, preparing to launch. With the pad catching the trickle of blood, I was buzzing and hovering, poised to take off for Angola.

The timing of my period struck me as entirely appropriate. I thought about how flat my chest had been when I came to Hartford, but now my breasts swelled tenderly in my bra. I felt an aching twinge in my breasts responding to the ache in my ovaries. I thought about my baby dolls that had fueled my childhood fantasies. I wondered if I was too old for them now that I perched on the edge of fertility.

In preparation for returning to Angola, Mom arranged eye exams for me, and I came home with glasses. Outside with my glasses for the first time, the details of life jumped out at me. The trees, which had been blobs of green, focused into intricate patterns of individual leaves. I could see that leaves and branches moved independently of each other in the breeze. The branches hummed slow, low notes while the leaves trilled along at a fast tempo like shiny piccolos. The edges of the leaves stood out, sharp and clear as trumpets, and behind them layers of leaves fluttered and overlapped like intertwining melodic lines. The bark, no longer an undifferentiated brown, groaned a bass line of striations, knobs, and holes. I had the sensation that I was not only seeing but hearing the earth for the first time, not America so much as nature itself. In a moment of revelation and awe, I picked out particularity and detail I'd missed before. My glasses brought the world into focus and helped me understand literally where I stood.

I caught a glimpse of myself a step removed from America, clutching my international citizenship in my hand. I was proud of the good things about America like democracy and equality, and I was inclined to forgive America its minor blemishes. Even I, I had discovered, had a few. "American kids don't know anything," I had complained to my parents. "Take it easy on your friends," Mom said. "They haven't had the same chance to travel that you've had." Maybe Mom was right. Looking down my nose all year at my American compatriots was giving me a stiff neck and a twinge of guilt. Wasn't I as limited as they were? Didn't I find them as incomprehensible as I imagined they found me? I had the feeling I should try to understand them. But I couldn't quell the overriding scorn I directed at ignorant Americans.

Before I left, I had one more task. School was already out. I wouldn't be seeing Mr. Donohue again. I'm not sure what impelled me to tell him my news. I fancied myself sophisticated about the world, but in my relationship with him I was hopelessly naïve, sure he'd want to know my intimate secrets. I called him on the telephone.

"Mr. Donohue? Hi, this is Nancy Henderson."

My heart thumped and my face flushed. Now that I had him on the phone, I had to go on. I couldn't just hang up. I was afraid someone in my family would hear me, so I talked quietly into the phone in my parents' room. I sat on the edge of their bed, jiggling my crossed leg.

"Um, I just wanted to tell you, before I leave, that I got new glasses so I can see much better. I couldn't believe what a tree looked like when I first put on the glasses. I could actually see the leaves!"

Mr. Donohue laughed and asked, "Were you having problems reading the blackboard at school?"

And I said, "Well, that's the funny thing, I didn't even know what things were supposed to look like. I didn't know leaves and words on boards were supposed to be sharp."

I smiled at him through the phone. His laugh echoed in my head. I had one more surprise for him, if I was brave enough. I crossed and recrossed my legs and felt my mouth go dry. Maybe I should just say good-bye and hang up. But I blurted on. "Um, Mr. Donohue? I started my period."

Thoughts gushed through me so fast I couldn't catch them. If only I could explain to him how alive I felt. But he jumped right in. I guess he could hear the excitement behind my quiet voice. He replied, "Congratulations! I'm so happy you called to tell me. Good luck to you."

I knew he was at home, but I imagined him there at his desk at school. He paused a moment with the phone in his big hand and his eyes wrinkled into a smile before he hung up. I smiled too, felt his warm voice sizzling through the phone lines, and whispered good-bye.

With Mr. Donohue's best wishes, I launched a new self back to Angola.

of the language, exaggerating each syllable, drawing out the vowels. *Ó pa, vá t'embora. Ai minha filha, dá me um beijinho, ai que riqueza.* I loved rolling my R's, letting my tongue vibrate against the roof of my mouth. Some R's were guttural, requiring a rasp. The shape of the language burned deep into my brain so that even now, though I hardly ever speak Portuguese, on the rare occasions when I travel in Portugal I am delighted to find the language flowing back.

Portuguese was the language of our home in Lobito. Within the family, of course, we spoke English, but even on those days when we had no guests, we shared the house with servants who spoke Umbundu and Portuguese. I chatted in Portuguese with our laundry lady, cook, houseman, and gardener. The language cemented my connection to the small city of Lobito. It was an expression of my inner knowledge that yes, this was my town, this was where I belonged. The shouts of the kids in the schoolyard up the street, the fisherman yelling *garopa, garopa* as they rowed by, Dona Isaura's shrill voice calling to her houseboy, formed the background of my life. Though my looks identified me as an *estrangeira*, I felt exquisitely at home riding the bus downtown or transacting my business with the storekeeper.

My first attempt to prove myself Angolan, oddly enough, was to take French lessons in a Portuguese school. It put us in sync with our Portuguese friends. At the small private *Colégio Luis de Camões* my sister and I supplemented our English correspondence lessons with French. On the walk home, we recited aloud our new conjugations. "*Je suis, tu es, il est, nous sommes, vous êtes, ils sont. Je finirai, tu finiras, il finira, nous finirons, vous finirez, ils finiront.*" The indicative, the conditional, the subjunctive modes. Imperfects, present perfects, pluperfects. French had such structure, such regularity, and such irregularity. Suddenly it dawned on me that language was organized. I'd never imagined that English and Portuguese had grammar and structure. French helped make sense of all languages.

Padre Alberto, our teacher and also a Catholic priest, was a short, tubby martinet of a man. Even so, he was intimidated by these two *estrangeiras* in his class. My sister and I were older than the rest of our classmates by several years, since Portuguese schools typically start French, German, and English lessons in elementary school. Not only did he have to deal with our being Americans; even more exotic, we were Protestant.

"You are excused from the Christmas lesson in the textbook," he told Kathy and me. Apparently he had no idea that Protestants as well as Catholics were Christians. In the insular Portuguese Catholic Church of the 1950's before Vatican II, it was not unusual for priests to be provincial or just plain ignorant.

Like most Portuguese teachers, he believed the ruler was the best enforcer of instruction. If our classmates messed up reciting the lesson of the day, Padre Alberto, with a satisfied smile, called them to the front, one by one, for a heavy crack or two of the ruler on the open palm. The ruler, a wide heavy piece of wood with holes drilled in it, sucked up the skin with each whack. We sat up front in the narrow cramped classroom, within a couple of feet of Padre Alberto. I'd watch him raise his meaty arm and would wince when he brought it down hard on the little boys' hands. With each smack of the ruler, the boys quivered, whimpered, and tried not to cry out. And when Padre Alberto finished disciplining them, they pranced back to their seats, full of macho swagger. Instruction by intimidation, teaching the love of French with a whack seemed to work for both teacher and students. Teacher didn't need to teach and students didn't need to learn.

I was quite sure that Padre Alberto wouldn't hit me, but to make certain I studied hard until the conjugations rippled off my tongue. Even if I hadn't been so studious, though, my exotic status protected and isolated me. I had returned to Angola glad to be home, knowing that I wasn't American, but Padre Alberto reminded me, in the way he gingerly trod around Kathy and me, that I wasn't Portuguese, either. Before furlough, Angola simply was home. I fit in as one of the mix of nationalities and cultures. Now back in Angola, I realized for the first time the power inherent in being different. The rules evidently didn't always apply to me, heady stuff for a teenager.

If French brought me closer to the outside world (right next door in the Congo they spoke French), learning Umbundu seemed like a lifeline, anchoring me to the cultural pool of home. Learning Umbundu was a good time-filler after I'd whizzed through my eighth grade correspondence course. But I'm certain that it was also a latent political act, proving my allegiance to the good guys, the Angolans, against the evil colonial Portuguese. I was even more judgmental of most Portuguese than of American teens.

I made a trade with my Umbundu friend Rebeca Valentim. I would help her with English conversation, one of the trio of European languages besides Portuguese that she was expected to learn in school, and she would teach me her native tongue. Rebeca, a couple of years older than me and the middle child of six or seven, came from an educated family. Her father was a nurse at the railway hospital and he had worked hard to gain the status of *assimilado*, an officially and legally recognized Portuguese citizen. Like me, Rebeca straddled several cultures.

We sat at a table on the upper verandah overlooking the bay on her weekly visits. She brought her English text from school. I used the Umbundu lessons my mother and father had once studied. I thought I would pick up Umbundu as easily as I had French. I was accustomed to hearing it spoken around me and could follow the gist of conversations. In the *sanzala*, after church or with my mother on an errand, I could make out what she and Dona Emilia, for example, were talking about. The language was easy to pronounce, none of those wacky spellings and unarticulated letters of French. But the grammar wasn't anything like French or Portuguese or English. Umbundu was tonal and had six classes of nouns. I had difficulty distinguishing one set of nouns from another and remembering how the adjectives agreed with the nouns.

Learning Umbundu was hard, but Rebeca was fun. When I saw her striding up our driveway from the bus stop in front of our house, I'd run downstairs to gather juice and cookies for our afternoon labors. If our mostly reliable kerosene-driven refrigerator were working, I'd clink some ice cubes into tall aluminum glasses. Rebeca, hot from the cross-town ride, mopped her face and traced patterns with her fingers in the condensation dripping down the glass, delighted by the icy intrusion on our tropical day.

"So what happened with Padre Alberto this week?" she asked in Portuguese.

"One of the little boys pulled away his hand just as Padre Alberto swung down the ruler. The padre lost his balance, pranced forward on one foot and almost fell over! I could hardly keep from laughing. But then Padre Alberto grabbed the boy by the ear and whapped him around the head. He went crying back to his seat and I was glad I hadn't laughed out loud."

With Rebeca eager to hear the latest Padre Alberto story, I could poke fun at his silly self, even when being in his classroom could feel scary. I'm not sure how long Rebeca and I labored over Umbundu and English, with occasional walks on the beach or in the garden. I never achieved even a basic level of fluency.

Our language lessons were cut short by the arrival of the orphan baby.

Technically, the baby wasn't an orphan. When her mother died, her family, unable to supply her with the milk she needed to survive, took her to the mission orphanage at Dondi, expecting to reclaim her when she was older. Despite regular feedings and care by the nurses, she had failed to thrive.

My mother had listened seriously to my daily badgering to "have an orphan," and had arranged for the baby to live with us temporarily. I knew several missionary families who were raising orphan children and I didn't consider the care of a baby out of the ordinary. Children in Angolan culture tackled adult responsibilities every day, lugging water from the well, and taking charge of their younger siblings. And even in missionary culture, children were given independence very early. It wasn't unusual for them to leave the family at age six or eight to attend school far from home and to see their parents only a few times during the school year. In addition, a couple of books I had read when I was around ten or eleven spiked my fantasies about orphans. Helen Doss wrote about her tribe of twelve multiracial, adopted children in *The Family Nobody Wanted*, a book that prompted me to contact the Dosses and develop a pen pal correspondence with a couple of the children. Dale Evans' descriptions of her Downs Syndrome child, in *Angel Unaware*, enflamed my desire to nurture. Dale Evans and Roy Rogers also had several adopted children. Both books were strongly Christian. I suspect the joining of abandoned children, Christian sensibilities, and my recent years away from home in Dondi made me fascinated with the whole topic of defenseless innocents.

The day the orphan arrived my mother drove me to the train station. We stood together on the hard-packed dirt between the station and the tracks, my heart beating so hard I could see the bodice of my shirtwaist jump. I carefully folded my arms to contain my unseemly excitement. We looked up the track into the distance, listening for the whistle to tell us that the train would soon arrive. Right on time, it chuffed and squealed to a halt, doors were flung open, and passengers disgorged. My mother pushed ahead through the crowd and I raced to keep up, a slight girl with golden brown hair a few days past my fourteenth birthday.

We spied Dona Clara walking toward us, cradling a parcel. She shifted it into my arms. I drew away the blanket to look at the baby and she winced against the bright light, crinkling her eyes and turning her face into my chest. She was tiny, an eight pound seven-month-old, named Maria Teresa. We immediately called her Teresinha, little Teresa, which soon shortened to Tezinha or simply Tez. Delicate as a newborn, she couldn't turn over or hold her head up. Like any new mother, I unfurled her fragile fist to count her fingers and let the baby grab my finger. I couldn't tear my eyes from her. I took in every detail from her tiny toes and fingers to her dark brown eyes, from her satin skin to her tightly coiled soft hair. I wanted to squeeze her, to meld her Angolan self to me. We drove home to introduce her to her new family.

I was ready for this project. I had no doubts about my ability to care for and love this child. Had I not babysat three children under the age of four when I was twelve years old? Had I not borrowed babies to jiggle on my knee and volunteered to work in the crèche at church on Sundays while the parents were attending the service? Had I not changed my baby brother's diapers when I was eight and carried him around on my hip?

I still had five months to fill before embarking on the long journey to my new high school in Rhodesia. My sister plowed ahead with her far more taxing ninth grade course. David, my eight-year-old brother, would soon be returning to Dondi, leaving only Mark, my five-year-old brother, at home. Dad's attention was directed at his administrative duties. Mom ran our household and church groups and occasionally checked on our studies.

I longed to cuddle a baby to absorb Umbundu-ness through Tez, skin to skin. The dailiness of bathing her slippery brown body, dressing her in clothes that I washed in the bathtub, and feeding her formula mixed by hand would entitle me to enter the Ovimbundu world of love. Angolan mothers carried their babies on their backs until age two or three, rocking them to sleep there, and bringing them around front to suckle when they awoke, in a natural rhythm of body connection. I'd never seen mothers impatient or angry with their small children. Through Tez, I would gain a family of my own.

Tez was ravenous. Day and night she sucked down the bottles of milk I mixed for her. As predictably as the tide moved in and out of the bay in front of our house, Tez cried for milk. Before I went to sleep I fed her, and midway through the night I stumbled to her crib to feed her. At church I heard the Portuguese ladies whisper to my mother, "Nancy has circles under her eyes like a new mother."

I paid no attention to my exhaustion. I was exhilarated by the miracle of Tez plumping up. Almost minute-by-minute I noticed plushy flesh where before she had painfully thin bones. Her skin turned a glossy brown as ounces added up to pounds on the scale. Even more exciting, she smiled. The little line of worry between her eyebrows smoothed out. She chortled. She held up her head without a waver. She reached out for the rattle I held and flipped herself over in amazement. I laughed and clapped at her great feat. She was nine months old. At ten months she sat by herself and at eleven months grasped the slats in the crib and pulled herself up, compressing her infancy into a few short weeks, like the chicks I used to feed. She crowed with delight.

I was glad for the infant care book, published in the 1940s, that my mother gave me when Tezinha arrived, because I wanted to bring her up correctly. I carefully read the instructions on how to put baby on a schedule, what to feed her, and how to potty train her. Its rigid approach to caring for infants, though, clashed radically with the relaxed Umbundu style. Should I follow the intuitive ways evident in the culture all around me or should I adhere to the categorical how-to approach of this authoritative book? Without an Angolan mentor to show me the way, I chose the way of the book. Its suggestion for placing the baby on a potty starting at age four months, struck fear in me that I had delayed too long with Tez. I was afraid she'd fallen way behind schedule and that she'd never be properly trained. While I knelt over the tub, scrubbing her diapers and clothes, she sat beside me on her potty until she pooped, chirping and playing, patient with me.

The book also mandated a rigid sleeping and eating schedule and advocated placing her in a playpen when she was awake, feeding my nascent moralism. Tezinha, I felt, should follow her schedule. She and I had our first clash when I insisted it was time for her nap and she was equally insistent that she wanted to stay awake. Why, I wondered, would she refuse to lie down? Why did she pop upright when I tried to put her down? She knew she was supposed to go to sleep. I rapped her once, twice, three times on her knuckles to force her to let go of the crib railing. With a great wail, she plunked down in bed but within seconds she pulled herself up again. I rapped her knuckles again, harder. Sobbing, she lay down. Suddenly I became aware that Mãe, our laundry lady, stood in the door. My room was just above the laundry area and Tez's screams must have been easy to hear. Crying babies in her culture were tended to immediately. Ashamed of my cruelty and embarrassed to have been found out, I froze in place. Mãe looked worriedly at Tez, who continued to cry, until she could stand it no longer. She rushed over to Tez, scooped her up, and comforted her.

The mission of bringing up Tez, the thrilling job I had pleaded my mother for, was rattling me. My longing to immerse myself in Ovimbundu-ness had been usurped by the strictures in the book my mother gave me. I no longer knew what was right. The book laid out in detail exactly the schedule baby should follow and I reasoned that this would also be my mother's advice. Mãe was showing me a different path, but one I couldn't intuit. The older Tez got, the more feisty her opinions, the less I knew how to cope. Full of shame, I sank into a discouraged gloom. Tez was here because I had insisted my mother find me an orphan. "OK," she'd said, "the rest of the family will love her and play with her, but you will be responsible for her. I don't want any extra work to fall on Tomás or Mãe or Cipriano." I would be charged with making Tez's food, washing her clothes, and watching out for her day and night. Now I was failing. I wasn't allowed to depend on Mãe and I had no right to ask Mom for help. I had learned from my mother's relentless cheer to keep bad news from her. I plodded through my chores and care taking, wondering how I could continue. Slowly, as I made Tez's milk and washed her diapers, walked with her on the beach and bathed her, the worm of melancholy burrowed in and made me question my very life. I wasn't taking good care of Tez. What use was I?

I brooded especially during the repetitive task of mixing milk in an empty kitchen. In the still space my despair had free rein, unhampered by the need to keep a good face on. I dipped cooled boiled water out of the pot on the stove. *I wish someone would help me.* I hadn't known, I just hadn't known how hard this would be. I measured the powdered milk and sugar. I mixed the milk and sugar with water, stirring them to a smooth paste. I dipped my finger in the mixture and tasted the sweetness. *I'm sure Mom and Dad will be sorry when I'm gone.* I pictured them stricken on the verandah, my mother clinging to my father, my father draped over my mother. I could almost hear their sobs from the kitchen where I lurked, invisible and ghostly. I thinned the paste and poured the milk into Tez's bottles. I sterilized the nipples and sealed the milk in. I was surely a failure.

The notion that I could bring my despair to my mother never entered my mind. She was always busy. Dramatic action, thankfully, also was foreign to me, and I had time to mull over my best course. I loved Tez fiercely and protectively, even as she baffled me. If I weren't here to care for her, who would? My sister loved Tez, I knew that, but she was too busy with school. My parents were occupied with their work, my brothers were too young, and Mãe and our cook and houseman had their hands full. In the end, it was Tezinha who kept me anchored in life. Leaving Tez alone seemed worse than the relief I imagined from dying. I stayed alive for her.

Early in January of 1960, just as Tez was on the verge of walking, she, my mother, sister, and I boarded the train. Kathy and I were on our way to school in Rhodesia, and Tezinha was returning to her family upcountry.

During the overnight train ride, Tez slept with me, snug on the inner side of my bunk. I recalled the scrawny bundle I'd been given at the train station in Lobito, how fragile she had been five months earlier. Proudly I stroked the robust child beside me now, with her muscled legs. Under my care, she had grown to a toddler, greedily eating her way out of infancy. I put my arm around her silky body protectively, even jealously. I had no idea what her family was like and was sure they couldn't love her as much as I. But if they didn't, what would become of her? She had seared herself into my soul, and I wondered if I could let her go, if I could undo the chemistry in the few hours I had left.

After we stopped briefly in Vila Nova, I started counting down the minutes until we would arrive in Bela Vista. Thirty, twenty-nine, twenty-eight... Tezinha's bag of clothes, diapers, and toys sat on the seat beside me, ready to be handed out the window. Tez stood gripping the sooty windowsill, watching the grasslands go by, not suspecting that she, too, would be passed through the window into another life. We were quiet in the cabin. I kept my hand on Tez to steady her from the rocking train. And then I could feel the train slowing down. I felt a burning in my gut and my head swirled. I didn't want the train to stop. I heard the squeal of the brakes and the whistle warning us that Bela Vista lay just ahead. I pushed up the window to look at the familiar red dirt of nearby Dondi. I could see the back of Fadário's general store a block away on the main street, where we used to stock up on gum on Saturdays. We stopped with a hiss in front of the brick station. The crowd surged forward, anxious to get on in the brief moments before the train chugged on to Chinguar.

"Mom, who's coming to get Tezinha?" I asked.

"Probably Aunt Lillian," she answered.

Aunt Lillian saw us just as we spied her, a large woman with short dark brown hair and a plump, smiling face. Knowing that she was a nurse reassured me about Tezinha's immediate fate. I smothered my fears about Tez's spectral family.

I picked up Tez for a last touch. Her soft hair tickled my nose when I nuzzled the top of her head and nibbled my way down her wide forehead to kiss her on her nose. She grinned at me and grabbed my face in an impulsive wet baby-kiss, as if she wanted to eat me. I wanted to hug her back, to squeeze the breath out of her, but Mom said we had to let her go because the conductor was already yelling *partida* [all aboard]. I passed Tez and her bags out the window into Aunt Lillian's outstretched arms. The train whistled, lurched, and moved on. I waved until I was simply waving at the African savannah, until Tez's kiss dried on my cheek.

"Well, on to Rhodesia," said my mother.

I sank back into the seat.

I stashed Tez inside of me with all my tenderness, guilt, attachment, and loss, and I carried on.

About a year after I left Tez, war broke out in Angola, a war that would last until the new century. It started as an anti-colonial conflict. In 1975, after fourteen years of fighting to preserve her colonies, Portugal suddenly gave them independence, handing Angola over to the socialist revolutionary government allied with the Soviet Union. In the ensuing chaos, the war for independence evolved into a decades-long grueling civil war, a war that split me off from my childhood and Tezinha. Had there been no war, I might have visited her village when I was home on holidays. I never saw her again.

As I look back on that time, the notion that we could simply hand Tez out the window of the train as we whistle-stopped in Bela Vista is absurd. But that is what we did, with little sense of the impact on her psyche or on ours.

Still, forty-five years later, all those afternoons learning Umbundu with Rebeca and those months of nurturing Tez count for something. I know now I could never be fully Umbundu or Portuguese, but my Umbundu lessons took on new meaning recently when I unexpectedly received a letter from Rebeca. She wrote in Portuguese that she intended to break the long silence between us. She reminisced about the good times we'd had at the Casa Missionária, as we sipped our cold juice, walked in the garden, and swam on the beach so close to the house. She remembered my stories about Padre Alberto. Finally she listed her seven children and their considerable accomplishments: Silvia was a doctor specializing in cardiology, Álvaro was a vet, Alda was in medical school, and her two youngest, Afonso and Felisimina, were in tenth and eleventh grades. But her notes about her middle sons Valentim and Gilberto, who were well past high school age but were both in twelfth grade, reminded me of the reason for the years of silence: the terrible war, that engulfed Rebeca's family, drove me from Angola and continued unabated for forty years.

I have little hope that Tezinha's life after 1960 will ever be revealed to me. From the time she was two Angola was at war. I don't know if she and her family were spared disruption, hunger, or even death, as hundreds of thousands of Angolans fled to neighboring countries and more were killed and maimed by land mines. By the end of the war, Angola was one of the most land-mined countries in the world. Through all the unknowns, though, she has remained a part of the child-mother in me, a profound connection with my Angolan childhood. When my own two sons were babies, the lessons I learned from her encouraged me not to go by the book and to trust myself.

As I stand on the American side of the Atlantic Ocean, I conjure up the bay in front of my Angolan home. I remember countless hours of building cities in the sand, diving off our tilting raft to touch the gently swaying tentacles of the anemones, collecting sand dollars to skip across the flat water, watching the ships steam by. I see Rebeca and me strolling along the beach and Tez crawling full tilt into the salty water. In my fourteenth year, I dove into their Umbundu culture. Forty-five years later, the salt of my love for Rebeca and Tez still glazes my heart.

Poem: Riches

English, at birth
The language of my mother
Portuguese, at two
The tongue of Vitelina
French, at thirteen
Taught by Padre Alberto
Umbundu, at thirteen
Coached by Rebeca
Latin, at fourteen
My Rhodesian challenge

Chapter 9 — Native Tongues

Nda ki siki, o pulungunja; wa tuna wa asa.
Embora não toque boa música,
improvise alguma coisa com os instrumentos que tem.
Even though it doesn't sound like good music,
improvise with the instruments you have.

                                                   Umbundu proverb

"East, west, home's best," the proverb says. Home is where everyone speaks your language. Home is where you learn your mother tongue, where you learn to think like a native. For me, who, at fourteen, understood four languages, home was language itself, a kind of sonar by which I made my way through the blind confusions of a dislocated life.

By adolescence, I had spent much of my life away from home. Despite my status as an *estrangeira* in Angola, I had always felt connected to the people, places, and languages of those around me. I had learned Portuguese along with English, then French, and then Umbundu from Rebeca Valentim. But at fourteen, I was split off from all that. My parents arranged for my sister and me to go to high school in English, with teachers and peers who would challenge us. The closest English school was a ten-day train ride away in Rhodesia. Perching by the window, leaning into the glass, I watched the landscape change from scrub savanna to woodlands until it all merged into a blurred negative streaking past my window. With eyes closed, I felt as if at any moment I might fall off the edge of the earth. Detached and disoriented, I reflected on the hard truth that in Rhodesia I would know no one but my sister. I was trading Portuguese colonial society for British, Angolan Umbundu for Rhodesian Shona culture, a warm temperate climate for colder southern air, American education for British, family and orphan baby for a dorm and school full of strangers.

I was acutely aware that, while I was gone, my family would move from our coastal home in Lobito to a remote and unfamiliar mission. Before, when I was away at school, Lobito had been my constant, my anchor. I'd daydream of home and know that was where I'd return. Now, when I stared into the distance, both future home and school hung featureless. There were no sounds of water lapping on the beach, no fishing boats gliding by, no palm leaves rustling, no images at all upon which to fasten my longings. And in Rhodesia there'd be no community of language, no melding and layering of Portuguese and Umbundu, to bind me securely to the people I loved or to the person I knew as Nancy Henderson.

Our long train trip included a layover at Victoria Falls, on the border of Northern and Southern Rhodesia. The Zambezi River, about a mile wide at the falls, roared as it plunged 355 feet into the channel below, giving it the name Mosi Oa Tunya, "Smoke That Thunders." The mist-shrouded grasses and trees, the majestic sweep of the falls were our welcome to the beauty of Rhodesia. But so were the heart-stopping force of the water and the rumble of thunder. When we sat on the Victoria Falls hotel patio for a cool drink in the evening, a troop of baboons sat around the edges, watching us. Occasionally they loped in to snatch a marmite sandwich.

Once we arrived in Salisbury, Mom stayed a few days to register Kathy and me at Hatfield Girls' High School and settle us into our dorms. As had happened our first year in Dondi, when I lived with the Collins and Kathy with the Tuckers, that first year in Rhodesia we stayed in separate dorms each run by a different missionary organization. Hatfield Girls' High was an all-white British public high school, in the American sense of public. Most of the students at the school lived with their British colonial families of shopkeepers, farmers, and mechanics in nearby neighborhoods of that rural district outside Salisbury. Only about twenty of us at Hatfield came from other parts of southern Africa, to board in the dorms set up to care for missionary kids. The school year, which began in late January and ended in December, was divided into three terms of approximately three months each, with several weeks of holiday between terms. When we said goodbye to Mom, she told us we could expect to return to Angola in May during the first term "hols," and also the Christmas holidays in December.

Hatfield's campus turned inward to a grassy, central courtyard, where we gathered for assemblies and ceremonies, presided over by Miss Humphries, our head mistress. A no-nonsense, but understanding and welcoming woman, she took special interest in the missionary kids under her charge. I would later hear her offer up one of us as an example of an excellent scholar to be emulated by her British students.

On my first day at Hatfield Girls' High School, I was ashamed to find myself placed in the lowest level of Form One, One-E, sitting among younger kids who didn't care about school. This was the challenge my parents had sent me thousands of miles to seek? It confirmed a secret dread: I deserved whatever I got. And so I kept silent. I felt at the mercy of the adults around me, as though I didn't have a say in my own life. That passivity developed at home first, where I was ultra sensitive to anyone thinking I was stupid.

Once I ventured the opinion that a little Portuguese girl we knew was "really spoiled." My mother sarcastically said, "Oh, you noticed, huh?" I decided it was better to keep my mouth shut than to risk saying something obtuse. By the end of the week at Hatfield, though, my teachers moved me from Form One-E to Form Two-A, with girls my age and academic level. I regained confidence in my parents' charge to go forth and compete. I was assigned the usual classes: English, Math, Science, History, French, and, most wonderful of all, Latin.

Working me into Hatfield's Latin syllabus had been tricky. Miss Humphries, who helped me set up my new schedule, told me that at Hatfield everyone started Latin in Form One. But she devised a way for me to stay in Form Two and still take Latin One. "Do you think you could learn two years of Latin in one," she asked me, " and catch up with your Form Two classmates by the end of the school year?"

"Yes! I'm sure I can," I said. I cleaved to Miss Humphries' charge. She was my ally in this strange land. If she believed I could tackle two years of Latin in one, then I would. If Miss Humphries had asked me to walk to Bulawayo, miles away, I would have put on my marching boots.

On my first day in Latin, Miss Moore handed me a Latin One book and instructed me to start working through it. She would be busy teaching Latin Two. I sat in the back corner of the classroom crammed with students, my desk scrunched up against the wall, staring at my teacher and the backs of my classmates. With a crisp British accent, Miss Moore explained the imperfect subjunctive passive, writing sentences in English and Latin on the blackboard.

"He ordered his soldiers to do this. Militibus imperavit ut hoc facerent."

Miss Moore's black academic robe billowed as she turned from the board to give the class a translating assignment. She shoved her glasses up on her thin nose. I shifted my gaze through the window to the hockey fields and to the pool in the distance, where I would join the swim team after school. I wondered if I'd be chosen to go with the team to the big competition in Umtali. Umtali would be an overnight train ride going east toward Mozambique, into the mountains of Rhodesia, turned lush and beautiful with the rains.

The sounds of Latin in the classroom carried me back to Lobito and the Latin on my sister's record player the previous year.

"Italia non est insula. Italia est paeninsula."

Each syllable pronounced clearly and deliberately. The p-a-e in paeninsula pronounced pay. The s-u in insula and paeninsula said with a long u. Pay-nin-su-la. We worked on our studies upstairs on the verandah, away from the commotion of the house, with my desk on the front side of the house and Kathy around the corner. I had wondered, as I listened to the Latin sounds, how the speaker even knew how to pronounce it, for wasn't Latin a dead language?

Now I was thrilled to be learning Latin myself. Every day I wended my way to the back of the crowded classroom. My classmates and I, dressed in light blue cotton frocks and dark blue blazers, fluttered like a flock of birds into our seats. But despite our identical feathers, I chirped a different tune. Leaving class one day, I tried to catch my teacher's eye. I stood near her desk, planning to tell her what lesson I was on, but she didn't notice me. I was too shy to speak up, perhaps a result of too many years living in dorms. I'd developed the habit of letting others, whether dorm parents or peers, make the decisions and I was usually content to follow. If I became angry, I usually expressed it in a sly and underhanded way, never openly. When Miss Moore continued erasing the board with long, slow sweeps of her arm, I didn't press the issue.

Every day in Latin, I tuned out Miss Moore, as she instructed the class, and the class, as it responded and recited. I opened my book and began reading. Latin had French beat when it came to regularity, structure, and complexity. I had to memorize six noun declensions, with ridiculous names like genitive and ablative, and four verb conjugations. I ignored the absurdity of it and concentrated on rote memorization. I made a virtue of learning the structure faster than any of my peers could have. I took note of where the class was in its lessons and each day I tried to gain ground on Latin Two.

When first term came to a close at the end of April, I set Latin aside, satisfied that I was on track. I was both happy to be going home and melancholy, knowing this holiday would be the last time I lived in Lobito. We were coming to help Mom and Dad pack up the house for the family's big move inland to Bunjei. The train passed Bocoio. It passed by Aunt Marjory's back yard in Benguela, and the sugar cane fields of Catumbela. It slid into the Lobito station. Dad and Mark, who was six, met us at the train. "Mommy's back is hurting her," Mark informed us, "so she couldn't come to the train."

We drove home to Tomás, clanking pots in the kitchen as he prepared a dinner of baked fish, smothered in onions, peppers, and tomatoes. Mãe was shaking the ashes out of her iron under the shade of the tulip tree.

In full bloom, the ragged fringes of the scarlet flowers opened bell-like to yellow throats. "Bom dia," I said to them in greeting. Though Mom was in bed, we could hear the warm vibrato of her soprano voice singing snatches from an aria. It felt good to find everything in order. Mom couldn't do any of the stooping, lifting, and hauling required, to prepare for the move, but she had no trouble directing Kathy and me. "The books in the living room need packing, then move to my office," she'd say. "You'll also need to sort through all your dolls, to decide which to keep and which to give away, and the same with all your books."

Between packing chores, I read a book, played the piano, wandered on the beach, took the bus downtown to immerse myself in the tumble of Umbundu and Portuguese. Our old friends Josinda, Belinha, and Rebeca visited. Chattering with them in Portuguese about life and school in Rhodesia helped soak the language back into my soul. But too soon, we had to retrace our steps back to Rhodesia for the second and third terms.

Latin came right back to me after the hols. I dug in deep, each day plowing a page or two closer to Form Two. Though I wished I were part of the class, by myself I could work faster. Learning Latin was what saved me from my perennial lack of confidence during my first year in Rhodesia. It gave me a meaty test of character and boosted belief in myself. I was certain I'd make my goal.

When second term ended in August, we stayed in Rhodesia. Mom and Dad couldn't afford to bring Kathy and me home so soon after the May holidays. We were invited to spend the hols with Gladys Merritt's family. Gladys, who had a happy grin and flaming red hair, was in Form Two with me, but I didn't know her well because she lived in Kathy's dorm. Barbara Schaad, one of my roommates who was also from Angola, was invited as well. Gladys's parents, missionaries in a fundamentalist denomination, lived several hours' drive from Salisbury. Mrs. Merritt once had been a guest in my parents' home and seemed delighted to reciprocate by taking care of Kathy and me. She let us sleep in late and fed us well. Mr. Merritt took us around to local villages to participate in prayer meetings. Gladys, Barbara, Kathy, and I formed a quartet to warble hymns for the gatherings. As a believer in bringing souls to Jesus, Mr. Merritt also pushed us forward to witness our faith.

Growing up, I'd never practiced witnessing. Publicly proclaiming Jesus as Lord and inviting strangers to embrace Him was a foreign tongue to me. I had recently been introduced to the language of redemption and salvation when Billy Graham had brought his crusade to Salisbury, but I still felt awkward talking about it. Mr. Merritt was a fluent evangelist and he wouldn't allow us to hang back. "Tell them how much you love the Lord Jesus Christ," Mr. Merritt would say. Along with the other three girls, I'd step forward, clearing my throat, clasping my trembling hands behind my back. "I'm happy to claim Jesus as my Lord," I'd say, brief and to the point, in my quiet voice. Mr. Merritt made me anxious to get back to the more comfortable requirements of Latin.

Back in Salisbury for our third term, classes resumed. "Only one more term to catch up with Form Two Latin," I said, giving myself a pep talk. Somewhere in the middle of second term, I had glided, without ceremony, from first to second year Latin. My teacher had given me my exam, a passing mark, and my new Form Two Latin book, as if it were an everyday event. My eye was so riveted on the goal that, even to me, it seemed insignificant. What was important was my final, triumphant entrance into full Form Two membership, when I finished that last page of the Latin Two book.

Toward the end of third term, I allowed myself to become excited about going home to Angola for Christmas. I had one small worry. How would I know if I had come home to *myself* on the new mission my parents had moved to, where everyone and everything would be unfamiliar? I wondered if my spirit still lingered in Lobito, for it surely hadn't migrated to Rhodesia. Somewhere, I believed that my true self roosted solidly, soared confidently, but not here. Here I fluttered on the edge of things, barely keeping my balance, afraid I'd lose my perch and free-fall into space.

I missed my parents. The closer we got to exams, the more the kids in my dorm felt sad, lonely, and teary. Mrs. Glegg and Miss Manson, our dorm parents, didn't understand why we were so crabby and on edge. I wrote home, "I've been feeling bad. I can't talk to anyone about it except Barbara and Ruthanne, and they feel just as sad as I do. The younger kids have been fighting about stupid things. Rosemary tells the slobbery dog to get out of her room, so Flora gets mad at Rosemary and kicks the cats. But don't worry about me, I'll get over it soon."

I was nervous about returning to my family, whom I hadn't seen for seven months. I wondered how I would fit in. My little brothers would be much taller. David, whose tenth birthday loomed, might even be bigger than me. I was afraid that, away from Lobito, I would feel like a visiting stranger. My stomach hurt when I thought about Mom and Dad. I had to will them away to prepare for finals.

I studied Latin furiously, staying up until midnight or waking up at four o'clock in the morning. Latin had seeped into every crevice of my brain. I was drunk on it. It banished loneliness and overwhelmed homesickness. By exam time, I was giddy with excitement. I couldn't believe that I was only a few lessons away from completing Latin Two. As I sat in the exam, though, a fog misted out the Latin. My brain, recently so agile and cooperative, became snared in a haze as sticky as cotton candy, and I sensed that all my Latin was an incoherent mess. In desperation I guessed at dozens of words in the English translation exercise. Stabbing wildly at answers cleared my viscous mind. I quit worrying about the results and let the Latin float free, and, by the time I had finished, I was exhilarated. I fought through the exam and came in third in the class! I was delighted with myself. I (and Miss Humphries) had known I could do it. I smiled and shivered with excitement as I wrote home to Mom and Dad to tell them the good news and let them know they had been right to be confident in me.

I could hardly wait for our year-end awards ceremony. The whole school crammed into the courtyard as Miss Humphries presided over the restless bunch of students. She recited the high points of the school year, the music competition our choral group had won, and the triumphs on the athletic fields. And then she turned the program over to the teachers to present awards to their especially worthy students. I sat on my folding chair, trying to appear nonchalant, but smiling broadly. I knew that very soon my Latin teacher was going to walk up to the podium and call my name. I was sure to receive the award for most-improved in Latin. After all, how much more improvement could you make than learning two years of Latin in one? My Latin classmates would look amazed and murmur their congratulations. Miss Humphries would smile at me as she shook my hand and we'd share a secret pride in my accomplishment. I only hoped my shyness wouldn't prevent me from acknowledging the best wishes of the audience.

My Latin teacher strode up front. She arranged the certificates and her notes on the podium and called out briskly, "Mary Keillor, please come forward."

Mary inched her way through the seated crowd, her wide hips knocking against the girls squeezed into the tight rows.

"Mary, I present to you the award for Best Latin Two Student."

Mary grinned as she walked back to her seat. I smiled and nodded. Mary deserved that award. Still I envied the easy way she approached life. I felt so serious in my work. True, my labor bore fruit, but I wished for a more graceful, carefree route to the harvest. More like Mary. Instead my life was full of struggle, doubt, and fear.

Now, I thought, my envy churning into anticipation, it's my turn. I sat forward, my heart beating so hard I thought my classmates could hear it, so hard that it muted the words my teacher was saying. It seemed like she was whispering.

"And now for the Most Improved Latin Two Student," I thought she said. I strained to hear my name.

"Sheila Blackwell."

Not Sheila! I couldn't believe it. I felt like standing up and yelling, "Unfair! I was better than Sheila. Don't you think that coming in third in the whole class deserves recognition?" I wanted Miss Humphries to know that her faith in me was well placed.

But they were on to other teachers and awards and I slumped back in my seat.

I didn't even care when my name was announced to receive a copy of *Wuthering Heights* in recognition of good work in English. I swallowed my disappointment and graciously accepted the book, even though I most coveted the Latin award. I didn't need an award in English. English hadn't prevented me from being a full-fledged member of Form Two. Latin had stood in my way, kept me struggling to prove myself. Until I could show that I deserved Miss Humphries' confidence, I'd never find my place—in class or in Rhodesia. Learning Latin, two years in one, was my price for joining Form Two, for being part of Hatfield Girls High School, and I knew I deserved the Most Improved award. It would have clinched my position publicly, for all to see that, yes, Nancy Henderson did belong.

Even well into my forties I struggled with the problem of belonging. I was a second-guesser, never confident in my own ideas, my own desires. The combination of adjusting to multiple cultures and homes, trying to fit in, and wondering how securely I was a member of my family drove me to search for identity and validation outside my self. My brother David has agreed that he didn't have a sense of individual identity within the family. He formed his once he left. My sister, who has been estranged from the family for years, once pointedly told me that she didn't consider me part of her family. And my friend Barbara told me that even in her late fifties, "I have not found my niche, either culturally or spiritually." Though everyone the world over is formed by the interaction of our genetics and our experiences, I think it is fair to say that many children who are raised outside their native cultures and away from their families develop typical patterns of feeling inept, outsiders even to themselves. One respondent to my survey said she "always feels different and like I don't quite fit in anywhere here in the United States." Another said she has "few ties to people and places." A 2003 doctoral dissertation by Patsy Shealy studied military brats. She identified as common themes "a conflicted inner sense of self, rootlessness and a sense of not belonging, and loneliness and detachment." Only in the last fifteen years, through writing, solitude, and therapy, have I located an authentic core. The discipline of sitting at my keyboard, recording the memories that bubbled up, has allowed the self to emerge. Extended periods of solitude have helped me make peace with my own beliefs, opinions, strengths, and weaknesses.

It felt odd going "home" to Bunjei for Christmas break. This time we flew all the way: from Salisbury, to Lourenço Marques in Mozambique, to Luanda in Angola, to Nova Lisboa, where our parents and brothers met us. From there, we drove the 150 kilometers south to Bunjei. Being in new surroundings helped mask the embarrassment I felt around my family. *What can I talk to them about?* I thought. *So much happened in Salisbury, but now I can't remember any of it. After a year, I barely know them.* I felt like I couldn't expect much more of my family than I could of this new mission. Bunjei, much tinier and more remote than Dondi, didn't call for much exploration. The church and the elementary boarding school for Angolan kids, who came from the surrounding district, were on one end of the mission. The hospital, where Uncle Bob McGowan worked, was on the other end. Interspersed along the red dirt avenue between school and hospital were the missionary houses: the McGowans', Aunt Betty Gilchrist's, and ours. Our house was built of the red-brick found in all the mission buildings, with the usual graceful arches on the porches. It felt like mine only because Mom had furnished it with familiar pieces, the glass front bookcases, my old blue dresser, and our beds, that they had moved from Lobito.

I don't recall leaving the confines of the mission in the six weeks of vacation, except to learn how to drive. Now that Kathy and I were sixteen and fifteen, Dad decided we were old enough to handle a car. He would drive our Land Rover out of the mission, safely past any pedestrians or bicyclists. Then he'd turn us loose on the empty, rugged road shooting straight into the distance, with scrub brush on either side as far as the eye could see. Driving was like learning a new language, building a vocabulary of clutches and gears, gaining fluency with the structure of the vehicle and the idiom of shifting. Dad would sit beside me, wincing, as I lurched and jerked the car from one gear to another. Once I reached cruising speed, I'd career down the road, paying little attention to avoiding the ruts or slowing down on the washboard. The vehicle took each bounce with a stiff clunk. I'd grasp the steering wheel with all my strength to keep the Land Rover, which was more truck than car, in the center of the road. Dad would grip his barely cushioned seat and try not to hit his head on the ceiling, speaking volumes with his body, hardly at all with his voice. Over time, I subdued the beast of a truck. I learned to shift more gracefully and to anticipate the rough road, to the great, though unspoken, relief of my father.

At the end of January 1961, we said good-bye to Mom, Dad, the boys, and Bunjei and flew back to Salisbury for the start of the new school year.

Finally in sync with my class as a Form Three student, I realized that while I hadn't gotten the public recognition I craved, I had been claimed by Latin, more deeply and completely than any public honor could have shown. No longer relegated to the back corner, I talked and joked with the kids around me, especially with Mary Keillor. Mary's family was from Scotland, but she had lived in Rhodesia all her life. After school, she went home and I went to my dorm. But, in school our shared love for Latin and surprisingly similar political beliefs scaffolded a friendship in some ways deeper than my bonds with my dorm mates.

One day, Miss Crowther-Smith, our English teacher, provoked a discussion about race relations. "Let's suppose that tomorrow black and white Rhodesians were to start going to school together," she said. "How would you react to that?"

"*Kaffirs* aren't smart enough to go to school with us," or "*Kaffirs* and whites aren't meant to be together," were the typical remarks of our classmates.

Mary, Gladys, and I were the only kids in the class who said we wouldn't mind going to school with black Rhodesians. Of course, I thought, Gladys and I should vote that way. After all, weren't we missionary kids? But Mary impressed me. Though she'd lived here all her life, she could see the injustice of white Rhodesians treating the Africans badly. We were political soul mates, and after I left Rhodesia, I corresponded with her for a few years.

But, more than her politics, I loved Mary's sense of humor. We both had this crazy notion that we should be able to speak Latin. Latin isn't a spoken language, but so what? Mary and I formed our own little society, our sisterhood in Latin. For us learning Latin wasn't odious drudgery. It made our spirits soar. It made us laugh. Latin connected us, the Rhodesian girl and the American girl. During class breaks we strolled along the breezeway that ran in front of our classrooms, trying to converse in Latin.

"Quam est puella cum corona?" [Which is the girl with the crown?]

"Non est corona, est barba." [That's not a crown, it's a beard.]

If we couldn't find the words to complete our thoughts, we would resort to French or even Pig Latin.

Then I'd look at her and we'd burst out laughing, clutching our sides, leaning over the banister and sending our giggles into the courtyard below. Our laughter lifted like birds into the African breeze, like the resourceful English swallows that migrate across Europe, over the Mediterranean Sea, to nest in Africa.

Talking to my Rhodesian friend, in dead Latin, I had found a home.

Chapter 10 — The Passion Years

Njupe kuvi, ku ka njupe komanu.
Corrija os meus erros, mas não me separe dos amigos.
Correct my mistakes but don't separate me from my friends.
Umbundu proverb

I found my intellectual home in Latin at Hatfield Girls' High. Teenage passions, though, could only be expressed in the intimate quarters of my dormitory, where, in the peculiar missionary brew of close female friendships, enforced segregation of the sexes, and youthful interpretations of religion, we explored our sexuality.

I stayed at the Africa Missionary Fellowship (A.M.F.) dorm, run by the Gleggs, a British couple who had been active in Christian youth ministry in England. They had immigrated to Rhodesia to open a dorm for missionary children. A.M.F. was the last house on a dirt road seven miles from the center of Salisbury. It stood on several acres with lawns, tall pines, gardens, and woods, and was surrounded by grasslands, boulders, and an occasional neighborhood store. A.M.F., T.E.A.M., my sister's dorm, and Hatfield Girls' High, a five-mile bike ride from our dorms, were the points on a more-or-less equilateral triangle in the same rural district.

An immense, round boulder immediately outside the fence signaled the turn onto A.M.F. property. It afforded a panoramic view of the Rhodesian countryside. Downtown Salisbury spiked in the distance, and closer by, the tall grasses changed from green to brown as we passed through the wet and dry seasons. A neighbor's house was just barely visible through the trees lining the road. Down the long drive, the entrance to the one-story, white stucco house was through a vine-draped porch, flanked by two bay windows with tile roofs. The house boarded twenty missionary kids ranging in age from eight to eighteen, about evenly divided between boys and girls.

The Gleggs supervised the boys' wing and lived in a small apartment with their three children, Alastair, Fiona, and Flora. Alastair attended University College in town. He was tall and handsome in an aristocratic way, and produced romantic crushes in some of the girls. I thought he was arrogant. Now I don't know whether that reflected my shyness and lack of confidence around boys or his actual personality. Fiona was in Form Five or Six at Hatfield and was nicknamed Pudding, perhaps because she was plump. I became her victim in a game that from a distance feels more like torture. She found out I was very ticklish and would set to work on me until I was rolling on the floor in the hallway of the dorm, almost sobbing with laughter and torment, and begging her to quit. Twelve-year-old Flora was tall and chubby and had a mean streak. I suppose that sharing her parents with twenty other children put her in a bad mood. Since she was younger, I ignored her. Their mother, Mabel Glegg, tall, sharp in manner, and intellectual, was a former medical doctor. Their father, Donal Glegg, a former minister, was almost blind from diabetes. His daily insulin shots left little spots of red on his white dress shirts and at meals he dribbled food down his front, leaving stains. We called them Magee and Pagee (with a hard 'g'). On the girls' side of the dorm we were guided by Miss Manson, a Scottish woman in her forties, whose soft brogue matched her gentle personality. She fluttered fussily about us and never liked to give us direct orders.

"Girils," she'd say with a trill, "don't you think it might be time for bed?"

We pretended we were oblivious to her hints, forcing her to be straight with us.

Soon after I settled into A.M.F., my roommates Barbara, Katherine, Jane, and I took up the habit of lying in bed at night before lights out, reading passages aloud from the *Song of Solomon* in the *Bible*. We dreamed of our beloveds ravishing our hearts. I was unclear what being ravished meant, but I loved the voluptuous language. We found ample food for thought there about the major puzzle of our lives, sex. I thought God was speaking to me when I ran across this passage in the *Song of Solomon:* "My beloved is like a roe or a young hart: behold, he standeth behind our wall, he looketh forth at the windows, shewing himself through the lattice. My beloved spake, and said unto me, Rise up, my love, my fair one, and come away."

Just the night before, the boys in the dorm had been at our window, talking, laughing, and enticing us to come outside. I already had my eye on Andrew, a tall, slim British boy from Bechuanaland.

Because religion occupied our lives, it seemed appropriate to be looking in the *Bible* for clues to sexual understanding. Besides church on Sundays, we attended youth group on Friday evenings, memorized Bible verses every Sunday afternoon, went to retreats, camps, and Billy Graham crusades. Even at our public high school we attended the extracurricular Scripture Union, led by Miss Greenshields, my history teacher. And when we imagined our parents at home, we knew they were wrapped up in church activities. God ruled their lives and, by extension, ours. He was the reason we were in

Africa. I hoped He could lead me through the sexual maze I had stumbled into at fourteen.

"Listen to this," I said. "'Let him kiss me with the kisses of his mouth: for thy love is better than wine...He brought me to the banqueting house, and his banner over me was love. Stay me with flagons, comfort me with apples: for I am sick of love.'"

"Sick of love. Do you think this really means she's tired of love?" I asked my roommates. "How could anyone be sick of love? Maybe what it means is that love has filled her so full that she feels she'll burst."

I imagined myself lying on the couch with a bloated heart, fed a diet of milk, honey and love. As I languished there, "his left hand is under my head, and his right hand doth embrace me." I nestled into my bedding, feeling warm and shivery.

The right hand embracing me couldn't possibly be Andrew's. Touching Andrew was a distant fantasy. One of the first warnings I received from my roommates, when I moved into A.M.F., was "Don't talk to the boys." Barbara cautioned that, according to Mrs. Glegg, we couldn't talk to the boys at the dining table, even if I was sitting next to one. Mrs. Glegg reminded me of Aunt Jean in looks and personality. They were both exceptionally tall women in their forties, with wide-set eyes, sharp noses, and broad faces. Like Aunt Jean, Mrs. Glegg was opinionated and showed little interest in learning about the kids in her charge.

One Saturday morning I stayed home from the swimming pool to finish washing my clothes in the tub. Mrs. Glegg chose that day to make a swing through the girls' side and she found me alone, busy at work.

"What on earth are you doing here? Why aren't you swimming? You'll never make a good mother because you take far too long to do everything," she pecked at me.

Her keen eyes searched mine and I silently looked down. But I thought angrily how she had never tried to find out anything about me. I had already been a mother to Tez for five months. Two and a half short months earlier I had handed Tez out of the train window and out of my life, but I found her in every baby I encountered in Salisbury. I cuddled the Thrussel baby, whose family gave me a ride to church on Sundays, and I worked in the crèche at church, tending the babies while their parents attended the service. I smelled Tez in the fragrance of the mimosa blossoms. These were secret losses and longings I would never share with Mrs. Glegg, whom I'd never seen hugging Flora, her own daughter.

You can go jump on it, I thought.

The boys were clearly favored by the Gleggs. Even the youngest boys, the "little boys," as we called them, had more freedom than the girls to roam outside after six o'clock in the evening. In my fifteen months at A.M.F. I was invited only once into the Gleggs' sitting room. For prayer, not because they were being sociable. In truth, Miss Manson was a far more palatable dorm mother than Mrs. Glegg, but I couldn't help feeling we were treated as second best over on the girls' side. From my adolescent perspective, Mrs. Glegg's defining characteristic was her obsession with the perils of sex, especially for the girls. Barbara had warned me, "Magee will stare right through you and interrupt your conversation, if she finds you talking to a boy."

Before I had even laid eyes on the boys, they had turned into scary creatures. I didn't know their names nor where they were from for days after I arrived. I didn't want to attract Mrs. Glegg's stare. When she drew up her already tall frame, she was a giant hawk. She'd fix me with her sharp eyes, scanning my soul for thoughts of boys, love, or sex.

According to the *Song of Solomon*, love (and sex, I supposed) consumed the beloveds. Love was sensual and beautiful. The *Bible*, source of religious understanding, told me that love and sex were wonderful. Mrs. Glegg, source of adult authority, disapproved of it. She even seemed to be scared of it. I was caught in a snarl of messages issued by the powers in my life. I decided to write to my father, my personal authority on religion, although I approached the subject very generally.

"Daddy, my roommates and I have been reading the *Bible* at night before we go to sleep and we don't understand the *Song of Solomon*. Can you tell me what it means?" But he never responded. By that time, after four years of living away at school, I no longer expected my concerns to be addressed from afar by my parents, and I didn't nag at him to reply. Still I thought, as a man of God, he must have some idea what the *Song of Solomon* was all about. I puzzled on, relying on my roommates' opinions and my own sense of right and wrong.

So when the boys came around to our window at night, I stood silently, afraid to say anything. I hoped that Andrew would be in the group; maybe I'd catch his eye. Talking to the boys didn't seem so awful to me. At home in Lobito the previous year, my parents didn't care whether we chatted with the Portuguese boys in our youth group. I had been secretly fond of Júlio, with his olive skin and thatch of black hair that curled in a thick and charming pile atop his head, but sensed that our cultural differences made him taboo. In Rhodesia, how could talking to fellow missionary kids be against the rules? I couldn't take these rules seriously. I hadn't lived at A.M.F. long before I concluded that not talking to the boys was unnatural, as ridiculous as trying to defeat the earth's magnetic forces. How dangerous could it be for me to chat with whomever was sitting next to me at the dining table? I wondered against what danger we were being protected, when the girls had to be inside way before the boys. When dark fell at six o'clock in the evening, Miss Manson would lock our outside doors, trapping us inside while the boys still played outside.

"Why can't we go out? What's so wrong with playing tag?" we asked. We hammered her with protests and questions, but she stood firm. I didn't hold a grudge against Miss Manson, though, because I knew she also chafed against the Gleggs' rules. The boys visited Miss Manson at her window at night and she winked at their visits to us. I never talked to her about it, but I could tell she was on our side. I saved my contempt for Magee.

I'd been at A.M.F. a couple of months when I had a taste of Magee's fears and narrow mind. As we were preparing to go to a co-ed camp during Easter break, Magee called Ruthanne, Barbara and me aside for a pep talk. "Boys don't like cheap girls. They only like decent girls," she told us, over and over. How dare she think I wasn't a decent girl? "Honestly, what does she think we are?" I fumed in my diary. I was looking forward to spending several days with my sister Kathy at camp. Oddly enough, although T.E.A.M. was more evangelical than A.M.F., the dorm parents at T.E.A.M. were much freer in allowing boy-girl friendships.

"I guess Magee thinks we'll get contaminated by the T.E.A.M. kids," I wrote.

Still, the Gleggs' relentless effort to keep boys and girls apart made me wonder if I'd really be able to tell where innocence stopped and cheapness began. The lush language in the *Song of Solomon* scared me a little. Was it really okay to talk so much about breasts and desire? To compare the breasts to clusters of grapes and to seek my beloved "by night on my bed?" I wasn't sure. At camp, I couldn't help noticing how openly Dick and Marilyn, two T.E.A.M. kids, hugged and kissed. Was Marilyn verging on cheapness?

But once back at A.M.F. I couldn't see anything wrong with talking to the boys at our windows at night. By midyear, I couldn't see anything wrong with sneaking out at night with them either. The girls had a tradition of midnight feasts, or midis. We'd wake up at midnight to gorge on potato chips, peanuts, chocolate, and coke we had bought at the neighborhood store. Occasionally we climbed out the utility room window to romp free as fairies in the moonlight. When the boys invited us outside one night, I stepped easily out the window, still sure of my innocence. Fifteen of us, all but the youngest girls and boys, played sardines in the pines far down the driveway, away from the Glegg's quarters. We darted as silently as possible in the night, looking for the hiding spot, and when we found it, we slipped in quietly and huddled on the soft pine needles. Once we accounted for everyone, we started over. Sometimes we finished the night with a game of leapfrog, trying hard to stifle our laughter. Miss Manson's bedroom window looked out on the driveway. I wonder now if she slept through all our night games or if she merely chose to ignore them.

"My, but you're all tired this morning," Mrs. Glegg would say at breakfast the next morning, and we'd smile at her with innocent, if droopy, eyes.

I tasted victory over the hawk, who scrutinized our every movement and flexed her claws, ready to pluck us away from transgression.

I'd been in Salisbury only a few weeks when the Billy Graham crusade arrived in town. Billy Graham represented a completely different style of religion from that of my parents. At home the church had "evangelical" in its name, A Igreja Evangélica de Angola, but it snared souls through social outreach. Education, health, and democracy were as important to my parents' mission as preaching. Adult literacy work and schools, promotion of public health and immunizations attracted members without crusades and aggressive proselytizing. An egalitarian structure, in which all members had a say in governing the church, appealed to and shaped my sense of social justice, but by the time I arrived in Rhodesia, set loose from family and home in Angola, I was open to Billy Graham's spiritual message of salvation and redemption from sin. My sexual energy, suppressed and distorted by Mrs. Glegg's rules, rose up in a desire to be saved. I was borne along by hymns of passion and connection.

Appropriately, Valentine's Day 1960 was the first day of the crusade. The A.M.F. kids piled into the minibus for the ride to the showgrounds where two huge tents had been erected. Kathy and the other T.E.A.M kids arrived at the same time, and we sat in our reserved seats until the crusade began. To his credit, even in 1960 colonial segregated Africa, Billy Graham insisted on an integrated crusade. The capacity crowd of black Africans and white Europeans rose to sing "Blessed Assurance."

"Blessed assurance, Jesus is mine! O what a foretaste of glory divine! Heir of salvation, purchase of God, Born of His Spirit, washed in His blood."

Jesus was mine! He had soared into my heart. The chorus allowed our lungs free rein. We sang the five simple notes of the first three lines of the

chorus at the tops of our voices. "This is my sto-ry, this is my song, Praising my Sav-ior all the day long; This is my sto-ry, this is my song." Then
we swooped into the last line with its own five lower notes, "Praising my
Sav-ior all the day long."

Our rich voices reverberating into the warm Salisbury afternoon
carried me back to the African church in Lobito. On Sundays in the Igreja
Evangélica hundreds of voices soared in four-part harmony, the basses
resonating under the melody. The whitewashed church stood stark and
austere on the salt flats, but the joyful voices floated to the rafters and out
the open windows, inviting the people to enter and participate. The music
was a magnet, pulling us in and setting our hearts buzzing with emotion.
Sitting packed on backless benches in Lobito, listening to the rustle of
shifting bodies, the occasional baby's cry, and the murmured responses of
the congregation, I felt enveloped in love and acceptance. As I sang with
the Billy Graham crowd, I was again part of an organic whole, drawn in by
the music. Rev. Joe Blinco led us in prayer following the hymn.

"Heavenly Father, we come to Thee today with fullness of heart, grateful
that Thou hast brought together all these people, all these sinners who are
ready to hear Your message and ready to throw down their cares before You,
ready to seek salvation ... in Jesus' name. Amen."

We all murmured "amen." The mayor of Salisbury welcomed the crusade,
followed by the sermon by Rev. Blinco, Billy Graham's warm-up preacher.
Rev. Blinco called to the unsaved to trust in the Lord. He called on us to
rise out of our seats and come to the front to declare the Lord our Savior. I
watched with curiosity the trickle of people turning into a stream, making
their way down front in response to his evangelistic fervor. I could feel my
heart, still swelling with the hymn, responding to Rev. Blinco's invitation. I
yearned for his recognition and for God's saving grace. But wasn't I already
saved, or at least hadn't I shared in our quieter version of being saved? I
had been confirmed in my faith at the Portuguese church in Lobito, which
had allowed me to take communion and become a full member of the
congregation when I was in eighth grade. I didn't think I needed saving, and
I didn't feel brave enough to physically stand up and walk to the front, to
make myself the object of attention. But when Billy Graham himself walked
forward in response to Rev. Blinco's call, I thought, "Well, he's already
saved and he's going up." That powerful and humble gesture stirred me and
scrambled my arguments with myself. I arrived home at A.M.F. in a daze,
wandering around the dorm, unable to concentrate on anything until supper.

That was a Sunday. I attended the crusade five more times in the next nine days. I watched as Karen, Peggy, Flora, Rosemary, and several of the little boys from A.M.F. went up front to be saved. On Monday, although it poured rain, both tents at the showgrounds were full. On Tuesday, the last night of the crusade, Billy Graham himself was scheduled to preach.

"It's not going to rain tonight," I told my friends. Even when it started sprinkling, I was sure it wouldn't rain on Rev. Graham's night, and it didn't. Throughout the crusade, I had felt a tension settling in my legs, a tension derived from wanting to say, "Yes" to the Lord, "Yes" to being swept up in the fervor of the crowd, and saying "I don't know" to myself. Each night my heart said, "Go ahead," but my legs hung inert. Each night the flow of people stopped, the crusade ended for the night, and I sat still in my seat. Tonight was my last chance to be saved. I wondered if I'd let my heart be touched and filled with the Spirit enough that I'd be able to will my body to stand up at the call.

At last Billy Graham took the podium. He looked out at us, his bushy eyebrows rising and falling as he laid out God's message of love and peace.

"The *Bible* says, 'For God so loved the world that He gave His only begotten Son, that whoever believes in Him should not perish but have everlasting life.' If God planned for us to have peace and abundant life right now, why are most people not having this experience? Because we are separated from God through sin. We choose to disobey God and go our willful way. There is only one remedy for this separation. We must receive Christ. We must trust Jesus Christ and receive him by personal invitation. For the *Bible* says, 'Behold, I stand at the door and knock. If anyone hears My voice and opens the door, I will come in to him and dine with him, and he with Me. And if you confess with your mouth the Lord Jesus and believe in your heart that God has raised Him from the dead, you will be saved.'"

I was sandwiched between Jane and Barbara, but I wasn't aware of them or the crowd around me. My attention was riveted on Billy Graham. Looking up at the podium, I remembered the hundreds of Sundays I had listened to my father preaching his sermons based on the parables and stories of the *New Testament*. I thought about the prodigal son arriving home, and how his father "had compassion, and ran, and fell on his neck, and kissed him." And the father said, "This my son was dead, and is alive again; he was lost, and is found." I imagined my father spotting me walking up our driveway in Lobito, his startled look changing to relief and joy that I was home. He'd call to Tomás to kill the fatted calf, for this his daughter was lost, and is found. And he'd hug me and lead me in to great rejoicing and I'd know I was loved.

"Is there any good reason why you cannot receive Jesus Christ right now?" Billy Graham asked.

No, no, no, I answered in my heart, I'm ready to be found.

"Here's how to receive him now. Admit your need, be willing to turn from your sins, believe that Jesus Christ died for you on the Cross and rose from the grave, and through prayer, invite Jesus Christ into your life as Lord and Savior. Let us pray. Dear Lord Jesus, we know we are sinners and need your forgiveness. Let us now turn from our sins and invite You into our hearts and lives. Let us trust and follow You as Lord. In Jesus' name. Amen."

"Amen," I said.

This time I stood up on wobbly legs, tingling with nervous excitement. I wanted Billy Graham to direct God to me, to find me and enter me. I made my way to the aisle, oblivious of the toes I might be tramping on. My arms bowed out at my sides; I tilted my head back slightly to create an open coffer of my chest, ready to be filled with God's love and forgiveness. I walked slowly down the grassy aisle with the crowd. We spread out in front of the stage where Billy Graham stood praying for us and encouraging us to invite God into our hearts. Bowing my head, I acknowledged I was a cipher, empty but eager for redemption. God's love didn't strike as a lightning bolt, transfiguring me. It descended as a drenching rain, soaking my soul and filling my heart with kindness. Love gushed from me, flowing onto those around me.

Afterward, in the milling crowd, I felt my arm being gently pulled. I looked up, surprised to see Miss Greenshields, my Scripture Union teacher from Hatfield Girls High School. She drew me aside, along with three other girls, and told us she would be our counselor and guide into the world of salvation. She gave us forms to fill out at home, pamphlets, and the *Gospel of St. John* to read, and told us she would check in with us. I floated through the rest of the week, suffused in light. I radiated a soft glow into the bedroom from my corner bed. I read my *Bible* and the pamphlets faithfully every night. One evening the Gleggs invited the kids who had stood up at the crusade for prayers and weighing in, a weighing in of our souls and bodies. Although I knew nothing about such a ritual, I said a joyful prayer of love and thanksgiving and weighed in at eighty-nine pounds, five feet one inches tall.

Then the light began to fade. The glow of warmth and love that had suffused me during the ten-day crusade dimmed and life returned to its usual shades of greens and browns. I hadn't welcomed Miss Greenshields' clumsy attempts, as my counselor, to horn in on my communion with God. Filling out forms and reading pamphlets hadn't helped me forge my own relationship with Him. Without the crusade to stir me up, God was a nebulous concept, too abstract to keep me charged with the electricity of love. I'd been attracted to the passion and intensity of the crusade just as I'd been captivated by the sensuous possibilities of romance with Andrew when I read the *Song of Solomon*. In real life, God and Andrew remained remote. They failed to live up to my fantasies of spontaneous connection. Perhaps, too, I was afraid of that spontaneity, afraid of losing control. In any case, I didn't know how to maintain the passion I'd so recently felt. As I came out on the other side, I walked in spiritual limbo, emotionally empty.

The Congregational Church near A.M.F. that I had been attending since arriving in Rhodesia now seemed tame and pallid. Of all the kids in the dorm, only Andrew, his sister Mary, and I went there. I wanted to attend the Baptist Church along with most of my dorm friends. I imagined it to be full of life and energy. Mrs. Glegg didn't think I should switch without consulting my parents, but she said I could go to the Baptist Youth Group on Friday nights. The youth group was lively and the Baptists knew how to sing. Their hymns were much more passionate than the Congregational hymns, with singable tunes and lusty lyrics, in which blood flowed and sinners were redeemed. They satisfied part of my craving for passion and belonging. Ultimately though, the Friday night programs of speakers and films bored me. I still yearned to be grabbed and shaken to my bones.

"Our motto will be 'Honesty Comes from Heaven' and our song 'The Bridge on the River Kwai,'" we decided at the founding meeting of the Merry Maidens Club. The song, whistled in the movie, was appropriately upbeat for the merry maidens. We didn't know that the lyrics associated with it were bawdy. We formed the club for mutual support and assistance. Katherine didn't want to join; she thought we were silly. She was very serious, wore her dark hair sensibly short, and had the breasts and hips I associated with a mature woman like my mother, even though Katherine wasn't much older than the rest of us. Every Saturday we planned to donate sixpence to the club's community fund to purchase necessary items like shampoo and goodies for midis.

"And let's each choose new names," I said. "I'm going to be Henry because it's my real name." On the train coming to Rhodesia I was looking at my birth certificate and other documents Mom had brought along. I discovered to my astonishment and delight that my actual legal name was Henry Lucile Henderson. My mother had never noticed the misprint.

We all selected boys' names. Ruthanne chose Ricky; Barbara, Bobby; Jane, Doug, and on until all ten of us were renamed. It appealed to our sense of the ridiculous that the Merry Maidens have boys' names. Everything about A.M.F. seemed off kilter: living so far from home, the Glegg attitudes towards sex and teenagers, the unspoken ways that religion defined us. Naming ourselves as boys allowed us to thumb our noses at Mrs. Glegg. If she wouldn't allow us to have boyfriends, we'd challenge the taboo by becoming boys and boyfriends to each other. Taking on boys' names was the daylight equivalent of sneaking out at night, in which we entered a fantasy world, tinged with risk and sensuality. Becoming boys lent us power and status.

In our romantic world, we knit ourselves together through song. We sang along with the hit parade on Saturday afternoon, as we gathered around the radio in the small sitting room on the girls' side. Any time three or more of us were together, we spontaneously sang "Greensleeves," or the first song I learned in chorus, "Rhodesia."

"Be firm in purpose, land of light/ Share your riches, gain in might/ Have faith like Rhodes and do the right/ for God and Queen, Rhodesia."

Hymns were our favorites, with their simple round melodies that invited us to blend in harmony. We sang as we rode together in the minibus. We sang as we walked up the hall to the dining room to eat supper. We sang while we washed our clothes on Saturdays.

In the safety of our little group, we declared our love for each other by pairing off and getting married. One night in late May 1960, Ruthanne, Karen, Barbara, Rosemary, and I crept outside for a marriage and midnight feast under the pines. The stars pierced the intense darkness of the southern African sky. No street lights or house lights shone for miles around to dim the clarity of the stars. The moon was a spotlight, bathing us in its glow. Ruthanne and I stood by the huge pines lining the long driveway up to our dorm, our shadows lost in the uneven darkness of the trees. We recited together our vows of affection and loyalty. "I, Henry, and I, Ricky, do solemnly swear to cherish each other and devote ourselves to the good of the Merry Maidens. Amen."

And then we celebrated with a feast from Widdecombe's Garage: candy, peanuts, chips, and bottles of Coke laid out under the pines. Our weddings, mine and those between other girls, were asexual unions, simple rituals, declaring our allegiance to each other and promising a closeness our faraway families and the Gleggs couldn't provide. We seemed to be acting out, in pure innocence, Magee's most dire fears of the consequences of affection between boys and girls, but without the resulting pregnancy or trashy reputation.

Like real families, we suffered divorce as well. One sunny afternoon after school, the Merry Maidens convened in the garden to formally enact Karen and Rosemary's divorce. Peggy, dressed in a black robe and wig, presided as judge. Mary, in bowtie and straw hat, acted as the solicitor. I, with the brim of my school hat turned up into a bowler and my glasses perched on the end of my nose, was the nervous country parson. As soon as the divorce was final, I performed the marriage of Karen and Barbara. Barbara (Bobby) was at her masculine best, wearing pedal pushers, white shirt, tie, and blue school blazer. She had stuffed her long blonde hair into her school hat. Karen had pulled her straight hair away from her face and it flowed over the shawl she had draped around her shoulders. Rosemary, discarded spouse, was folded back into the family as Karen and Bobby's child. Rosemary, the child, reminded me of Magee's dig that I was far too slow to be a mother. Despite Magee's disparaging remark and her attempts to keep me from growing out of childhood, I was a Merry Maiden. I was free to be boy or girl, woman, and mother, all the roles she would have denied me.

Through our marriages and divorces, our midnight feasts, escapades, and songs we connected and reconnected, weaving our strands more securely. I had tested other bonds: my intellectual friendship with Mary Keillor, my sexual yearnings for Andrew, my fervor for Billy Graham. None delivered the affection I craved, nor did Mrs. Glegg and my father talk to me honestly about sexuality. In the end, the girls in the dorm, the Merry Maidens Club, provided me with the real stuff of love, its prickles and its tenderness. We blended our voices in harmony, irreversibly entwined.

Bread peddler at a small market in Canata, with pigs rooting in the garbage dump

Cooking in front of
her house

Pounding corn in
front of her house

Lining up for water in Canata

Large and small piles of salt by the saltpans

Public outhouses in
Canata

Tezinha on the verge of going back to
her family, December 1959

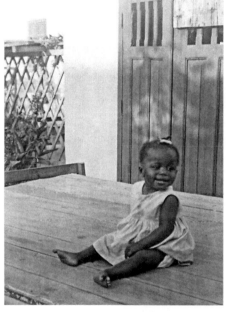

The beggar with elephantiasis, mistaken for
Chicucuma

With Tezinha

At Victoria Falls on our way to school in Rhodesia

Our Christmas 1960 vacation at the new home in Bunjei, three months before the Angolan war for independence started

The Merry Maidens at AMF

Friends in Lobito including Rebeca Valentim, seated second from right

My freshman Carleton friends

Back in Angola to visit my family in the summer of 1966

With Doug James on the Minnesota prairie, 1970

Chapter 11 — No Reservations

Ka pali etende, pa ende ocine.
Se não tem o que se quer, use o que tiver.
If you don't have what you want, use what you have.

Umbundu proverb

At the conclusion of our first year in Rhodesia in December 1960, Kathy and I flew to Angola, this time not to cosmopolitan Lobito but to the remote mission of Bunjei, where the family had moved six months earlier. By late January 1961, the end of Christmas hols, I felt as though I'd endured six weeks of confinement. I craved action and excitement. I expected I'd find some on the looming cross-Africa flight back to Rhodesia via Mozambique. We'd traveled back and forth enough to know that even meticulously made plans could go awry. Neither did our final destination in the Glegg "lock-up" diminish my anticipation, because I had my eye fixed not merely on the continental trip, but more precisely on the strange and curious landscape of two teenage males—Melvin and Jerry—who boarded the lumbering DC-7 plane in Luanda on a Saturday with Kathy, Barbara, and me.

The day before, Kathy and I had flown from the central Angolan city of Nova Lisboa to Luanda on a tiny commuter plane, which had bounced with every air current and whose droning engines hadn't been able to mask the sound of someone vomiting behind us. I stared, rigid, at the back of the seat in front of me, holding my breath to shut out the smell and to short circuit my jumpy gag reflex. In Luanda, we met Melvin, Jerry, and Barbara, who had arrived by train from the Methodist mission of Malange, hundreds of kilometers to the east of Luanda. The children of the Methodists in northern Angola and the Congregational missionaries in central Angola rarely had opportunities to mix. But now we were together on the plane, five teenagers, ranging in age from thirteen to sixteen, making our way to Salisbury for the start of the new school year.

I was excited about exploring Mozambique's capital city of Lourenço Marques during our layover with Melvin and Jerry. Boys alive and within reach! They set off a tingly, illicit feeling in me. The boys were traveling for the first time to Rhodesia and they seemed like young innocents, marching unawares toward the perversity of the Magee mind. I had the urge to shelter them and warn them of what lay ahead. Above all though, I wanted to laugh.

I wanted to prance through the trip and show off to the boys. I wanted to savor the sexual yearnings reverberating deep down.

The DC-7 flew smoothly and steadily southeast across southern Africa. We must have looked as though we were playing a game of musical chairs, constantly popping up and down, switching seats, laughing. I perched on the arm of the chair beside Barbara, aware of Jerry in the seat behind her. My eyes caught his for a brief second. I turned back to Barbara and asked, "So how was Christmas? How's your family?"

"Oh, they're fine," Barbara replied. "I didn't do much…"

"Well, Kathy and I learned to drive the Land Rover and how to play the Portuguese national anthem four-handed on the piano," I said. "We banged out the chords as loud as we could and sang along at the tops of our voices! It was so great." In Luanda, Kathy and I had successfully searched the bookstores for a copy of the sheet music, to continue playing A Portuguesa in Salisbury.

Then we stood up and Barbara and Kathy leaned over to tease Jerry while I took a seat by Melvin, tall, slim, and sixteen, the same age as Kathy. I tried not to look too dopey when I stole looks at him. Straight nose, straight, dark brown hair, cut short and parted on the side, handsome in a conventional way.

"Want to play gin?" I asked and I shuffled the cards Mom had given me to help pass the time. "If only Magee could see us now," I said, "together with you guys. She'd have a fit." How delicious, although a little scary, to conjure up her face. We were safely out of her reach, but after a year at A.M.F. her moral censorship sometimes sat like a self-righteous judge on my conscience. I felt the urge to stick out my tongue and recklessly chant "nya-nee nya-nee nya nya," at her.

"But what's wrong with what we're doing?" Melvin asked. I couldn't answer him, but I knew I felt invigorated and little dizzy.

I ate dinner seated next to Jerry. He was shorter than Melvin, because he was only thirteen. I wanted him to be older than thirteen. I wished he were closer to my fifteen because merely looking at him made me flush. His light brown hair curled around the edges of his face, his lips swelled, his nostrils flared, and when his wide-set eyes wrinkled with a sudden grin, I felt gooey inside. I couldn't think of anything to say.

"I think we're getting ready to land," Jerry told me. I could feel the airplane tipping as we circled over Lourenço Marques, and I caught a glimpse of the Indian Ocean in spite of the dark night. We walked down the steps of the plane into the muggy heat. By the time we went through customs, no one was at the desk to verify our flight to Salisbury on Monday. We caught a cab directly to Hotel Avis, where we had reservations. At least we thought we had reservations. The hotel manager insisted our reservations were for the following night, but they had enough room for five traveling teenagers. Barbara later wrote her parents that the manager "almost had kittens when he heard us speak Portuguese so well." We fell into our separate rooms and beds. I at least was completely unaware of the sexual possibilities in our arrangement.

Sunday morning the sun seeped through the shutters. I pushed them open and looked down at the bougainvillea vine, bursting with pink blossoms, shading the front walk into the hotel. The day stretched before us, a day to relax before our final flight to Salisbury on Monday. Over breakfast of chewy Portuguese rolls and hot milk, we talked about what we wanted to do.

"First let's phone the Methodist church to find out when services are," suggested Barbara. Lourenço Marques struck me as very modern; perhaps this was because it was next door to South Africa. We couldn't have picked up a phone to check on services in Angola. My father had futilely put our name on the phone list for a number in Lobito ten years earlier. Barbara discovered the services weren't until 8 o'clock in the evening, allowing us time to roam the city in the daylight. Lourenço Marques, or L.M. as we called it, was a coastal city like Lobito, on Delagoa Bay, situated to catch the breezes off the water. We headed east toward the bay, past stucco houses in pastel pinks and greens and yellows, all topped by red tile roofs. As we approached the bay, the street descended to the downtown and a promenade that meandered along the bay. On Sunday morning no one moved downtown. On the palm-lined promenade we seemed alone, five teenagers set loose in an empty city.

"Everyone! Only walk on the black lines," ordered Jerry. We followed the undulating pattern of black stone set into the white stone sidewalk, teetering in our effort to avoid stepping off our path.

"I know," Melvin said, "let's find a movie theater."

"Hey, good idea," we chimed in. "There's time for a matinee before dinner and church." We didn't care what movie was showing and now I only remember that I thought it was stupid and overdone. But I clearly recall fluttering in anticipation of a couple of hours in a dark theater with the boys. Would I get to sit beside Jerry, or even Melvin, without seeming too obvious? Would we fall in place naturally or should I position myself deliberately? We handed our tickets to the usher, who showed us to our seats.

"I have M-14," I announced. Please let me sit beside Jerry, I prayed. I thought I might levitate when I realized I had a boy on each side. The house lights dimmed, the velvet curtain drew back, and the screen sprang to life through the sheer curtain as it opened. The movie flickered on and on, but I was paying more attention to the drama of my beating heart and how closely to hold my arms to my body in case I inadvertently nudged Melvin or Jerry, and how discreetly I could turn my head to sneak a look to left and right. The boys leaned forward slightly, their attention riveted on the screen, and Melvin snorted with laughter. I relaxed and settled back into my seat, happy that I could glance at them unnoticed.

"Oh boy, was that ever great!" said Melvin, when we emerged from the theater. All the girls groaned. But still, the glow that had kindled in the darkness of the theater stayed with me through dinner and church.

First thing Monday we had to find the travel agency to check on our afternoon flight to Salisbury. We had noticed on Sunday, as we wandered the city, that Barbara had an unerring sense of direction, and we called on it again on Monday to get us to the agency.

But when we arrived, the clerk asked, "What reservations?" He ran his finger down the list of passengers, shaking his head. I thought maybe he couldn't read English names. We craned over the counter to look at the list ourselves. He was right. We weren't on it.

"How can that be?" we asked each other. "First the hotel reservation was wrong and now this..." I hoped this mix-up would be as easily solved.

"When is the next plane we can catch to Salisbury?"

He said, "Oh, not until a week from tomorrow. It only flies on Mondays and Tuesdays and we're booked through next Monday." Stunned by the news, I looked at Kathy and then over at Melvin. I hoped they, as the big kids, had some ideas about what we should do. I turned to see if Barbara and Jerry had heard.

"What did he say? We're here for a whole week?" they asked.

The trip our parents had arranged for us had fallen apart. Who could we talk to? Who would extricate us? How would we get to Salisbury? The minor hitch Saturday night at Hotel Avis all of a sudden seemed an omen of larger problems. The sense of carefree adventure I'd carried into the trip turned to dread. What else might be lurking just beyond view? What else could go wrong? I felt a little dizzy, as if this high adventure had deprived me of oxygen. We gathered close to each other for strength.

I reminded myself that we had each other and I *had* been hoping for excitement. I felt giddy and bubbly and erupted into nervous giggling that spread like contagion among the five of us. The more we looked at each other, the more we snickered and guffawed, and soon we were laughing so hard we had to wipe the tears from our eyes. Maybe things weren't so bad after all.

"Know what?" someone said. "We're going to miss the first days of school!" Enforced absence. Can't do anything about it. What better excuse than being stranded in Lourenço Marques for a week? I worried about one thing, though. Our choir was rehearsing to sing for the Queen Mother's visit to Salisbury and I could imagine Miss Smith, my teacher, not being amused. Would she still allow me to provide the piano accompaniment to the Pretty Polly Pellicote duet? Since living in Rhodesia, I had caught the royalty fever. I closely followed the birth and naming of the new little prince: Andrew Albert Christian Edward. I fervently hoped I could perform for his grandmother.

In the meantime, we had to make a plan. The clerk offered to reserve space on next Tuesday's plane or tell us where to find the truck transport station.

"*I* don't want to travel by *carreta*," Kathy was quick to inform us. "First of all it will take forever because the truck will stop often, and we'll be squished, and we'll have to sleep overnight somewhere." We all agreed.

"We also don't have enough money to wait a week for the plane," Kathy continued.

"I know. Let's try the train," said Barbara. We marched buoyantly over to the train station, with the triumphant feeling that we were on our way to a solution. The next train to Salisbury left on Wednesday.

"That's not bad. We only have two days to kill," I said. "But how will we pay for the tickets?" When we added up our combination of Portuguese *escudos*, American dollars, Rhodesian pounds, and South African pounds, we didn't have enough money for living expenses and tickets.

"Now what?" we all said, looking listlessly at each other.

"One thing's for sure," said Kathy. "We can't continue on at Hotel Avis. It's too expensive." She seemed to be taking charge and I relaxed. As usual, Kathy applied her analytical reasoning to the situation, and I knew I could trust her to get us through. Wasn't it funny, though, that I didn't look to Melvin for direction? He was Kathy's age and he was a boy, which should automatically have lent him authority. But he was so goofy. Kathy could go into a dreamy, far-away state when she read poetry or a novel and nothing

I said to her would penetrate. Nonetheless even at sixteen she knew where she was headed and she didn't tolerate fools. Melvin was enthusiastic about right now and didn't seem to care what lay ahead. When he called our hotel Ajax instead of Avis, I was completely charmed, but his imprecise way of looking at the world was exactly why I couldn't quite trust him to lead us. Kathy became our treasurer and financial advisor.

"Well, if we have to leave Hotel Avis, where will we go?" I asked.

"Remember yesterday we passed by the Swiss Mission? How about trying them?" suggested Barbara. Yeah, kindred souls, I thought. Whenever I traveled I played a game of spotting missionaries. They invariably wore dowdy, out-of-fashion clothes, no make-up, plain haircuts, but they had kind, open faces. I couldn't imagine that the Swiss would turn us away. Even the oppressive January sun didn't slow us down in our quest for new lodging. We walked briskly over to the Swiss Mission, which seemed huge compared to our Casa Missionária in Lobito. Three or four houses were scattered under the trees of the lot, enclosed by a wall that appeared to be at least a city block in size. We walked through the gate as if into another world, a hushed world, empty of people, far from the honks and shouts of the streets. A breeze off the water and the deep shade of the compound cooled us. We approached the largest house, knocked on the door, and were greeted by a tall, thin African man who said he would get the *dona da casa*. Soon, a young white American woman, holding two little children by the hands, came and introduced herself as Janet Mondlane. I recognized her name. In fact, Kathy and I had met her and her husband Eduardo three years earlier in Boston. I knew that Eduardo Mondlane, Mozambican and black, was a leader in the emerging anti-colonial movement in Mozambique. We explained our predicament to Mrs. Mondlane, but she seemed hesitant to take up our cause.

"My husband is away," she said. So what? I felt like saying. I thought about my mother who had helped hundreds of guests through their transitions in Lobito. She had never shrunk from the task. Mrs. Mondlane had a big two-story house that looked as if it had room for five stranded teenagers. We continued to stand at the door, hoping she would soften because we couldn't think where else we could turn. Mrs. Mondlane reminded me of the Portuguese woman who lived across the street from us in Lobito. When Mom invited her over for tea once, she had to refuse because her husband wouldn't allow her to come. I hoped I was more like my mother and my sister than Mrs. Mondlane, that I shared their willingness to take charge, manage details, and solve problems. Mrs. Mondlane finally said, "Why don't you talk to Mr. Claire. He's the Swiss missionary in charge."

We found Mr. Claire at his house on the compound and, after hearing our tale, he said, "Well, yes, we happen to have an empty house right now. Why don't you move in there? Do you want to go look at it?" Relief washed over me. I felt like cheering but instead I grinned. All the way to the Hotel Avis and back we chattered. "That's a great house! Did you notice the verandahs that wrapped around it on two sides? Just like missionary houses in Angola."

"How about sheets and towels? Did Mr. Claire say he'd lend us some?"

"Yes, when we get back they'll be there."

"What about meals? Shall we cook?"

We were hot and sticky from carrying our luggage across town in the stifling humidity, but when we walked in the front door of our house, the cool of the brick walls and floor tiles was like a cold-water plunge. We staked out the bedrooms we wanted, the boys in one and the girls in another, and I suddenly felt less shy with the boys. Moving from bare acquaintance to living together in the brief span of three days had transformed them into something more akin to brothers. The sexual edginess I'd felt around them softened into comradeship.

The large eat-in kitchen was equipped with utensils, a stove, deep sink, and table. The uneven, well-worn tile floor and the dozens of pots and pans stored in the cupboards suggested that some family had eaten heartily from this kitchen. But rather than cooking, Mr. Claire had suggested we order in our meals from the *pensão* around the corner.

"One of the young boys here at the mission can bring the food over for you." For the noon meal that day, he carried in *caldo verde* [potato kale soup], *batatas fritas* [fried potatoes], and *bifes* [beef steaks]. He stacked one pot after another on our counter.

"Oh my gosh, look at all this food. How will we eat it all?" we all exclaimed, peering into the pots. "And did he say it only cost twenty *escudos*?" That translated to eighty cents. For supper he brought potatoes, cod, and cabbage, with boiled potatoes left over to turn into hash browns at breakfast the next morning. Breakfast wasn't available from the *pensão*, so we bought milk, eggs, and bread and planned to supplement them with leftovers.

That evening we relaxed in the living room, with a luxuriously competent feeling.

"We found a free place to stay, thanks to Mr. Claire, and cheap food," I said. "Now all we have to figure out is how to pay for the train."

"Let's get out all our money so we can see what we have," said Kathy. We emptied our wallets and purses onto the coffee table.

"Hey, look! I forgot we had this." Kathy pulled out the fifty dollars Mom had given us before we left Bunjei to buy clothes in the Salisbury department stores. I looked longingly at that bill, imagining the shoes, blouses, and skirts it would purchase. For a moment I thought about snatching it back, hoarding it for Kathy's and my pleasure. I hankered for a pair of heels for church and dressy parties and some nylon stockings, nylons to make my legs sleek. But when I looked around at our group, I knew I was dreaming. Of course, the money would have to be used for getting us back to school. I rather loved the drama of sacrificing for the group.

"Even with the fifty dollars," Kathy figured, "we're still going to need a *conto* [about forty dollars] for train tickets. Maybe we can borrow that from Mr. Claire."

This detour in Lourenço Marques reminded me of the Famous Five mystery adventures I used to read when I was a kid. *Five Run Away Together, Five Get into Trouble, Five Go Adventuring...* Barbara, Melvin, Jerry, Kathy, and I had landed in the middle of our own mystery, the mystery of life really. While we sorted out the problems of room, board, and travel, we were learning about each other, especially how boys and girls interacted. I had wanted to rely on Melvin to figure out how to solve our predicament, just as Julian in the Famous Five took the lead. But I realized I had a whole lot more sense than Melvin did. Even Barbara, who was younger than Melvin and me, took charge of guiding us around while the boys acted like useless appendages. It made me wonder again what Mrs. Glegg was sheltering us from and why the boys at A.M.F. were allowed so many more freedoms than the girls.

Since the train didn't depart until 6:30 in the evening on Wednesday, we had another two days to spend in Lourenço Marques.

"I know, let's go to the movies again," said Melvin.

"We still have to get through today and tomorrow here in L.M., buy food for two days on the train, and pay the taxi to the station," Kathy, Barbara, and I leapt to remind him.

I thought to myself, "Where's your brain, Melvin?" Jerry was wisely silent, in pleasant contrast to his burbling brother. Another point in his favor, I thought, glancing at him with a little smile.

With the money we borrowed from Mr. Claire in Kathy's pocket, on Tuesday we walked back to the train station to purchase our tickets for Wednesday. Juggling the different currencies, we tried to buy beds on the train for both nights, but we didn't have enough money. In the end, we bought beds for the first night and decided we would sleep in our clothes on the bare bunks the second night.

We also telegraphed the Gleggs. "Complications. Arriving Friday by train." We also had wired them on Monday when we realized we had no plane reservations, so they wouldn't go to the airport looking for us.

"It's a thirty-seven hour train trip," I figured out loud. We were to leave at 6:30 in the evening on Wednesday and arrive at 7:30 in the morning on Friday. "So that's four meals if we let Gleggs feed us breakfast on Friday."

"What should we get to eat, then?" someone asked.

Wednesday morning we walked to the market for peaches, oranges, and guavas. We picked up a round of Gouda cheese at Casa Holandesa, chewy Portuguese buns at the *padaria*, cans of tuna and British soda crackers at Casa Inglesa. We purchased can and bottle openers and a sharp knife. Part of the fun was figuring out how little we could spend. I remembered all the overnight train rides Kathy and I used to take on our way to Dondi. Eating in the dining car had always been one of the pleasures of riding the train in the old days. Olive oil and garlic aromas used to greet us as we approached the dining car. The tables were draped with starched white tablecloths, set with heavy silverware and crystal. The waiters dressed in white jackets would hurry over to take our order. This time, though, we'd be picnicking in our cabin. Roughing it added to the adventure. We'd spread the food out on the table, letting the bread crumbs fall, dribbling orange stickiness onto the floor, proving we had the inner resources to fill ourselves despite dwindling funds. The picnic would seal our journey with a ritual, a celebration of our ability to persevere independent of adults. We'd made it through the surprise layover in L. M., and I had the feeling I could take care of myself anywhere.

In the late afternoon, we lined up our luggage on the verandah of the guesthouse. As we waited for the taxi to arrive, we listed everything we should have done before we left. Yes, we'd stripped our beds, cleaned up the kitchen, thanked Mr. Claire for his kindness, said good-bye to Mrs. Mondlane and the kid who had brought us our food, gone through the house one more time to check on hairbrushes and tooth paste. We were ready, but the taxi was half an hour late. Dusk descended.

"Where is he? I know we told him to come at 5:30. Didn't we?" Every minute that passed made us more frantic that we'd miss the train.

"When's that taxi going to arrive?" worried Barbara. "What if the train leaves and we have to wait another week? Then what will we do?"

"Don't even think about it," Kathy said. "Phone the cab place again."

Just then our taxi drove up.

It delivered us to the train station with no time to spare. We raced down the platform, our suitcases knocking against our legs and food jumping out of the bags. We jostled down the narrow corridor of the train looking for the two side-by-side coupes we had reserved and when we found them, we fell with relief into a pile on the seat in the girls' cabin. The coupe was half a cabin, with one long seat, one window, and a hinged table that lowered down over the small stainless steel sink. The train lurched then chuffed out of the station. We were off!

"Why don't you take your stuff to your cabin," I told the boys, "then come on over to eat." In the coupe we were squished up against each other, practically on each other's laps. I just knew that being so close to Melvin and Jerry would horrify Mrs. Glegg. I shivered with delight. I could see her glaring at us, shooting warnings through her dark eyes. Oh, I wish she weren't so suspicious, I thought. I dreaded the moment we'd actually have to face her. I wished we could ride the train forever.

Right now, no one truly knows where we are or what we're doing, I thought. Kathy and I had sent a letter to Mom and Dad from Lourenço Marques. "I guess we were made to get into trouble," I wrote, as I described our series of missed reservations and how we'd taken care of ourselves. But they wouldn't receive the letter until well after we arrived in Salisbury. Maybe because we were cut off from our parents and the Gleggs, the five of us wanted to be together every waking hour on the train. We were our own little world. Out of reach of everyone but pleased with ourselves, we sat crammed on the train seat, eating our picnic dinner.

Later that evening, the steward moved our luggage off the top rack, which doubled as the third bunk, and made up our beds. I lay up there, sandwiched between the rich brown wooden ceiling and the hard mattress he had brought in, gently rocked by the clacking train. The train climbed steadily from the coast up to the inland plateau and later into the hills and mountains of Rhodesia. Curves in the track made the car creak, luggage shift, wheels squeal in protest until the track straightened and the train clicked forward.

When Barbara turned fourteen on Thursday, we felt as though we'd all bloomed in the past five days. Now we had an excuse to feast and sing "Happy Birthday."

"Hey, look," said Kathy during one of our stops, "let's get some *bolos* for the party." She had spied a vendor walking beside the train, balancing a wide glass-topped wooden case on his head, full of custard-filled tarts, crispy elephant ears, coconut tarts, slices of sponge cake, bite-sized ultra-sweet egg pastries.

"I'll have two elephant ears and a custard tart," I said, and nibbled at the flaky pastry, savoring each crunchy and creamy bite. We washed them down with bottles of Coke and wonderfully juicy peaches. Kathy and I gave Barbara a card, which we signed "Love from all of us." But Melvin and Jerry protested, "Why did you write *love?* Don't sign my name to that." Barbara had grown up with the brothers and didn't pay them much heed. My sister and I also dug out two little Portuguese vases, exuberantly hand-painted with flowers, dogs, and deer.

"Oooo, mushi, mushi, I love them," Barbara squealed, when we presented them to her. "Thank you, thank you."

"*É o seu aniversário* [It's her birthday]," we pointed out to the conductor, when he passed our cabin.

We were still chugging through Mozambique and were hard to miss, with our height and blonde hair, fair skins, and silly behavior. The conductor seemed to understand that we were poor students scrimping as much as possible, because we never ventured forward to the dining car and we didn't buy beds for Thursday night. We didn't tell him our whole story. Nonetheless soon the surrounding passengers were giving us understanding looks. Once we passed into Rhodesia, our American accents made us stand out. An old woman passed by our compartment to wave good-bye and smile encouragingly at us. "I heard you are university students. Good for you!" We were too amazed to contradict her.

"Did you hear what she said? *University* students?" we laughed, feeling flattered and grown up.

On Thursday evening, we had to change trains in Bulawayo. We hoped our reservations for the Salisbury train were in order. "If they're not, you know what that means—we're out of money so we'll be sitting up all night in the station," I said, trying to prepare myself for the worst. We were greatly reassured when we made a smooth transfer, but we discovered that the new train was full of British men and boys. Here at last, Melvin and Jerry lived up to my expectations. Their male presence fended off the unwanted attention we girls were getting. Without bedding, the night was cold and long. I slept fitfully, worried about not waking in time for our 7:30 arrival. If I lay on my back, my shoulder blades and backbone pressed into the bare seat. On my side, my hip bruised. I balled up a dirty shirt for a pillow and gave myself a stiff neck. I was anxious about seeing the Gleggs. I dreaded the end of our freedom. And I thought about being late to school. How much had I missed? Could I make it up easily? Would I get to sing for the Queen Mother? Friday morning none of us could sleep past 5 o'clock.

"Do you think the Gleggs will meet us?" I wondered aloud. We got up and stood in the corridor until the train pulled into Salisbury. I searched as we approached the station and spotted the Gleggs together far up the platform, looking so small and insignificant that I almost wondered why I had dreaded returning. The train crept forward until I saw Pagee's ubiquitous bow tie and suspenders and knew, without seeing, that his white shirt had food stains on it. I felt a surge of pity for him. He had the habit of tilting his bald head up when he listened. It gave him a look of open expectancy and innocence. The train wheezed and came to a stop. Magee, who had grown into her full stern self, brought me quickly back to feeling defiant. She leaned forward slightly, I suppose from the effort of looking for us, her lost charges. She strode down the platform to meet us, pulling Pagee along like an injured kite.

We climbed down the steps of the train to the platform, lugging our suitcases and empty food bags. I was suddenly aware of how close I was to Melvin and Jerry, bumping and touching them in plain view of the Gleggs. I could sense myself withdrawing, embarrassed about being seen in what moments before had been a comfortable companionship. The sight of the Gleggs bearing down on us made me luff and flap like a sail losing its wind.

"The complications have finally arrived," joked Magee. "We wondered if we'd ever see you again. We've been going to the airport everyday since Monday looking for you."

"Didn't you get our telegram last Monday saying we missed our plane reservations?" we asked.

"No! No word until we got your wire about the train!"

With some reluctance, we picked up our suitcases and climbed into the minibus for the ride home to A.M.F. and the new school year. As I'd feared, Miss Smith didn't allow me to perform in the concert for the Queen Mother.

But the sparkle of our L.M. adventure continued to flicker in my mind.

We soon resumed our midnight escapades with the boys, despite finding that our windows had been fitted out with bars while we were gone. It didn't take us long to figure out that the bars on the kitchenette window were easily removed. But our adventures began changing from group games to pairing off. Before the end of my first year I had lost interest in Andrew. He's too British, I wrote in my diary; too shy, too reserved, too tongue-tied. Too much like me, in fact, although I couldn't have seen that then. Jerry arrived at the right time for me, and our travels together made me feel like we were already good friends. Sometimes Jerry and I sat in the back seat of Miss Manson's little Austin Morris and another couple sat in front. But when no one else had claimed it, we sneaked across to the Gleggs' Jaguar, with its large, elegant seats. We whispered and didn't dare slam the door, parked, as it was, close to their apartment.

I sat straight with my hands in my lap, looking at the heads in the front seat, excited about being out at night. Sitting so close to Jerry, I tensed in anticipation of what was ahead. Would he "kiss me with the kisses of his mouth?" I felt my thudding heart go soft around the edges, its warmth oozing into my body. I breathed deeply, relaxed into the leather seat of the Jaguar, and allowed my left shoulder to touch Jerry's shoulder ever so slightly. Our conversation and the music on the radio loosened us so that our hands slid off our laps. Jerry's sweaty hand clasped mine; I didn't pull away. For two hours, while we held hands and talked, I leaned into Jerry's shoulder, my stiffness melted away. Even as I bent into his warmth, breaking all Mrs. Glegg's rules, I never felt indecent, vulgar, or any of the feelings Mrs. Glegg had warned me against. I was sure that her rules were ridiculous, so sure that I wrote home to Mom and Dad about the midnight forays. Kathy, who had moved to A.M.F. that second year, also wrote home. We blithely told our parents how we climbed out the window and met the boys outside for hours of talk, explaining also how benighted the rules were. In one of the few letters that Dad wrote us, he indicated clearly that he was worried about us. He was afraid we were getting into predicaments we couldn't control, and even offered to leave Africa if that would help.

What is he saying? I thought in alarm. I couldn't imagine leaving Africa and I couldn't understand why Dad didn't appreciate our situation at A.M.F. I wanted him to come visit, so he could see for himself and I could explain to him in person. But he was a ten-day train trip away. Rather than disturbing him anymore or pushing him into a reckless decision to leave Africa, I quit writing home about sneaking out at night.

Now, as a parent, I can see he was caught between wanting to stop a potentially dangerous sexual situation and wanting to trust us to make the right decisions. I also know now that when the family moved to Bunjei, he and the single woman on the mission had initiated an affair. My mother has described to me Betty's aggressive appropriation of my father and his eager acquiescence; it greatly distressed her. Our letters, I imagine, put my father in a moral quandary. How to reconcile his feelings about his daughters' confessions with his feelings for Betty and their equally risky position? In later years, I observed that when confronted with an emotionally charged problem, Dad would simply not say anything. His way of dealing with a dilemma was not to deal with it. Although I didn't realize it at the time, I doubt that further revelations of mine by letter would have prompted him to pack us up and leave Africa and his lover.

Chapter 12 — Against My Will: Losing Africa

Cimbapo copeka, cokutima ca tila.
É mais fácil largar o que está na mão do que o do coração.
It is easier to let go what is in the hand than what is in the heart.
Umbundu proverb

Four months later, a couple months shy of sixteen I was thrown out of Africa. Against my will.

One second I was sitting at my desk completing my first term exams in Salisbury and the next, it seemed, I was sitting on a French train heading for Paris. I pushed myself into the corner of the seat by the train window, silently weeping over the sudden end of my life.

How did this happen so fast, without warning? I wondered. I turned toward the window, hoping no one, especially my adventurous mother, would see my tears. Rows of grape vines greening up after the winter and freshly planted fields whizzed by, but I turned my vision inward.

Maybe I should have anticipated it. Maybe I should have realized that the tensions I had felt building throughout southern Africa in the past two years would end with my sitting on this train. But I couldn't or hadn't wanted to read the signs of upheaval in Congo, Rhodesia, and finally in Angola as actually affecting *my* life. I had my life planned out. I would finish Form Four in a year and a half, take the O-level Cambridge exams, and return to America for college. I would have plenty of time to bid Angola farewell. I would loll in the bay, looking up at the verandahs where I had played with Tezinha, studied eighth grade, had cambric tea. In Dondi I'd smell the sharp scent of the eucalyptus trees, hear the crunch of fallen bark under my feet, climb the granite rocks, and drench myself in the waterfalls. I'd visit everyone I knew, tell them my plans, and receive their best wishes. I'd grasp the Portuguese women and pull them forward for a quick air kiss, one-two, beside each cheek. The Angolans I'd thank with a clap-clap of my hands and a *kalunga* [thanks]. They'd reply *ku-ku* [you're welcome].

But instead nightmare.

The previous year after first term exams, Kathy and I had gone home on vacation to help Mom and Dad pack up the house for their move to Bunjei. But this year was different. We stayed in Rhodesia because Angola was at war. Or maybe the news just indicated unrest. I didn't know. In March 1961 we began to hear brief reports about Angola on BBC radio:

"Luanda prisons attacked."

"Bands of Angolans attack Portuguese traders."

"Coffee plantations come under attack."

My parents were worried enough about the situation to tell us to spend our May holidays in Rhodesia at Mt. Silinda mission. I worried about them too, but in an abstract, distant way. The fighting sounded like it was taking place far from where my parents lived, and I hadn't heard enough details to pin my fears on.

Well before war broke out in Angola in 1961, more than a year earlier, during my first year in Rhodesia, murmurs of freedom and liberation had been buzzing around colonial Africa in anticipation of the June 1960 independence of the Belgian Congo. No one dared ask, at least out loud, how an independent country so close by would affect life in Angola and in the rest of colonized southern Africa.

The July 1960 riots in downtown Salisbury gave me an inkling when they disrupted our school choir's Drill Hall concert. Before the final rehearsal for the concert, Miss Smith had called an emergency meeting. "How do you feel," she asked, "about traveling downtown?"

For me and the rest of the choir, the riots still seemed more like stories on the radio than real events. We wanted to proceed, but she had trouble getting a bus to take us downtown. When she finally succeeded, we were dropped at the bus terminal. We had to walk past the Rhodesia Regiment headquarters to the school where the rehearsal was being held. I wrote home about the "hundreds (literally) of soldiers sitting around waiting for trouble to arise." Like a pride of watchful lions resting in the shade of a baobab tree, the relaxed soldiers with their lethal rifles slung casually over their shoulders wouldn't hesitate to lunge and kill if provoked. We were quiet as we scurried by, trying not to stare or draw attention to ourselves, and we arrived late for the rehearsal. The next day Miss Smith was told that the concert had been postponed indefinitely. Not enough schools would attend.

The effects of Congo's independence impressed me even more when refugees began to ooze out of every corner of the Congo. "Salisbury is teaming with refugees, including loads of missionaries," I wrote my parents. "I'm just wondering how many we know."

The Gleggs, as part of the missionary community, volunteered their space and hospitality in the crisis. A Belgian mother and her four children lived with us at A.M.F. for a while. I treated them as my live-in French tutors. I complained to my parents, experts at operating a hostel for missionaries, that I didn't understand why the Gleggs didn't take in more refugees.

It was not until the Gleggs hosted a series of Sunday afternoon prayer meetings and teas for the refugee families that I actually understood the Gleggs' predicament. One Sunday Mrs. Glegg had asked my girl friends and me to sing a hymn during the service. We stood together in a tight bunch, looking at the crowd of more than two hundred gathered on the lawn, more people than I'd ever seen on the A.M.F. grounds. "Leaning, leaning, leaning on the everlasting arms," we sang, and I could sense we were all succoring each other. My girlfriends and I swayed as we harmonized, mingled our soprano and alto voices, and sent them out to the crowd, who listened attentively to us. Mothers pulled restless children into their laps and hugged them close. For the moment, we softened the uncertainties of the crisis with the promise of comfort in His everlasting arms. But the reality of feeding the huge crowd limited the Glegg's boundless hospitality. After the service, we shuttled trays of hot tea from the kitchen, poured and served it, dodging the little kids who were happy to be released from the constraints of worship.

In the bustle of preparing for two hundred missionaries, Mrs. Glegg forgot my fifteenth birthday. I felt like a refugee myself, lost in the crowd. Only Kathy and Miss Manson remembered. Kathy had come over from her dorm to present me with a picture of herself along with English Lavender powder and soap. In my hierarchy of sophistication, English Lavender ranked up there with Chanel No. 5. Miss Manson gave me Nivea cream and a *Bible* bookmark. I didn't feel I could say anything to Mrs. Glegg about my birthday; I didn't want to bother her with extra responsibilities or act like a pouty child when she was so busy. After all, I was fifteen.

Even so, when I attended the party that T.E.A.M. threw for Kathy's birthday a few days later, I had to beat back envy. Kathy's dorm parents remembered things like birthdays. We drank coke and ate chocolate birthday cake, then watched Kathy hunt for the presents everyone had hidden for her.

Someone, maybe Miss Manson, eventually told Mrs. Glegg my birthday had passed uncelebrated, so when Heather Wilson, one of my dormmates, turned sixteen a couple of days after the tea, I was hurriedly incorporated into her party. I agreed to participate, but I'd never much liked Heather. She was loud and bossy. I didn't want to share her party. Besides, ours was a puny party compared to Kathy's. Heather and I each received a small antelope pin from Mrs. Glegg and played Parcheesi and Twenty Questions until we gathered for refreshments: orange juice, period, full stop. No cake with frosting and candles to blow out. Not even a cupcake or a cookie. I suppose, in reality, A.M.F had exhausted its resources hosting the refugee teas, but I was too fixed on self-pity to understand that.

Six months later, in early 1961, we'd been back in Rhodesia only a few weeks, after Christmas break and our adventure in Lourenço Marques, when we began to hear ominous reports about Angola on the radio. They couldn't give me the real news I was after though, the news about my family. It took weeks to arrive. When letters did come, my mother, constrained by Portuguese censorship and not wanting to alarm us, wrote only the most mundane details. I wanted to know if my parents and brothers were near the fighting and if PIDE, the political police, had arrested anyone we knew. She simply described the fawn and puppy my brothers had adopted, and who had come to dinner. The hard reality of the war and its consequences still eluded me. A couple months later, as I sat on the train hurtling toward Paris, I had to face the truth that the war had catapulted me into a future I couldn't imagine.

With the war, my family had become separated for what evidently would be considerably more than a few months. Dad was still in Angola with the men while the women and children had been told to leave. We were in France, and we had no idea when we'd see him again. Between Christmas and the May vacation, Kathy and I had waged a mini-campaign in our letters home to entice him to visit us in Rhodesia during our holidays. I grudgingly understood it would be best for us not to venture into Angola right then because of the war, but Dad, in his new job as secretary of the *Aliança Evangélica*, traveled all over Angola and especially to Luanda. I didn't see why he couldn't fly to Salisbury during one of his trips.

"Mom's been here; now it's your turn," I'd say. Or "Please, please, please come visit us." Or "I hope you know you're coming to see us in May." Mom's letters came sporadically and she didn't respond to our pleas. Dad never wrote. I wasn't sure if he even considered coming and now, with the war in Angola breaking out, he couldn't.

In May 1961 at the end of first term, suddenly everyone at A.M.F. was packing a bag and leaving for home, or, like Kathy and me, for vacation in Mt. Silinda with a family we didn't know. But I was unconcerned. I'd be back in Salisbury soon enough for next term. Meantime, I had a new place to explore.

Mt. Silinda was the central Congregational mission in Rhodesia, just as Dondi was in Angola. The Belairs welcomed us to their rangy, one-story home, with vines crawling up the stucco walls and around the windows.

Their four kids showed us around. Before I'd really settled in, within days of arriving at Mt. Silinda, Kathy and I were called back to Salisbury.

"We've had a wire from your father," Magee told us on the phone. "You're to prepare to leave Rhodesia and Africa." The news knocked me dizzy. I was half deaf from a ringing in my ears. I couldn't have heard right.

Kathy and I were driven back to Salisbury the next day and returned to an empty dorm. As I wandered from room to barren room, I was nauseated with feelings of uncertainty and homesickness. I wished I could snatch all my friends back and say good-bye. I wanted to sing with them again. "Leaning, leaning, leaning on the everlasting arms," I quavered, but my voice was no good alone. The place echoed with the casual "byes" I'd said then, when I thought I'd be seeing them again in three weeks.

"Good-bye, Barbara, Ruthanne, and Karen," I now said to their empty beds. "Good-bye, Mary, Rosemary, Flora, and Peggy. Good-bye, Heather, Sheila, and Katherine. Good-bye to all the Merry Maidens."

I hadn't said good-bye to any of the boys either, not Andrew, Melvin, Jerry or the little boys. Sensual, languid, laughing Jerry. Leaving Jerry was like pulling the beginnings of a sweater off the knitting needle, unraveling us even before we had taken shape. I lay on my bed, wistful, disconnected, and sad but, when I imagined brushing my lips against his and touching his arm, also relieved that I didn't have to live through an awkward farewell.

I remembered the year before when Jane's mother arrived from Mozambique on a Saturday and told her to pack, ready to leave on Monday to return to America. Jane was in shock and so were we. Now I knew what Jane must have felt, but no one was around to send me off. The dull lump of homesickness stayed with me as I threw out my school papers. I wished school were in session so I could drop in at morning break, the way Jane had, for a final good-bye. I wrote Mary Keillor's name in my address book and reminded myself to get her address. I smiled a little when I recalled how we had buzzed along on the same wavelength speaking Latin, and if that failed, Pig Latin. If only I could say good-bye to her, face-to-face, I'd promise to write, no matter what. I looked at my school uniform: a Wedgwood-blue wool blazer, matching blue felt slouch hat, and two ugly light-blue and white striped cotton dresses with square necklines. I decided to throw out the hat and leave the dresses for Mary Seager, who was about my height. But I packed the jacket, with the falcon crest of Hatfield Girls' High School that I'd sewn onto the breast pocket.

I pulled out a shoebox of letters from Mom, Pauly, my brothers, and everyone else. I reread the one from Pauly telling me what classes she was taking in high school in Canada and the one from Mom describing Mark's seventh birthday party. Robin and Bobby, the McGowan kids, had come over to help him eat his chocolate cake. All my life, letters had threaded across continents and oceans, connecting me to my mother, father, brothers, and my friends. I'd stashed some of them away at home and carried some with me. I couldn't imagine leaving them behind in Africa, so I squashed the letters into the top pockets of my suitcase. The cream suitcase with blue trim had been my twelfth birthday present. With the top open, it made me think of a saggy-breasted bikini. I picked up my diary, a slim hardback notebook, black with a red cloth spine that had cost two shillings and six pence at the Widdecombe store, and opened it to the first page, the day I moved in to A.M.F.

"Woke at about 6:15. Hopped out of bed and got dressed... Went to bed at 10 to 9:00 but I lay awake till about 10:00." Just the barest of details. I mourned the letters, diaries, and books I'd stored at home in Angola. Would Mom, I wondered, leave them there when she left? If she did, what would become of them? If Dad left, would he think to pack them up and bring them? In fact, I didn't get my diaries back, but my mother saved the letters I'd written home over the years and has continued to return them to me as she sorts through her boxes and trunks.

In Salisbury, my sister and I took breaks from packing to hang out by the phone in the central sitting room, down the hall and past the dining room from my bedroom, waiting for a phone call from Dad to tell us where and when to meet Mom, David, and Mark. For several days we jumped at every ring of the phone, hoping Dad was on the line. Because the Gleggs' phone was on a party line, shared by several households, we had to learn to screen out all the signals but our three short rings. To complicate matters further, Dad's call was coming from Portuguese Africa to British Africa via telephone operators who couldn't understand each other. Over a period of several days, Dad had tried to contact us. The phone would ring.

"Hello," I'd say, grabbing the phone up, anxiously leaning into the receiver, and smashing it tight onto my ear.

"Hold, please, for a call," the British operator would say. I'd hear distant operators talking, sometimes in English, sometimes in Portuguese. I wanted to dive in and translate for them, to get things moving. Minutes ticked by. Then someone on the party line would pick up the phone, listen, sigh audibly, and clang down the receiver. Long minutes later someone again would pick up the phone but this time she wouldn't give up.

"Get off the bloody line," one of our neighbors would hiss, "I need to use it." Or she'd threaten to call the police. My face would flush, my heart bang and I'd quickly hang up. Minutes or hours later the phone would ring again. "Hold, please, for a call," the operator would say, and we'd start over.

Since the call in Mt. Silinda, I'd hardly been able to focus on packing. After sorting through my clothes for a few minutes, I would wander down the hall to find Kathy. Or sometimes I'd sit in the sitting room waiting for Dad to call and, when no call came, I'd go for a walk up the long driveway, wondering where we'd settle in America. I stood on top of the granite boulder outside the gates, warmed by the sun and the tans and golds of the savannah grasses, drying, now that the rains had stopped. The red dirt roads and the rustle of gray-green eucalyptus trees reminded me that I might never again see Dondi, fifteen hundred miles to the northwest. The air was so clear, I could see the tops of the tallest buildings in downtown Salisbury. I wished I could see all the way to Lobito. I wished I could stand on our verandah feeling the damp ocean breeze stir my hair and walk barefoot along the beach all the way to the end of the spit. I wished I could have a Portuguese meal of *canja* [chicken soup], and little cod balls, crispy and fragrant of olive oil, and fried potatoes. I wished I could hear a mournful *fado* from Dona Isaura's radio next door and the call of the fishermen rowing by. Losing Africa was like gouging everything rich and vibrant out of me.

Every day I hoped that we would pick up the phone and Daddy would be on the line. I wished it so hard that I dreamed he finally got through. I heard Dad's voice as clear as if he were in the next room.

"Get on the plane. Mom and the boys will meet you in Léopoldville. I'm staying behind in Bunjei."

"But why?" I protested. "Why do we have to leave? Are you O.K.? Why can't you leave, too?" I cried in frustration, afraid Dad couldn't hear me. I was pushing against something dense and murky, trying to make my way to him.

"Nancy, wake up," my sister called to me. "It's time for breakfast."

My eyes were filled with tears and I realized I'd only dreamed about Dad. He never could reach us by phone and finally sent a telegram, a terse, impersonal message, telling us what flight to take to meet Mom in Léopoldville. Years later as I reconstructed the details of leaving Africa, I firmly believed that Dad had reached us by phone. I clearly pictured the scene and heard his voice. Only when I reread some old letters Mom had saved did I realize the truth, that I had indeed left without talking to my father.

When the airplane lifted away from the Salisbury airport, my heart swooped down, a dangling yo-yo unable to snap back. Africa wouldn't release me, and I couldn't let go.

In Léopoldville, where we met Mom and my brothers, I floated along like the swift and wide Congo River. I caught snatches of Mom's grandiose plans for us and let her carry me along on her current. "We'll see Pudding in Geneva ... the Bakers in Le Chambon ... Paris ... Brussels ... still don't know where we should go to wait for Daddy ... Boston? Tacoma?" I didn't care. One place was as good as another.

Mom dragged us along at a listless meandering pace through Europe. We visited the Glegg's older daughter near Geneva, where she was attending a Bible college. Mom marched us around Geneva to admire the United Nations-affiliated buildings and Lake Leman. We huffed up one of the foothills of the Alps, in the company of a Swiss missionary woman we'd known in Angola. She spent the whole afternoon exulting over the beauty of the green hills, the blue cloudless sky, and the dazzling, white wildflowers. All I could see was gray.

From Geneva, we caught a train to the mountain village of Le Chambon in southern France, to the home of the Bakers, old Yale Divinity friends of my parents. They invited us to spend as much time as we wished with them and offered us the use of their car. I was grateful to be able to hunker down and lose myself in *Gone With The Wind*, a long book as far from my present life as I could get. After a few days reading, though, Mom pried us loose for an eight-day tour of historic southern France... Agde, a Phoenician town, medieval Pézenas, the beach at Palavas, the walled city of Aigues-Mortes, Roman Nîmes.

"Go ahead, girls, ask the waiter for our check. Girls, ask the clerk where the nearest market is. Nancy, go ask that man across the street where the beach is," Mom pushed and prodded Kathy and me to speak French, but I refused. I died with embarrassment when Mom, in frustration, stepped forth to speak in Umbundu, the first language that presented itself.

At the Palavas beach, a bracing wind whipped off the Mediterranean straight to my marrow, molding my skirt to my legs, and giving me an earache. I resisted my mother's plans for swimming there and again at Le Pont du Gard. She wanted to swim in the river Gard, sparkling in the sun, and spend a night at the inn perched on the cliff overlooking the Roman aqueduct. But we were within a few hours of Le Chambon.

"Let's just get there," I said.

"Gad, where's your sense of adventure?" she asked.

I missed Africa so much. I missed Dad. I missed the friends I'd left behind. I knew Mom was disappointed in me, and the way I silently hung back, sulky and sad. But I couldn't understand how she could throw herself so enthusiastically into touring. Didn't she miss Dad, too? We returned to Le Chambon in a cold rain and caught the train to Paris a few days later.

I stared out the train window, unable to stop the tears. I cried for myself and my lost life. I cried for my father alone in Bunjei. I cried in anger at my mother for enjoying several glasses of wine with the Bakers. Every evening at dinner, they had uncorked a bottle of wine, and she had accepted their offer of a glass, as if it were her daily habit. The more she laughed, the more I shrank from her. In my view, she was betraying my father whom we had abandoned. He was alone in warring Angola, facing unknown dangers, and Mom was whooping it up with friends in France. Even more, I knew drinking alcohol and smoking cigarettes were bad. Period. Missionaries didn't do that sort of thing. I'd seen the painful expressions on Dad's face if we happened to be in a situation where alcohol was being served. Forces "out there" had torn me from the African soil, and now my mother was lightheartedly dismembering the moral principles I relied on. She didn't seem to care.

Decades later, as a wife and mother myself, I understand that life was considerably more complex for my mother than I could grasp. She handled the uncertainty of being heaved out of Africa by "holding her chin up," as she described it to Dad in a letter, and making it into an adventure. She adopted an almost manic determination to experience it all. Privately though, in the letters she wrote to Dad during the year they were apart, she expressed her anguish over having taken down their bedroom curtains before she left. She kept apologizing. She thought he'd be moving... the room must be so bare and ugly.... The barren bedroom seemed emblematic of their situation. A few days before their eighteenth wedding anniversary, she wrote, "I wish you would write me a brief explanation of why I am here, in view of the fact that the Coles and Woodmans are still there." She went on to question the Mission Board's hasty recommendation to evacuate women and children, when it soon became apparent that the war hadn't enflamed the whole country.

"I keep telling myself I am not worried about you ... but I do miss you terribly," Mom wrote. "I wish we had sat down and talked things over a bit more rationally. If I'd gone to Salisbury, I could have parked the kids in school and gone back to see you." Even more than the uncertainty of the war, Mom was worried about the attractive single woman missionary still in Bunjei with the bachelors, Dad, Uncle Bob, and Uncle Robin. She had shown an obvious interest in Dad even while Mom was there.

"How is the mission attacking this problem of the single ladies?" Mom wrote. "Specifically, how is Betty going to get along in Bunjei? Really, I'm so cut off here." Jealousy gnawed at Mom. Perhaps it prompted her to break free of Dad's constraints when she was in France, to enjoy a glass of wine and a laugh with her friends. Maybe she wanted to show the world that she could handle the tension. But then in her letters she returned again to how sorry she was about the bedroom curtains.

Sitting on that train in France, I was unaware of my mother's complicated emotions. She hid them behind her cocked chin and called to her children to be curious and daring. In the years ahead, I came to appreciate her fearless embrace of adventure and unhesitating readiness to say yes. But at that time, in that place, I wanted her sympathy more than her challenge. I needed to cling to Dad and Africa. I needed her to confide in me that leaving Africa was hard for her, too. Instead, I saw unfeeling bravado.

I turned into the train window, knowing that she wouldn't see my tears.

Chapter 13 — Lost in America

Nda endele-e-e-e, ndi tāi!
Não tenho pressa de ir onde só há estranhos!
I'm not in a hurry to go where there are only strangers!
                    Umbundu proverb

Africa, Europe, America... giant steppingstones but where were they leading me? Whisked away from Salisbury on a week's notice, now just two months from my African life, and from the continent I carried in my soul, I wasn't prepared to like anything about America. Mom pointed the used station wagon she'd bought in Boston, loaded with four kids and the possessions we'd carried out of Africa, west to her hometown of Tacoma. I pined for my old home.

"Hello, hello," said my Aunt Marcia, as we piled out of the gray Chevy and stood awkwardly in her front yard. She smiled and said, "Welcome to God's country!" She meant the Pacific Northwest. I cringed. Driving into town, the acrid smell of sulfur from the pulp mills had permeated the damp air, infiltrated the car, and wrapped its stifling cloak around me. But, confronted with Aunt Marcia, I was certain that the smell wasn't the only thing that would make living in Tacoma a trial. I dug my heels into her lush lawn and braced myself against her enthusiasm. I resisted her certainty that the Pacific Northwest was God's country, the only place worth living. She had rarely traveled outside the region and for her it was inconceivable that it was not the greatest place on earth. But for me, still tenuous about leaving Africa without a proper goodbye, I couldn't buy into her zeal. I couldn't even appreciate the beauty of the Puget Sound and the Cascade mountains, let alone transfer my allegiance from Angola quite so quickly. Equally afflicted with the certainty that Africa was God's continent, I held Aunt Marcia at bay, and rejected anything she said or did.

Aunt Marcia, my mother's sister, was, I thought, like America itself, contradictory and irritating. I found her excessively friendly to us but a snob to anyone outside her social circle. As society page editor for the Tacoma *News Tribune*, she covered parties, debutante balls, and weddings with sixteen attendants and cakes with five layers for those who could afford to live in the north end of Tacoma with views of the Puget Sound. My mother and aunt, whose father had been a lawyer, had grown up in north Tacoma. The focus of her profession on the social elite shouldn't have been a surprise. But in my contrariness I thought, "Being society editor just proves she knows nothing about the world."

Actually, I couldn't imagine her nibbling a canapé at a cocktail party. She had a loud voice, wide shoulders, and the aggressive manner of the newspaperwoman she was. I thought she would look more at home tackling a controversy or downing an Olympia beer at the local newspaper hangout. I suppose that, a generation later, she wouldn't automatically have been relegated to the women's pages. But as a teenager with an attitude, I assumed this assignment demonstrated her deep moral failure.

The trivial stories she covered infuriated me, especially when I didn't see stories about Angola in the paper. In her world, the war against Portugal didn't exist, Angolans weren't being arrested and killed for wanting their independence. I held her responsible for the ignorance of Americans and any danger Dad might be in. In Tacoma, I felt as if I'd stepped out of the world into the confines of a closet. The niceties of sending wedding announcements in the correct number of envelopes, accompanied by slips of tissue paper, appeared to occupy her to the exclusion of what I considered life's real problems.

The attitudes I carried then I've discovered to be typical of many children who have been brought up outside their parents' culture. When reintroduced to America, they can be hypercritical. In response to the survey I had sent out, one U. S. Foreign Service brat expressed it this way, "(Living abroad) has sometimes made me overly impatient with what I consider parochial opinions on the part of others." A missionary kid said, "It's a worldview that gets into you and you become impatient and view with a type of contempt, people who cannot see beyond their city, county, state, country." My brother David said, "It can be easy to become cold and negative about things that matter to a lot of people. We had very clear messages about political and social values. The issues of imperialism, colonialism, and various sorts of aggression were realities, not ideas or television images."

My notion of Aunt Marcia's society world clashed radically with the missionary world. Even in Lobito, my mother had always felt a divide between the missionaries and the other expatriates in town, who were businessmen. She often felt snubbed by them. It was hard to miss the cheers and groans of the weekly badminton games going on next door, and Mom probably sneaked an envious look from our upper verandah at the happy hour gatherings. She was never invited by the Gants, and later the Bensons, and the Sidebothams, to join in. Although Mom didn't express her disappointment to me at the time, I could sense the difference between our neighbors and us. The fact that they smoked and drank, and missionaries didn't, were the trivial distinctions between us. According to Mom, the biggest obstacle to friendly relations with the expatriate community was the constant presence of Angolans in our house, eating at our table, having tea, attending services and meetings. Back in America, confronted not only with Aunt Marcia's enthusiasm for the Northwest, but also with her society connections, I found her too reminiscent of the expatriates next door in Lobito. Her values clashed with the values I'd grown up with; Africa was pitted against the Northwest; and a worldview that included Africa and Europe was pitted against what seemed to be the narrow concerns of Tacoma's upper middle class.

There is a certain irony that children brought up abroad look back on their foreign experiences in glowing terms but find their home cultures hard to take. I include myself in this incongruity. We claim to be tolerant of different cultures, embracing of diversity, able to look poverty in the face, but we are impatient with what we deem to be the parochial attitudes of Americans. We are unable to treat our own countrymen with the same generous spirit that we extend to others. And so it was for me with Aunt Marcia. I regret that she died young, before I could approach her with compassion. If I'd been less of a snob myself, I would have noted that my aunt and uncle made their bedroom in the cramped basement of their house so that my uncle's mother could have the airy master bedroom upstairs. I would have recognized that as the act of a generous person.

My mother loved the Pacific Northwest and thought of it as home. Aunt Marcia was her closest living relative and they had a friendly relationship, but Mom has told me that she had often felt dominated by her sister. When they were children, my aunt, who was a year or so older, bossed my mother around, and got out of household chores, leaving them for Mom to do. My mother told me an amusing story of revenge against her sister. "I guess I was about thirteen and there I was stuck again with the dishes. Marcia just had a knack for getting out of them. I found a can under the sink with a big poison sign on it. I think it must have been lye, and I spread it on one of my arms. Soon the arm was covered with festering blisters. It hurt, but I temporarily got out of washing dishes and Marcia had to do them! My family was very sympathetic to me; they assumed that I had contracted some skin disease going around school. And as a bonus, I attracted additional attention at school when I showed up wearing bandages and a sling."

Perhaps Mom was willing to leave the Pacific Northwest in part to make her own life away from her sister.

My mother loved to travel. I think she inherited the excitement of discovering places and learning intriguing customs from her father. One of his law clients was a railroad company, and his work called him to travel frequently to the Midwest and east coast. She romanticized travel despite the fact that her father's trips caused him to be absent from many of her important rites of passage, such as her graduations. When I asked her about her father's absences, my mother shrugged them off, unwilling to feel sorry for herself.

For reasons I couldn't discern, Aunt Marcia called my sister Kathy the "jewel of the Woods family." Did she have a sparkle that I lacked? Certainly she had smoother social graces than I and she had a quick wit like Dad. Soon after we arrived in Tacoma, Aunt Marcia invited "the jewel" to show her luster in the debutante season. Kathy declined the invitation, and we added the "jewel of the Woods family" to our fund of stories about Aunt Marcia that particularly amused us. The next year Aunt Marcia didn't invite me to be a deb, the result, perhaps, of a decision I had made about where to live when my mother made plans to return to Angola. "Nance," Mom had said, "with the boys and me going back to Angola, and Kathy going to college, what do you want to do? Do you want to move in with Aunt Marcia?"

"Oh, sis no," I had replied, in Rhodesian slang. "I can't live with her. She hacks me. And anyway, she isn't in the Wilson school district. I'd have to switch schools." At the time, I didn't want to deal directly with Aunt Marcia and I let Mom make my housing arrangements. I don't know how the conversation went, but my aunt may have felt both slightly insulted and greatly relieved that I wasn't going to move in. Her daughter, Janice, was leaving for college that year. If my aunt was at all like me, I looked forward to a house without children when my sons went away to school, and wouldn't have welcomed an unplanned guest who was also a prickly teenager.

When we arrived in Tacoma, we stayed with my aunt, uncle, and cousin Janice Lee, who was Kathy's age, while we looked for a house to rent. I had to get used to Aunt Marcia's husband, Uncle Ewan. He was a steel worker with large hands, blunt, stubby fingers, and the big-boned, well-padded look of a linebacker. When we were around, he was taciturn, preferring to putter in the basement or take care of the neverending chores required to keep his salmon fishing boat afloat. At meals with them, I sat as far from Uncle Ewan as possible because he always seemed annoyed with Aunt Marcia or the rest of us. "Huh," he grunted in answer to almost any question. To me they were an incongruous pair, Aunt Marcia, a conservative Republican, hooked up with this union man.

On our furlough when I was six, I must have looked frightened around Uncle Ewan because Aunt Marcia had reassured me, "Don't mind him. He sounds gruff but he's really a nice man." I remained unconvinced, but much later, on a trip back to Tacoma with my husband and two-year-old son, we attended a party at my cousin's house. Her spacious house, with large rooms, high ceilings and hardwood floors, was crammed with guests, mostly family, milling around, drinking beer and eating hamburgers and potato salad. Uncle Ewan stood off to the side by himself, smiling but looking as though he'd rather be on his boat. I finally empathized with him and realized that his gruffness masked a shy and gentle nature.

When Mom found a small, two-story bungalow she could afford to rent on North Verde Street, I was relieved to move out of Aunt Marcia's orbit. In the fall I enrolled in eleventh grade at Woodrow Wilson High School. I hoped to slip into American high school life as though I had lived in Tacoma forever. I'd had to make transitions from Angola to the United States in seventh grade, and from Angola to Rhodesia in ninth grade. I expected I'd make a relatively smooth transition again. In retrospect, this was an unrealistic expectation, a hope based in knowing intellectually that I was American and that my future lay in America. I was my father's daughter when it came to neatly divorcing my logical left-brain from my right-brain feelings. I didn't bargain on the strength of my unease, a sort of culture shock, the intensity of my disaffection with America, and the long-lasting trauma of losing Africa. In school I felt like an outsider and a stranger, stiff and jerky with my classmates. My hair, without warning, curled up instead of down. My nose was too big for my chin. My left and right profiles didn't match. My shoes were clunky saddle shoes instead of the ultra-cool penny loafers. I talked with a whisper of a Rhodesian accent. I said I reckon instead of I guess. I called my tennis shoes plimsoles. I said something was putsy instead of really easy. I had Africa on my brain. I was sure all those oddities gave me away. No doubt too, I cultivated them to keep America at arms length.

In Rhodesia I'd been a racer on the swim team, so in Tacoma I joined the closest equivalent, the Doll-Phins synchronized swim club. I earned points to join Varya, the girls' honorary society, by baking cakes, selling milk and doughnuts in the morning before school, and, of course, by working hard on my grade point average. I joined the model United Nations club to declare my interest in the world. We researched our assigned country's positions for hours after school, but on the weekend of the conference, a blizzard prevented us from driving across the Cascades to eastern Washington. The cancellation relieved me. I hadn't wanted to admit my fear of public speaking and public humiliation.

My activities alone couldn't integrate me into American life. Learning the correct leg extensions and how to hold my breath under water and how to create flawless patterns with the Doll-Phins temporarily assuaged my unease. But then I had the rest of my life. I wasn't good at initiating conversations and was easily put off if saying that I was from Africa wasn't followed up with interest. I assumed my classmates weren't curious, instead of realizing that they were as buffaloed by me as I was by them. All the ambivalence I'd felt toward the United States in seventh grade came surging back, as if the three intervening years were mere seconds. As much as I wanted to belong, I still saw Americans as pallid and provincial. You're so uninformed, I'd think, looking down my too-big nose at the other students.

Tarzan was what popped to mind when American kids thought about Africa. On furlough, when I was six, a child in Sunday school had asked Kathy and me if we'd ever seen Tarzan swinging by our house. We pretended we had. Now, at sixteen, I interpreted disinterest in or ignorance of Africa to mean that I personally was unworthy of attention. I became embarrassed to admit that was where I was from. It felt too weird. Since I didn't feel free to talk about Africa, I couldn't think what else to say to people. I might have asked what they knew about the world outside of Tacoma, or what excited them, or how they liked to spend their free time, or what ideas grabbed them. But I didn't and I felt myself becoming as boring and shallow as I imagined Americans to be.

Anatol Lieven's book, *America Right or Wrong: An Anatomy of American Nationalism*, sheds light on my persistent youthful feelings that Americans didn't care about the rest of the world. He says that in 2003 well more than half of Americans believed that American culture was superior to the rest of the world, compared to only a third of French people's sense of superiority. He cites a poll from 1999, in which 72 percent of Americans had pride in their country, while 53 percent of the British, with the next highest score, were proud of Britain. The figures were consistent with a poll taken fifteen years earlier. If our country is the greatest, what incentives do Americans have to be curious about other places? Flying the American flag, reciting the Pledge of Allegiance, and singing the national anthem at public gatherings foster the conviction that our nation has been chosen to fulfill a special destiny. I certainly found the Pledge of Allegiance to the flag in seventh grade a powerful motivator for my patriotism and pride in our democracy, while at the same time I felt estranged from the insularity of Americans. Lieven points out that the American creed, including faith in liberty, adherence to the Constitution and the law, belief in democracy, individualism, and cultural and political egalitarianism is what binds our nation of diverse cultural, religious, and ethnic groups together. It allows immigrants from around the world to become Americans. For me the creed was the crux both of my attraction and my resistance to America. Having grown up under an authoritarian Portuguese regime, I found America remarkably free and open. My spirit soared in the air of equality. But it plummeted when I realized that my childhood experiences had no meaning for most of the people I met in school.

Borrowing from my past, I found an antidote to my loneliness. I immersed myself in schoolwork, just as earlier in my life I'd focused on learning French, Umbundu, and Latin. Researching, reading, and writing became my passions. I comforted and entertained myself by working hard. My goal was straight A's by the end of senior year, and this was a target I could reach, regardless of the approval or disapproval of my peers. The only people I had to convince were my teachers.

Mr. Rhule, my English teacher, was a slight, balding man with glasses and a right eye that wandered. His students called him "Rockin' Robert" because he made us laugh.

"Your homework for the weekend is Donne," said Mr. Rhule, pausing to made sure we got his pun. "John Donne, that is. Write an essay based on his poem 'No man is an island.' " Decades later, I still remember this routine assignment, I suppose because it reconfirmed my connections to other people and to the world. I wasn't an island, separate from the rest of Wilson High School or my father in Angola or my friends in Rhodesia, even when that's how I felt. I read the poem over and over until I had it memorized. Its language soothed me and tugged at the part of me that longed for Africa. When I was lonely and in a distant place, I'd whisper to myself, "Any man's death diminishes me, because I am involved in Mankind; And therefore never send to know for whom the bell tolls; It tolls for Thee."

When Mr. Rhule read my essay aloud to my classmates, I knew I had proven myself, at least in an intellectual sense, to belong to my class. Through Donne I could admit that my fellow students were people just like me, despite not knowing how to talk to them. "Never send to know for whom the bell tolls," it tolled for all of us.

In April 1962, toward the end of eleventh grade, my mother's one-year visa was about to expire. She decided to take David and Mark back to Angola to rejoin Dad. The war had settled into a sporadic and mostly livable course, with the fighting largely away from central Angola. Massive numbers of Portuguese troops kept it from escalating, at least temporarily. Kathy and I remained in Tacoma. Kathy finished twelfth grade and then prepared to go to Antioch College in Ohio. With only one more year of high school, I recognized that it made more sense for me to stay in Tacoma than to return to Rhodesia. My reason told me I should stay in Tacoma; my heart wished I could have returned with Mom. Had I gone to Africa with her, I still would have been far from home in Salisbury. I don't recall any conversation with my mother about my choices. My sister and I continued living in the house on North Verde Street, and were joined by Hazel Lundeen, a widow Mom had engaged to watch out for us. When Mom left, I had an odd sense of relief that more of my family would be back in Angola, anchoring me, in spirit, more securely to home. As happened when I took on the care of Tezinha, I felt perfectly capable of a more independent life. Left to fend for ourselves, though, we soon ran into problems.

After Mom departed, the support money from the mission board arrived several weeks late in May and June. "We can't pay Hazel till we get some money," Kathy told me and her boyfriend Larry, who spent much of his free time with us. "I think we are even going to have to ask Hazel for food money," she said, "and take a little out of savings for my graduation fees." Larry and we debated our options. "I'll help you write a letter to the Board," Larry said. We hauled out the typewriter and politely explained our predicament. It took a couple of letters to begin receiving the checks on time, but not before we had to scrap our plan to take driver's training in summer school. When she left, Mom had handed over the household responsibilities to us. Not wanting to burden Hazel with more than the cooking, Kathy and I paid the bills, mowed the lawn, mopped the kitchen and bathroom, and wrote thank you notes to a church for sending us second-hand clothes. "Most of them, though," I wrote my parents, "are too old, too big, or too old-fashioned."

At the beginning of June, Hazel moved home and Dad's brother and family arrived from El Paso, Texas, to spend the summer with us. Uncle Dick and Aunt Joanne brought along their four young children. Although I barely knew them, I was happy to let them fill in for my missing family. "Uncle Dick looks so much like Dad," I wrote my parents, "and he talks the same too."

I'd sit at the dining room table, watching Uncle Dick make reeds for his oboe. He taught in the music department of the University of Texas in El Paso. He was tall and skinny, and, if he'd grow out his crew cut, I thought, he could be the father I hadn't seen in a year and a half. My four cousins, ranging in age from seven to one, filled the small house with noise and energy. While Aunt Joanne cooked dinner, I would talk with her and distract the baby from clinging to her legs. One night the baby, slung on my hip, and I were blowing bubbles and vibrating mouth farts at each other. Aunt Joanne was stirring the spaghetti sauce and washing lettuce for a salad. The radio, droning in the background, caught our attention when the newsman announced the suicide of Marilyn Monroe.

"Oh, she was such a dumb blonde," I said, sticking my nose as far in the air as it could go. To me she *was* shallow America. She was society, flash, and sex. I didn't have any sympathy to waste on her. But Aunt Joanne startled me when she said, "Marilyn Monroe had a tough life." My aunt saw the real and complicated woman behind the image, and showed genuine sorrow for her death. I was ashamed of myself.

I didn't want summer to end. I wished the Hendersons didn't have to return to El Paso. I didn't want Kathy to go off to college in Ohio and leave me alone in Tacoma.

Aunt Marcia had invited me to live with her family my senior year, but I had visions of being sucked into the maw of America where I'd be transformed into an acceptable American girl. True, I fervently wished to pass but I didn't want to become Aunt Marcia's sort of American girl. I wanted to disentangle my American conundrum on my own turf. When Kathy went to Antioch, I moved out of the North Verde house and around the corner with the Graham family whom I had known through church and baby-sitting for their children. In exchange for doing house cleaning and baby-sitting for Jeannie and Janie, their eight-year old twin daughters, and Jack Ed, who was three, they charged almost nothing for me to live with them.

They carved a bedroom for me out of a sliver of space at the top of the stairs in the converted attic. Jeannie and Janie's room filled the rest of the attic. My room, windowless with slanted ceiling, was a cozy golden-brown cave, just big enough to hold a bed, bedside stand, small bookcase, desk, and me. The dresser was built in to the wall. There, shielded from the yells and giggles of the children and the manic laugh tracks on the television downstairs, I retreated most evenings to complete my homework and work on college applications.

"Dear Mom and Dad," I wrote one evening, leaning against some pillows on my bed, "I thought being on my own would be easier as I got older, but for some reason it's harder. Angola seems so far away." At seventeen, I understood I'd left Africa for good, but I didn't know where to find a new niche. Africa had been my center, a part of my identity, where I'd lived my life. Tacoma was just a temporary stop on my way to... where?

From the solitude of my tiny room, I dreamed up plans to escape. The most promising route, the road I could follow without consulting map and compass, was to concentrate on school. The sheer momentum of deadlines, reading assignments, and reports propelled me. I tackled chemistry and philosophy, subjects that I understood far better than the turmoil inside me. Both disciplines forced me outside my comfortable ways of thinking. I was confounded by the mathematics of chemistry and spent long hours on the phone at night with my lab partner, Diane, figuring out, sometimes even concocting, our lab results. Since neither Diane nor I were able to clearly explain our results, the A I received in chemistry first semester shocked me.

Philosophy was life changing for me, clarifying questions about my religious beliefs, and challenging my assumptions about what was real and true. Aha! I thought, Christianity represents but one out of dozens of ideas on how to live. I could aim to be a good person, someone my parents would be proud of, without believing in their God. Philosophy and the Liberal Arts Seminar for honors students I attended in the spring set me free intellectually. During a weekend in May, we retreated to a camp near Mount Rainier to discuss existentialism, images of the self, and the theater of the absurd. Our instructors were four University of Washington professors of psychology, philosophy, and literature. When I arrived I was surprised to find that only twenty-five students from around the state had been invited.

"We talked about anything under the sun," I wrote my parents. "What shocked me most was that some of the professors advocated free love. But it was the most fascinating, stimulating, enjoyable, exhilarating, invigorating, bewildering weekend I've ever spent. I'm all charged up and ready to really study and LEARN. I discovered so many things I knew nothing about so now I want to read, read, read."

I came home after that weekend determined to write my philosophy term paper on whether hedonism is consistent with Christianity. Earlier I had planned to write about duty and conscience. Suddenly that topic seemed dull, dull, dull. I felt like throwing off those straitjackets and diving straight into passion and enthusiasm. I wanted to dance and play with the ideas: Can free love be reconciled with Christian faithfulness? Can a Christian be a pleasure-seeking sensualist? I no longer remember what conclusions I came to in my term paper, but at least in the life of my mind, I was free of constraints and open to possibilities.

Searching for the right college to attend became a tangible way to imagine myself out of Tacoma and into my own future, toward a life of my own choosing in America. Kathy was at school in Ohio. To make it easier for us to spend vacations together, I focused on Midwestern schools. My guidance counselor at Wilson, Miss Moyers, helped me select several small liberal arts colleges, including Oberlin, Grinnell, and Carleton. As a back up, I also applied at Lewis and Clark in Oregon. I respected Miss Moyers' advice; I didn't at all trust the judgment of Aunt Marcia and the Grahams. Marge Graham, my temporary mother, used to tell me, "Your high school years are the BEST years of your life!" I'm sure she repeated that four or five times that year. I didn't try to contradict her, but thought to myself, "God help me if this is the best it's going to be." My parents, although interested in my choices, were too far away in miles and time to offer help. Phone service in Angola still wasn't available and letters could take three weeks to arrive.

Beneath my public assurance, I was sad, with a Dondi and Salisbury sadness, a hollow missing-my-family sadness. In the quiet of the night, I dreamed disturbing dreams and yearned for connection to people I loved. I had a series of dreams about my father. By then I hadn't seen him for two years and I idolized him. My mother had encouraged us children to venerate him, perhaps so we wouldn't see his all too human qualities. I kept a picture of him on my dresser. He stood so tall and handsome, shaking José Chipenda's hand in front of the new Portuguese church. Dad, in his light blue suit that accented the blue in his green eyes, looked down on the shorter Pastor José, who was wearing a white suit made even more dazzling by his dark skin. . . Dad at work, at church, smiling but purposeful. I missed him so much that he drove into my dreams once in a dilapidated car, another time in a dream about the end-of-year party for the *Banner*, the school newspaper. I said I didn't know he was on the staff and he said, "Well, if you had read the *Banner* this year you would have seen my name." I used to read the paper every week; how had I missed him?

One night Dad crept into my dreams and died.

That fall at the Grahams' house I had another dream about death and dispossession. "Dear Mom and Dad," I wrote, "I had the most awful dream last night," and I recounted it to them. "I'm in an enormous rambling Victorian house, owned by a group who takes in cancer patients. The house sits on an island in the middle of a lake and is surrounded by a high wall. At the end of the year, the current residents have to leave to make room for the next group. We are driven away by cyanide pellets dripping from the attic and spreading throughout the house. As the residents burst out of the house, the owners shoot at us. I am escaping with a little boy on my back, climbing the high wall and swimming across the lake. Along the way, I lose the boy but dodge the bullets."

I didn't receive any response from my parents, and at the time it simply seemed to be a terrible nightmare. But, it would recur for years, and I now understand the dream as a way for my unconscious to work through losing Angola. I had felt driven out of Africa, just as I was repeatedly driven out of the house in the dream. And the child may be the lost me, or it may be the lost Tez. After living in America for over fifteen years, the nightmare finally ceased its occasional visits. By then I had married, given birth to two sons, and moved into the house where I still live.

Around the same time as the nightmare, an ugly, red, suppurating boil erupted on my right cheek, as if the disease in my dreams had spread to my body. It grew alarmingly fast and developed a hard, deep core that pulsed and ached. Day after day I soaked my cheek with hot salt water and pushed out the pus. I wore a Band-Aid over the boil when I went to school in a futile effort to hide the festering sore. Out of kindness, perhaps, or embarrassment, no one at school asked about it and I didn't speak of it either. But even when it subsided and healed, it left a scar and a lump in my cheek.

April 23, 1963 marked the first-year anniversary of my mother's return to Africa. In commemoration, I made myself a small badge with a simple "1" crayoned in red. I wore it to school pinned to my dress, a tiny scrap of paper barely visible to anyone else. I hoped someone at school would ask about it, but no one did. On me, it burned with infrared heat into my chest, a small flame against the darkness of loss, the loss of family but, more essentially, the loss of Africa. I wrote my parents that I was all tied in knots. "I feel like crying," I wrote, "but when I cry I don't know what I'm crying about. I need someone to talk to but no one here really understands."

How was it, I asked myself, that I'd ended up alone in Tacoma, coping with a chilly damp climate? How had I taken root with the Grahams, who tended me tolerantly but who thought me rather odd and I in turn thought them odd? Marge Graham would say, "You need to get out and have fun!

These are the best years of your life! How can you study all the time?" I thought studying *was* fun, but couldn't convince her. Jack Graham, the father, was a traveling insurance salesman. I was glad that he was gone most of the week, because I found it repulsive to watch him stuffing mashed potatoes and gravy into his grossly fat face and hear him tell the same joke at every meal. Its punch line always included Piggly Wiggly and Hogly Wogly. I would force out an unconvincing, "Heh, heh." Despite my teenage eye rolling, the Grahams were easy to live with, just the latest in my string of surrogate parents. I appreciated their purchasing a piano for me to continue my music lessons, and I liked reading stories to the three kids.

The Grahams were kind, but I didn't fit into their lives. Unlike previous furloughs when I was six and twelve, I couldn't lull myself with the anticipation of returning to Angola after a year. I was here for good. Only fantasies of college promised an escape.

Despite my sadness, I accomplished my goal of finishing twelfth grade with straight A's. I had been accepted at all the colleges I'd applied to, and, when Carleton offered me the best scholarship, I accepted. Aunt Marcia and my cousin attended my graduation and soon afterward I set off for the summer, visiting family and friends. I wandered through California, Texas, Ohio, and Illinois, until in September 1963 I arrived at Carleton College in Northfield, Minnesota.

From my bed in Gridley Hall I looked out the enormously tall window at the arriving freshmen and their families crossing the Bald Spot in the middle of campus and dispersing to their dorms. My room, though it had a soaring twenty-foot ceiling, was just wide enough to hold two beds, dressers, and desks. I had unpacked my clothes, made up my bed with linens given to me by a church in Chicago, set the high school graduation gift from my parents, a portable Olivetti typewriter, on my desk, and now I waited for my roommate, Judy.

Judy was coming from Milwaukee where her father was an Episcopal priest. I could guess why we were put together, although it made me worry that someone at college thought my religious background my most salient quality. I wondered if Judy would expect me, a missionary kid, to be pious or devoutly Christian or a goody-goody. In my previous dorms, our parents' religion was our reason for being there, but not why I felt most comfortable with my dormmates. We had cheered each other with laughter. We had claimed each other as family. I hoped Judy and I could forget our religious childhoods and just be friends.

I needn't have worried about fitting into Judy's preconceptions of me. "Oh, excuse me," she said, as she bumped the door open and entered our room. "Oh, sorry, these are my parents, Rev. and Mrs. Gaskell." Her father looked stern and somewhat forbidding. I thought I'd probably keep apologizing too if he were my father. After they left, she made up her bed and we pondered the dilemma of what sort of curtains could cover a sixteen-foot window. "What do you think?" she asked.

"I don't know; what do you think we should do?" I said.

"Well, I don't think they make curtains that long," she said. In the end we agreed to look downtown for café curtains that would cover the bottom few feet of the window.

On the first night when we prepared for bed, Judy suddenly disappeared. I hadn't heard the floor creak, indicating she'd left the room, but she was gone. "Jude, are you there?" I asked. I heard a rustle in the closet. "What are you doing?" I asked.

"Oh sorry," I heard her muffled voice say, and she emerged, red-faced, in her nightie.

"Don't be embarrassed to undress in front of me," I told her. "I won't stare. I've lived too long in dorms to care about that."

"Well, I don't know," she said. We were weeks into first term before she ventured to dress and undress in front of me, but well before then I realized she wasn't any more pious than I was.

On the first day at Carleton I went next door to meet our neighbors, Marti and Raquel, on one side, and Rena, on the other. Where Judy was reticent, Marti, a Californian, was boisterous and friendly. I was immediately intrigued to find that she had attended boarding school in Colorado and I thought we might have common experiences. When I discovered that Raquel was a Spanish-speaker from Panama, and Rena was Greek, my international antennae went up and I felt at home with them.

Marti, Judy, and I bonded during freshman orientation. We along with the rest of the freshmen had been summoned to meet on the Bald Spot. "What are we doing?" I asked. "I don't know. Something about beanies," Marti said. Our resident assistant, Anne, handed out beanies to each of us, and instructed us to embroider our names on them. "Oh my god, have you ever heard of anything more stupid?" we all chimed in. To make it worse, the girls were also expected to embroider the boys' beanies. "Dumb, dumb, dumb," we said. We did as we were told, but not without deriding this hallowed tradition. When Anne passed on the word, "Carleton students must not be seen downtown in jeans," we immediately plotted how we could thwart the rules we thought ridiculous, and wondered if maybe we'd come to the wrong college. I had visited my sister at Antioch on my way to Carleton and it has been on Marti's list of colleges. Well known for its bohemian atmosphere, Antioch had become my standard for freedom and independence. At Carleton, our 10:15 curfew left us barely enough time to get back from the library in the evening before our dorm mother locked the front door. Meanwhile, the freshmen boys were allowed to have breakfast at the Ideal Café downtown at 1 o'clock in the morning. We made fun of the restrictions on inviting boys into our rooms. Twice a month on Sunday afternoons, we had Open House. The rules were, "The door must be six inches ajar, and there must be three feet on the floor at all times." "We should have gone to Antioch," became our mantra. Still, in my bones I knew life at Carleton was a vast improvement over Tacoma. Freshman year, living in a dorm within a small closed community, transported me back to familiar ground and shored up the confidence I'd felt slipping away in Tacoma.

Everything changed sophomore year. At the end of the summer of 1964 my family came to spend their furlough year in Chicago, and I fell into depression.

For years I've wondered about the connection between those events. That year, I was seeing my father for the first time since January 1961 when I had been fifteen. Now I was nineteen. I had last seen my mother and brothers in April 1962. My new Carleton friends had buffered my loneliness, but that hadn't kept me from writing, as a freshman, a tongue-in-cheek letter to my long lost parents on "the delicate matter of desertion. Since that tragic date when we became separated, I have been unsuccessfully attempting to seek you out." I don't recall a reply. On their actual return, I expected to be and thought I should be happy to see them, but instead I felt increasingly estranged.

I was living in Chicago with Kathy, her husband, Larry, and their newborn son, Christopher, during the summer of 1964 when my parents and brothers arrived. Christopher was the most wonderful baby I'd known since Tezinha. He was bright, responsive, and smiled with his whole squirming body. And he cushioned the reunion with my family. All our attention was riveted on him.

"Oh, look, he's smiling."

"Hi Christopher, what a sweet baby."

"Aww, d'you want to eat? Are you tired? Do you need a clean diaper?"

This new little Henderson mesmerized us and diverted our attention from each other.

Around the fall Parents' Weekend, I started to feel sick. A lump curiously like homesickness settled in my gut, but what was I homesick for? I felt off-balance, as though I were standing on a swinging bridge, trying to steady myself and quell the nausea, while the bridge threatened to break loose from its moorings and fling me off.

"I don't know what I'm going to do," I said to Judy. "My mother and father are coming for Parents' Weekend."

"Why not take them to the football game?" she said.

I grabbed onto that suggestion. I no longer knew them well enough to tailor the day to their interests. Although spectator sports bored me, entertaining my parents with football seemed like a good way to spend several hours. Our attention would be focused on the players running up the field and slamming into each other. I could watch the crowd and spot people I knew. We could buy hot chocolate to warm us up. We'd hardly need to talk. During the week leading up to Parents' Weekend, I'd seen reminders to "Buy a corsage for your mother." I couldn't bring myself to buy her one. Buying a corsage seemed sentimental and sappy, like something Aunt Marcia would want me to do. And I was afraid the flowers would signal a love I didn't feel. But, as we walked across campus to the football game that Saturday afternoon, the red carnation on every other mother's chest flared, dazzled, demanded my attention. I knew my mother couldn't be blind to them either. And, as we sat in the stadium, the sweet, rich scent of the carnations rose warm and cloying around us and mixed with the chocolaty smell of the cocoa. I knew Mom could smell it too. I wanted to gag. I was ashamed to even look at her.

I despaired of loving my parents. They were nearer to me than they'd been in years, but I wished they would go back to Angola where they belonged. In the United States, they left me rootless and lost. They were too uncomfortably close for the only love I could conjure for them; a nostalgic pining that wasn't robust enough for the reality of their living, breathing bodies. The love I'd nurtured in my attic room in Tacoma, a distant childlike devotion to abstract parents, had somehow to be transferred to a mother who seemed too nosy and a father too aloof.

I didn't know what Christmas vacation would be like in my parents' Chicago house. It turned out that I found myself in the uncomfortable situation of feeling more American in some ways than my family. I had become enamored of Bob Dylan, and I took all my Dylan albums to Chicago to play over vacation. "Hey, who is that?" my brother David asked. "He sounds stupid." A look of amazement and disgust came over his face, when he heard Dylan's nasal, insistent songs. David was fourteen.

But something in me responded to Dylan's poetry, his political messages and alienation. His whine made me nostalgic for a Portuguese *fado*.

My mother registered her complaints about me as well. I was certain I'd found just the right Christmas present for my father when I walked into a bookstore and was drawn to the luminous reds and blues of stained glass on the cover of a coffee table book of Christian art. It brought together my love of art with Dad's love of books and his Christian vocation. (I was thinking about majoring in art history after taking the introductory course that fall.) But Mom was horrified by my gift choice.

"$20 is way too much to pay for a book like that," she said. "What use is it? What can he do with it? It's a waste of money."

In 1964, $20 was a lot of money. I suppose Mom was despairing of her college daughter's lack of financial sense. Mom's practical nature must have wished I had spent the money on a useful present, like a tie that Dad could wear to work, or socks to replace the worn out supply he'd left in Angola. On the other hand, Dad seemed pleased with the book, although it wasn't the sort of academic book he would have chosen for himself. It's possible that I gave it to reveal something of my own interests to him. The glossy book of photographs of Chartres Cathedral's asymmetrical spires, Notre Dame's luscious rose window, the otherworldly quality of early Christian sculpture, and the Ravenna mosaics dazzled me. I could almost smell the sharpness of incense and feel the cool hush of the dark interior of the cathedral when I looked at the book

I didn't know how to respond to either David or Mom.

By spring term of my sophomore year at Carleton I had no interest in my classes. I couldn't concentrate on them. They all seemed irrelevant and pointless. I avoided working on them by attending every campus flick that came along . . . "Richard III," "The Last Bridge," "Raisin in the Sun," "Black Orpheus." I conversed into the night with friends. I ignored the class-assigned books and read *Black Like Me* and *The Fire Next Time*, hoping to blot out the queasiness in my gut. The smallest setback or nothing at all made me cry. One Friday night, I fought back tears the whole time I was setting up my wait station in the dining hall. The girl who had said she'd fill in for me had reneged on her promise.

"Leah," I said to a friend and fellow waitress, "I'm going to cry."

And to my embarrassment I did. After Leah helped me get a "conditional," an excuse from waiting that night, I retreated to my room.

I wanted to gather in my sorrowing self, to make myself whole. And the next minute I wanted to escape, scatter myself in the wind. But where would I go? What would I do? My parents' house was no refuge. Angola was a distant fantasy. For four years I'd tried to be a cheerful and purposeful American girl. On the surface I looked and sounded like I belonged. Inside I hid a desperate longing for home.

I yearned to lie in bed on a Saturday night listening to the steady pounding of drums, floating across the bay from the *sanzala*, overlaid by a swell of calls and responses.

I yearned for Dondi's air, with its head-clearing sharpness of eucalyptus, and Lobito's salt air.

I yearned for mangoes, ripened soft and orange, their juices dribbling down my chin and dripping off my elbows.

I yearned to climb a nespra tree for clusters of fruit that hung like fat yellow droplets.

I dreamed of Portuguese friends and Angolan friends, British, Dutch, Canadian, and American friends; missionary aunts and uncles who played musical saws and pianos, recited poetry to help us go to sleep, popped out their false teeth to make us laugh.

I was full of a sorrow I could not speak.

The Africa I had sequestered in my soul had no voice here. How would I find my way home?

Chapter 14 — Finding My Place

Caku suñama, cu ku upa vendo.
Quaisquer acontecimentos que se destinam para nós,
não escolhem o tempo e o lugar em que nos encontremos.
No matter what events are destined for us,
their time and place will be a surprise.

Umbundu proverb

In the spring of 1965, when I was a sophomore, I wanted to drop out of school. I made an appointment to talk with the Dean of Women. In tears I said, "I just can't go on." Dean Phillips, whom my friends and I called Mean Dean Jean, because we blamed her for the annoying *in loco parentis* rules we were actively rebelling against, soon ferreted out the information that I had no plan, no idea where I would go, or what I would do. I wept and she shoved a box of tissues my way. I blew my nose, looked at her out of bleary eyes, and was surprised to find a sympathetic face gazing at me. "Perhaps a better solution is to simply drop one of your classes," she suggested. "O.K." I said, taking a minute to think about it. I managed a grin of relief because that plan would keep me at Carleton and on track to graduate. As much as I resisted the curfews and the protective rules directed especially at the girls, and as much as I still occasionally announced the superior virtues of Antioch over Carleton, I had made friends at Carleton and I liked that I recognized the faces of all 1200 students. Dean Phillips helped me with the paperwork for dropping my course, and with a lighter spirit I thanked her and said goodbye.

In the bright sun of a chilly Minnesota spring morning, the tension and anxiety that had been gripping me for much of the school year loosened its hold. In the pressure cooker of a 10-week term, dropping one class out of three enormously diminished my stress. I walked to the student union to get my mail and stopped at the announcement board to check on upcoming events. "Action Party meeting tonight at 7:30 to organize a teach-in on Vietnam," caught my eye.

Until now, Action Party had mainly organized protests against on-campus "atrocities" that violated the students' sense of independence. Carleton's orientation materials had promised to develop us into critical and independent thinkers, and students in the early to mid 1960's grabbed hold of that pledge to push the school administration to its limits. We protested the dismissal of a dorm counselor for badly enforcing the open house rules, and the indefinite suspension of the staff of Truth, Ltd., which published satiric rags under the names of True Romances, The Happy Times, and Field and Scream. The Field and Scream issue had run a tongue-in-cheek ad for "Troiani. Live it up with the lively ones! 35¢—tipped or plain." The offending edition also included a special yellow Arb Extra, with articles such as "Advice for those hung over," and "How to get two in a one-man bag." As usual, I had read that issue of puerile humor and hadn't thought much of it. Suddenly the staff was sent home, but I didn't understand what the uproar was about. Someone had to explain, "Troiani is a perversion of Trojan, as in Trojan-brand condoms." I must have looked perplexed. I had no idea what condoms were. Obviously I was titillated and embarrassed by the whole idea of condoms, because soon I dreamed I was walking along the sidewalk toward my dorm, with my winter coat pockets so full of condoms that they threatened to spring out. I looked up to see Mean Dean Jean approaching me, and I madly, but unsuccessfully, tried to keep the condoms from leaping out as I passed her. She gave me a sour look.

As my dream suggested, sex and the male animal occupied a portion of my thoughts. After a couple of dry years in Tacoma, when the only boy with whom I had struck up a friendship was a loner alcoholic, I came to Carleton very attuned to attractive males. One of the first items on our to-do list, when Judy and I met, was to pour over the zoo book, a booklet issued to each freshman with a picture of the new students, along with names and hometowns. "So, who do you like?" I'd ask Judy. "Look at this guy, John. He's cute," she'd say. "Hmm, yeah, I think Victor is REALLY cute!" I'd say. We tried to spot our likely boyfriend candidates on campus.

I didn't succeed in capturing my choices. Instead that year, I dated a freshman boy who wanted to become a minister. We met a few times in the Tea Room of the Student Union until I realized how bored I was. I hung out with a big, brash upperclassman who conferred a bit of his fame on me; he was well known as a wild man, staying out all night at parties with his girlfriend of the moment. I wasn't especially attracted to him as a boyfriend, but he was far more exciting than the little freshman boy. He took me for walks around the arb, the arboretum that surrounded campus; we talked about campus politics and he teased me about my love of Beethoven. He was from the mountains of Tennessee and liked what I thought was hillbilly music. In the spring of freshman year, I dated a senior who courted me with bottles of Chianti on picnics in the arb. We lolled on a blanket, I sipped my first tastes of wine, and we breathed in the intoxicating sweetness of blooming lilacs. He took me to the only formal dance I've ever attended. Using a purloined key, he introduced me to the extensive maze of tunnels connecting campus buildings, warm retreats on cold Minnesota nights. And then he graduated and dropped out of sight. None of these relationships went beyond casual kissing. Meanwhile, I was honing my sexual theories with the help of my dormmates.

The *Playboy Philosophy* and the newly published *The Feminine Mystique*, by Betty Friedan, became the sources of endless discussions. Marti, Judy, and I, and our friends Danna and Leah, sat in a pile on the couch across from my room. Resting our legs across each other, turning toward each other, we were full of the liberating ideas that Hugh Hefner and Betty Friedan offered. In December 1962, Hugh Hefner had begun running a monthly editorial in *Playboy*, answering criticisms of his magazine. The *Playboy Philosophy* was resolutely male-oriented, but we applied his arguments to ourselves.

"Look," Danna said, "sex is O.K. for us too. We're as free as boys, as long as we're not hurting anyone." Danna, our *Playboy* authority, had copies of the magazine. She pointed out a section dealing with free speech and free love that quoted a professor at the University of Illinois. "With modern contraceptives and medical advice readily available at the nearest drugstore, or at least a family physician, there is no valid reason why sexual intercourse should not be condoned among those sufficiently mature to engage in it without social consequences and without their own codes of morality and ethics."

I had little doubt about my maturity. I was a college woman now and a critical and independent thinker. I was the cream of academic society, or at least the college officials had repeatedly told us so in our freshman week convocations. They recited how many of us had come from the top ten percent of our high school classes, how many were National Merit Scholars, and how many of us had unusual talent in athletics, music, drama, and student government. "This is a real lean, hard class—there is no fat. There are no dullards," the director of admissions told the student newspaper. I wasn't convinced those superlatives applied to me. Could I somehow pass for the crème de la crème? The whole notion made me timid in class. I kept my mouth shut in case my professors discovered I was mere skim milk.

"Yeah, The Pill keeps us from getting pregnant," said Leah. The birth control pill, Enovid, had just come available in 1960 and was poised to eliminate much of the fear and shame of pregnancy outside marriage. I knew about the pill but not about condoms.

We responded to the intelligent reasonableness of Hefner's arguments and his optimism about the "Upbeat Generation." "After 20 years of stultifying conformity," wrote Hefner, "a new generation has awakened America's natural optimism, rebel spirit and belief in the importance of the individual." Our rebellion against petty school rules and in loco parentis certainly allied us with the Upbeat Generation.

The Feminine Mystique gave us reason for optimism from a woman's perspective. "See, Betty Friedan says women should have the same futures as men. We don't have to be satisfied with just being housewives," said Marti. "In fact, she says just being housewives and mothers without other interests is making women feel empty and dissatisfied. I'll read what she says, 'It is my thesis that as the Victorian culture did not permit women to accept or gratify their basic sexual needs, our culture does not permit women to accept or gratify their basic need to grow and fulfill their potentialities as human beings, a need which is not solely defined by their sexual role.'"

"You know what this college recruiter asked me?" I said "Last year when I was in high school, he asked me why I wanted to go to college. I said I wanted to get an education so I could get a job, and he said I bet you want to go to get a husband. I didn't know what to say. Of course, I want a husband, but that's not why I wanted to go to college!"

On the one hand, *Playboy* was telling me to embrace sexual freedom, a heady message for an eighteen-year-old college student. On the other hand, *The Feminine Mystique* explained that the problem for women was that we had been exclusively defined by our sexual relations with men, and we were not encouraged to think about the world. I intended to have both man and world, but I had no clear idea how to get them.

I started sophomore year without a boyfriend in sight with whom to practice my theories of free sex, or with whom to work out who I might be in this world. A boyfriend seemed a necessary collaborator for me to get on in life. I didn't have a sense of myself as a freestanding, independent adult who could choose my own future.

In the past, I had looked for self and home in religion and Africa and school. Working hard at school had been my solution when dealing with difficult social and emotional transitions. Studying had always offered a familiar and comfortable refuge from inner conflicts and questions such as, "Where is my home in this world? And how can I make myself home with myself?" Now it felt odd but necessary to slack off on academics. Instead of feeling liberated by school, I had become frustrated with the time it took away from discovering more about America and my place in it. My family's arrival on furlough had put me into a deep funk where I stayed until my appointment with Dean Phillips that spring.

I had poked fun at Dean Phillips and Dean Jarchow, the men's dean, for restricting our freedom, had indignantly marched on the college President's house, and had signed petitions to abolish the weekly chapel requirement. The teach-in on Vietnam presented me with an altogether more serious matter. One I wanted to investigate, now that I was relieved of some academic pressure. With Dean Phillips' support, I jumped at the chance to get out of the library and into a real life problem with international implications. Now politics and love seemed the most fruitful ways to find my self and home.

I attended the Action Party meeting that night and began educating myself about Vietnam. The *Carletonian* newspaper ran editorials and articles about Vietnam, and the faculty of the college volunteered to run weekend teach-ins about its history and why we should be concerned about the United States' recent engagement there. And when Action Party started recruiting people for a march on Washington, D.C. to protest the Vietnam War, I signed up, along with Marti and Judy.

Carleton students shared buses to the march with University of Minnesota students. On the long bus ride to Washington I met Tom and Larry. They both attracted me enormously. Tom, a University of Minnesota student, was our bus leader. He was slim, not very tall, casual and easy. We both sat at the front of the bus and I surreptitiously watched him from across the aisle, in charge but relaxed and friendly. All the way to the march and home again I fantasized. We'd flirt, he'd find me irresistible, we'd bond over our shared political views, we'd talk on the phone, and we'd visit each other in Minneapolis and Northfield. He pulled his guitar out of the battered case on the seat next to him and led the riders on the bus in singing "Study War No More." He was the ultimate in cool.

In Washington DC, I hung out and marched with Marti and Judy and other Carleton students, but on the bus ride home, I was back near Tom. He called over to me, "Why don't you come sit with me so we can talk?" I lost no time in moving over. I told him I was from Angola and to show how cool and exotic I was, I relayed a story about my pet *ongongolo*, a giant millipede. "When I went away to school in fourth grade, I captured this *ongongolo* and kept it in a shoebox. It must have been five or six inches long and half an inch in diameter, with a hard dark brown shell sort of thing and tons of legs." Tom seemed fascinated. "I fed it leaves when I remembered. It must not have needed much food to keep it going because it seemed like it lived for a long time." I floated along, in my romantic daydream, wishing the bus would never arrive in Minnesota.

"Listen," said Tom, "I'm a member of a coalition that is planning a Minneapolis teach-in and march this spring. Why don't you join us when we get home? We need more help," Is that his way of saying he wants to keep seeing me, I wondered? "I'd love to," I promised.

Larry was another member of the coalition on the bus. He was a Carleton student whom I'd seen around campus, and a serious labor radical. After the Washington march, I used to go to Minneapolis on the bus with him, hoping to see Tom at coalition meetings. At one meeting, Tom spoke to me, smiling and sociable, "Guess what? I met a girl from South Africa—a doctor's daughter." An Africa connection. I was convinced that proved he had been thinking about me. At another meeting, he asked, "How's that caterpillar?" More evidence, obviously, that I was on his mind. But after the coalition march, the school year ended a few weeks later and I didn't see Tom again.

I saw more of Larry through the spring since he was on campus and I rode the bus with him, not only to the coalition meetings, but also to Young Socialist Alliance meetings. Larry was a member of Y.S.A. and no doubt saw me as a potential recruit. He would recommend books to me and take me to lectures on labor history. I liked his slightly rumpled, scholarly look, his tousle of black hair flopping into his glasses. Along with teaching me parts of American history of which I was completely ignorant, Larry gave me an inside look at the factionalism of left wing and socialist politics. I dreamed of turning our intellectual attraction into romance and even love.

"I personally favor Lenin over Trotsky," Larry told me. He went on to compare Y.S.A. to the Students for a Democratic Society.

"Y.S.A. is a much better organization because it's rigid and disciplined. It has a definite point of view. S.D.S. attracts all sorts of people who all believe different things, so, in a red-baiting investigation, S.D.S. will fall apart."

"I can see your point," I said, "but I like that the Minneapolis march coalition was made up of members of all those groups... the Dubois club, Women's International League for Peace and Freedom, Y.S.A., the Friends Society, and S.D.S. I like variety." As much as I liked Larry, I remained skeptical about the Y.S.A. information he fed me. I didn't question him, but I did wonder how much was propaganda and party line. Perhaps the experience I'd had with Salazar's right wing authoritarian rule in Angola warned me against the rigidity of the Y.S.A.

All spring we rode the bus back and forth to Minneapolis, pulling into Northfield late at night. In the dark coach, I rested my head on his shoulder, hoping that he'd put his arms around me, but he was single-minded about his future. He planned to move to the Twin Cities the next year, transfer to the University of Minnesota, and organize for Y.S.A. I wasn't part of his picture, but neither was he part of mine, I realized.

In the midst of working with the coalition in Minneapolis that spring, and dreaming of romance with Larry and Tom, I met a boy at an Action Party meeting who was impetuous and ardent. I wasn't at all sure how seriously to take Doug's first phone call to me. Though I'd met him at the meeting, and he had attended the Washington and Minneapolis teach-in and marches, he seemed to be a partier. He called me late one weeknight.

"Hi, Nancy," he said, "This is Doug. Remember me? I just met you at the Action Party meeting." I could tell he was drunk. He was loud and obnoxious.

"How about sneaking out at midnight? I'll wait for you behind Nourse and we can go to a party."

He definitely didn't attract me but his proposal intrigued me. For two years I'd been hearing about all night arb parties, and I decided this was my chance to experience one. I still had the reckless streak I'd had in Rhodesia, where I wanted to do the exact opposite of the Glegg's rules. You want to keep me in? I'll find a way to get out.

"I don't know," I said. "I have to wait breakfast and I have an 8 o'clock tomorrow morning. It's too late."

"Oh, come on, let's go. It'll be fun. We can get you back to the dorm in the morning in time to set up breakfast."

After a moment more of hesitation, I said, "Well, OK, I'll meet you behind my dorm in a few minutes." A casual friend lived on the basement floor of Nourse in a room facing away from campus. She had offered her window to anyone who wanted to sneak out at night. Here was my chance! Her light was out when I knocked on the door. "Can I use your window?" I asked. I got a groggy yes. Hers was a generous offer because the head of her bed was just below the window. She made an inadvertent steppingstone. As I hoisted myself up out of the window I tried not to walk on her. Doug was there in the dark and I said hi.

We joined a party going on at the farmhouse, a college-owned, but unoccupied house, which was only a short walk through the arb. When we arrived, we could hear the drunken laughter of a small group coming from the dark house. Once I adjusted to the dimness, I was startled to find two couples cavorting in the nude in a room bare except for a litter of beer bottles rolling across the wood floor.

Wow, I thought, am I expected to join them? What have I gotten myself into? I hated to be a prude, especially since Doug had seemed so uninhibited, but I kept my head even after a couple of beers. We sat on the floor, leaning against the wall, talking. "I can't understand," I said, "why so few kids showed up at the Action Party meeting tonight. Don't they care about the war?" I took a long swig of Pfeiffer beer.

"Everyone's too busy booking, I suppose," Doug said. He didn't badger me to remove my clothes nor make any moves to strip his off. I began revising my opinion of him. Maybe he wasn't as rash as he first appeared.

"Are you dating anyone?" he asked.

"Mm, no, not really," I said, wishing I could say yes.

For the next three weeks until the end of the term we picnicked, partied with friends, and defied curfew when we weren't reading, writing term papers, and studying for finals. The waiter-waitress-scully picnic, thrown annually by the college for those who worked in the dining halls, was one of the last parties of the year. Doug was a waiter in one of the men's halls. Armed with blankets, we walked down to the lower arb by the Cannon River, and staked out a place with some friends. We feasted on gristle-burgers, delicacies we adored in spite of their name. They were thin cuts of cheap beefsteak, dripping in grease and juices and eaten in buns. We drank freely from the kegs of beer and soon Doug loudly proclaimed, "I always propose to girls on the fourth or fifth date. Just to see their reactions."

"In case you want to know, no, I won't marry you," I said.

"If they take me up on it, I tell them I'm joking," said Doug with a laugh.

Norma, a friend from my floor, was sitting with us. I'd been confiding in her during that difficult year. She was a junior and therefore much wiser than I. "You'd better treat Nancy right," she told Doug. "I am," he said.

I was uneasy about his marriage joke. It seemed weird, and I didn't like his announcing it to the whole group. During the three weeks we dated, we had had a few conversations about sex. "I don't think sex is sacred," Doug said. "You don't even have to like the person to enjoy it."

Despite my theoretical belief in free sex, I was shocked. For me, free sex meant not feeling guilty about having sex with your steady boyfriend, not that you'd have sex with just anyone. "We're so different," I said, "You're cavalier about relationships. And you think that somehow you can stay detached from someone even when you're spending lots of time with them."

"It's easy to just be friends and not get involved," he said. I couldn't imagine us as a couple. As far as I was concerned, when the term ended so would our relationship. I had met him, it turned out, at the zenith of his sophomore irresponsibility. He had spent most of the year playing bridge, drinking, and not going to class. That summer the administration invited him to leave Carleton because his grades were so bad. It was the kick he needed to get serious about school. In his negotiations with the college, Carleton told him he could stay if he got a B average during fall term; for the next two years he earned nothing but As and Bs. It took me a long while to realize that Doug's boldness was a cover for shyness. That spring before meeting me, his girlfriend had broken up with him. He told me later, "I was trying not to let you catch me and I tried to be indifferent so I wouldn't hurt you."

I took the train to Chicago to spend the summer with my parents and brothers until they went to Angola and I worked at Wesley Memorial Hospital as a nurse's aide.

Only a few weeks into the summer, a letter from Doug arrived, just a short note. "Hey kid, I miss you. I can say with all honesty that I like you. The involvement happened and I cannot say that I am sorry!" He was lonely, working as a lifeguard out in Montauk, on the tip end of Long Island. For the rest of the summer, we wrote back and forth almost daily, long letters about our families, where and how we'd grown up, and our views on music, politics, religion, love, and commitment. Doug was the first person to ask me in a serious way what I thought about a multitude of issues, and he hadn't been afraid to hear what I said. I liked him for it.

In late summer, I went my cousin Janice Lee's wedding in Tacoma. The wedding was an ironic counterpoint to my burgeoning sense of what sort of woman I wanted to be and what I wanted in a relationship. Betty Friedan had convinced me that society squelched women's ambitions and funneled them almost exclusively into the domestic arena. Her ideas had set off a steady electric hum radiating from my center to my fingertips, the hum of possibility and growth, the buzz of surprise and the unknown. My cousin's wedding, on the other hand, promised to be a celebration of fashionable society, with the aim of pushing Janice, at twenty-one years old, firmly into domesticity. I wasn't opposed to marriage. In fact, I fervently hoped I would be a wife and mother one day. But I also dreamed of traveling, joining the

Peace Corps, and taking intellectual journeys. I wished such dreams for Janice too.

Earlier in the school year, Mom had called me at Carleton to say that Aunt Marcia wanted me to be one of Janice's bridesmaids. I was willing to attend the wedding, but I was sure I didn't want to be part of the parade of bridesmaids. I felt, unconsciously, that agreeing to be in the wedding would have meant acquiescing to an American life. Three years after being ousted from Africa, I was still angry and my anger centered on Tacoma, the place I was supposed to call home, and Aunt Marcia, the woman who declared Tacoma God's country.

"No thanks." I said. "Just tell her I prefer not being a bridesmaid." And I put it out of my mind. Only later did I think it odd that my invitation came not directly from my cousin, but in a roundabout fashion from Aunt Marcia to my mother to me. Had Janice invited me directly, I suspect my answer would have been the same. In my mind, she was not a separate actor in this drama, nor even the main actor. She was caught up in my storm of anger toward her mother. I didn't think about how she might feel about being turned down.

That summer before the wedding, Mom announced, "We have to arrive in Tacoma in time to adjust your gown." I couldn't believe what I was hearing.

"But I'm not going to *be* in the wedding," I protested. Perhaps my mother had never relayed my refusal to Aunt Marcia. Or maybe my aunt and my mother had assured each other, "She'll change her mind once the wedding is imminent. She just has silly ideas."

"She's a child and doesn't know what she wants," I could hear Aunt Marcia say to Mom. But I *did* know what I wanted. Many years later, my mother gave me a batch of old letters, including one to her from Aunt Marcia written in July 1965.

"Drat Nancy's negativeness," she'd written, "where is the respect for another's pleasure when it is such a little thing to appear in a wedding?" From the distance of forty years, it *was* a small thing. At the time, my stance toward the wedding was part of complicated emotions that I couldn't have spelled out. I was irritated with my aunt, Tacoma and America; I wanted to exercise my right as a woman to make up my own mind; and I felt urgency about politics that differentiated me from my Tacoma relatives and trumped a conventional family wedding. Besides opposing the Vietnam War, I was caught up in the excitement of hearing Martin Luther King, Jr. and John Lewis at rallies in Winnetka, Illinois that summer. Vietnam and civil rights were important, it seemed to me. The wedding was trivial. I didn't think I was negative; I saw myself as pro peace, women's rights, and civil rights. In her letter, Aunt Marcia also acknowledged, "If this is the only area in which we are disappointed I guess it is a little thing. In the main, [Nancy] is honest, forthright, sensitive to suffering and unhappiness and so eager to do her part about correcting these."

On the trip west, though, I only felt my aunt's pressure and disapproval. I watched the endless desert from the car window as we drove to Tacoma and mulled my options. They can't force me to be a bridesmaid. I thought with distaste about the bridesmaid's dress. How immoral to waste money on a dress I'd never wear again! I'd much rather have sent the money, spent on the dress, to support open housing on the North Shore of Chicago. My scorn echoed my mother's attitude toward the coffee table book of Christian art that I had bought my father for Christmas. Mom was eminently practical and could be dismissive of people she didn't agree with. Evidently she passed along that trait to me.

The highway through North Dakota and Montana, a straight shot west as far as I could see, bisected a scrubby brown land. Occasional dirt tracks veered to left or right without warning, sometimes with a faded, wooden sign announcing a distant ranch. I brooded on the wedding. I dreaded appearing in public, marching up the aisle and standing at the front of the church in the midst of strangers. I hated the thought of my long, free-flowing hair plastered into a beehive. I didn't want to be tamed. I refused to be false to myself. I was as uncompromising as the land we drove through.

But, before I'd even climbed out of the car upon arrival in Tacoma, my aunt had enlisted another cousin to talk me into complying. She joined me in the back seat and, with barely a hello, launched into her assignment.

"You're being selfish," my cousin said. "This is Janice's day and we do what the bride wants. She wants you."

Janice hadn't actually invited me to be her bridesmaid. But after listening to my cousin oblige and coerce me for half an hour while we sat in the car, my resolve weakened. I started sounding petulant even to myself. My aunt, mother, sister, and cousin stood on the lawn in front of the house, watching the minutes tick by, anxious for me to capitulate before the dressmaker closed up shop for the night. My cousin must have sensed that she had penetrated my resistance.

"Well, why don't you at least come along to watch Kathy get fitted?" she asked. I went along to observe the dress-fitting, but once there I realized I had been corralled. The fitter bustled over to measure me. And when

Janice asked me if I was going to be a bridesmaid, I helplessly surrendered. A couple of days later, I overheard a conversation between Aunt Marcia, Janice, and Keith, the groom.

"Nancy wasn't here more than five minutes before she was ready to go to the dressmakers," Aunt Marcia gloated. "I guess all the excitement just caught up with her." And Keith chimed in, "Yeah, she caved right in. From far away she could claim she didn't want to be in the wedding, but bam! as soon as she arrived, she caved in. I suppose it all looked so fun."

Janice said, "I even gave her a chance to back down at the dressmaker's."

I wanted to yell back, "No, I was out-maneuvered!"

The day of the wedding I told the hairdresser, "I'd like my hair to look natural, not ratted and all lacquered with hair spray."

"Sure, Hon," she replied, as she sprayed it into a stiff beehive.

Zipped into the white gown, with a fitted bodice, cap sleeves, and long floor-length organdy skirt with lavender bow and sash, I stood with the bridesmaids, groomsmen, candle lighters, ring bearers, and a flower girl, forming an arc around Janice and Keith. I tottered on high heels that pinched my toes. I'd been having back trouble that summer and I muttered a mantra to get me through the service, "Oh my back, oh my back, oh my back." The supper and dancing at the Tacoma Lawn Tennis Club lasted forever, a tortuous evening of chitchat.

A couple of days later, I flew back to my summer job in Chicago. As a final, futile, after-the-fact protest, I left my gown in Tacoma, hanging in Aunt Marcia's closet.

When I returned to Chicago, Doug and I made plans to meet before we went to school in September. To join him, I concocted the perfect scheme, or so I thought. My mother had suggested that I go to New York to see them off. My parents and brothers were about to return to Angola. "Oh, and then I can meet Doug at his mom and stepfather's in Brooklyn and we can go back to Minnesota together," I responded.

Doug had grown up in Minnesota with his father and stepmother. Conveniently for me, they lived near St. Paul, close enough to Carleton to provide me, at least in my daydreams, with the luxury of a family to stay with during school vacations. Doug and his family loomed in my imagination as a safe rock to stand on in this American wilderness. But my plans precipitated a struggle with my mother. She had been observing with some concern my intense correspondence with Doug that summer.

"No," she replied, "You can stay with cousin Jill. I don't want you to stay at the boyfriend's mother's house."

The boyfriend? Couldn't she even call him by his name? Mom accused me of being negative and selfish. I suspected Mom was afraid of the sexual potential in my relationship with Doug, on her mind since my sister's unplanned pregnancy. But at twenty, I wanted to be given credit for some common sense and the ability to make my own moral decisions. The idea of getting pregnant horrified me as much as it did her. I couldn't understand why Mom was opposed to my staying with Doug's mother. Even without having met her, she seemed the safest person possible.

Suddenly Mom changed her mind about my going to New York. "We don't want you to go to New York. Why doesn't Doug go through Chicago to see you on his way home to Minnesota?" Mom suggested. I recalled how small my sister's two-bedroom apartment was, just big enough for her family of three. I knew I'd be camping out on the foldout couch in the living room. Mom was as familiar with the apartment as I was, so I wondered where she thought Doug would sleep. In with the baby? She's as disturbed about sex as Mrs. Glegg was, I thought. Dad was silent or absented himself from the ongoing conversations. If he said anything, it was as a reluctant mediator between my mother and me.

"I think what she means, honey," Dad would sigh to my mother, "is that staying with Doug's mother would simplify things." To me, he'd say, "Mom wants you to stay with the Tuckers in New Jersey if you don't want to stay with Jill." I felt that Dad understood and supported me, but as I told Doug, "He usually remains silent." Did he care whether I saw them off in New York or was he also afraid of my fledgling friendship with Doug? Going to New York was an excuse to see Doug, but I genuinely wanted to say goodbye to my family there at the moment when they actually left this continent. From Chicago they planned to stop in New England before going to New York. Saying goodbye in Chicago weeks before their departure seemed to accentuate the distance between us.

Before my parents and brothers left, they drove me south to Hyde Park, the neighborhood between the University of Chicago and Lake Michigan, to leave me with my sister Kathy, her husband, and baby, until it was time for me to return to Carleton.

"We won't see you in New York, will we? We won't, will we?" Mom insisted. I shrugged and said, "I don't know."

But I did know. I had made up my mind not to go to New York. They didn't want me there. Just go ahead, go back to Angola, and leave me alone, I thought.

After writing to each other all summer, I knew Doug far better than I had at the end of school in June and I looked forward to seeing him in Chicago. I knew his father was an ex-labor organizer, who had been featured in *Life* magazine as "young radical of the year" back in 1941, but now was a television salesman and repairman. I knew his parents had divorced when he was about two, that his stepmother was a nurse, that his mother, who was a teacher, lived in New York, and that his stepfather was a cancer researcher. I knew that Doug had a passion for teaching and history. Influenced by his father's example, he wanted to contribute to society. "A good teacher combines knowledge with liking kids, and they must like him in return. Education is how we are going to change society and give everyone a chance at what we've had," he wrote me. He wanted to teach high school, although the young kids he was teaching to swim that summer made him rethink his goal. The ninth grade black girl I tutored that summer had made me think about teaching as well, or possibly social work.

Doug and I wrote each other about music and the war. "I really like jazz, K.C., New Orleans, and Chicago jazz of the 20's and 30's, Modern Jazz Quartet, Monk, Charlie Parker, Woody Herman... Folk music of the good type—Bob Dylan (not for his singing but his songs), Pete Seeger, Leadbelly." We discussed how Doug would handle the war and the draft. During the summer, President Johnson had doubled the draft quota and eliminated the marriage exemption. Would he serve in the military, or declare himself a C.O., now that the Supreme Court had ruled "that one does not have to believe in God to be moral," as Doug put it? Or would he move to Sweden?

I knew that, despite Doug's flip comments the previous spring about sex and commitment, he had a softer, more compassionate side. "I like people just because they are people. Everybody has something right with him if you are willing to look for it." Even so, I thought about the mail-order bride we'd met in Angola, a young girl who came from Portugal to marry a man she'd been corresponding with, but had never met. Now that Doug and I were meeting face to face again, would we find as much to talk about? Would we like each other in person as much as we had in our letters? Would he like Kathy and Larry, and would they like him?

Doug and Larry instantly discovered a mutual love of games. Chess, Go, Bridge, any game occupied them endless hours. The domestic chores of cooking and tending to year-old Christopher fell, for the most part, on Kathy and me, but they were leavened by conversations, among the four of us, that I characterized as intellectual. I had been accustomed to the political stew of Carleton, where we agitated over campus politics, the Vietnam War, and civil rights. Politics had a real-world way of making me feel weighted down by anger and the frustration of railing against an unresponsive government and society. Here in Chicago, the no less serious discussions of history, philosophy (Larry's major) and literature (Kathy's major) left me bubbling with joy and stretching for more. I relished Doug's zest for argument and ideas, and savored the chance to learn more about him. After a few days, when Doug returned to Minnesota, I accompanied him to meet his family.

The James family included his parents, brother Ric, who was in high school, sisters Kathi, who was in junior high, and Barbara, who was seven years old. When I met Bud and Rita, Doug's father and stepmother, I recognized where Doug had come from. Sitting at the dinner table in the James house was like finding myself in a verbal combat zone, about as far as I could get from the understated, unresolved conversations I'd been having with my parents. Nourished by Rita's beef-vegetable soup, fresh bread, and salad tossed with her blue cheese dressing, Bud and his children yelled at each other about the Vietnam War, about art, about yogurt, no topic too trivial to be tackled.

"Now yogurt is the miracle food," said Bud. "First they say yogurt does this wonderful thing for you, and then they say it has that amazing quality. But pretty soon they'll find that if you eat it every day it'll give you cancer! You won't find me eating yogurt." I began to see why Doug was prone to making off the wall comments and jumping to what to me were odd conclusions.

"Bud, no," said Rita. "Yogurt is fine for you." She was the family conciliator, keeping, without much success, Bud's wild statements in check. The family clashed and jangled, in what I took to be anger. Then they roared with laughter and went on as if no swords had been raised. I sat by, absorbing not only the full flavor of the food, but this new way to communicate.

The contrast between Aunt Marcia's sentimental ideal of womanhood and the James free-for-all convinced me that I could be as independent-minded and outspoken as them. It would take me considerably longer to figure out how to fit gracefully into my family. First, I needed to find a mooring of my own.

I believed in my bones Betty Friedan's warning that women were too often relegated to the domestic realm, but after graduation and an unsatisfactory stint in the wrong program in an Indiana graduate school, I moved back to Minnesota to marry Doug. He and his family felt like the solid anchor I required to blossom in America. My brothers have happily lived their adult lives outside the United States; I found a man who had never traveled abroad. Where many adult missionary kids lead restless lives, moving and traveling constantly, I needed stability and family, somewhere reliable to stay and someone to show me I was home. Doug was the quintessential American man, limited by income, but smart and motivated to move up. In attitudes and education though, his family were voracious and eclectic readers, argumentative, well versed in world events. Though he hadn't traveled, he was aware of the outside world, eager to learn, and not at all provincial in his ideas. I liked his confidence and optimism. I liked the way he boosted my spirits when I was laid low, certain that I'd never get out of the blues. I liked having his family to celebrate holidays with, to feel their warmth and love, to eat turkey at Thanksgiving and sinfully rich prayer bars at Christmas.

I hadn't forgotten Friedan's lessons. Early in my dating relationship with Doug, we had our first fight over whose responsibility it was to wash the dishes. We were visiting his mother in Brooklyn and we had brought along another Carleton couple. After dinner, the men went into the living room and the women cleaned up the kitchen, a fact that did not sit well with me. I figured that since this was his mother's house, Doug should pitch in to clean up. It was the first of many skirmishes on the way to equitable distribution of household labor.

Despite some disagreements, I zeroed in on Doug as the key to unlocking America for me. The irony, perhaps for all missionary kids, certainly for me, was that my deepest sense of home for so long was Africa. But in the end, the place that fostered my true homecoming to my self was my bete noir, America. I began to claim it as my adult home. Doug and his family were there to welcome me.

Three years after we'd met, Doug and I married on a hot Minnesota June day. My parents weren't able to travel from Angola to attend, but Kathy, Larry and Chris drove from North Carolina where they then lived, and my cousin Janice and her first son Kenneth flew in from Tacoma. We fashioned a homegrown, do-it-yourself 1968 wedding in the backyard of the James's house in Afton. I designed and silk-screened our invitations and sewed my own gown, a white linen mini-skirt splashed with bright yellow daffodils, orange tulips, and other generic red, blue, and green flowers. Doug wore a white turtleneck, a peachy-orange jacket, and a white carnation boutonniere. Our wedding reflected both the prevailing 1960's ethic of simplicity and informality, as well as our recent-student poverty. We decided to make do without floral arrangements, except for bouquets of yellow and white daisies carried by Doug's little sister Barbie and me. I wore a matching wreath atop my hair, which fell long and straight to the middle of my back. We let the grassy slope be our aisle, the giant oak we stood under be our altar, and the low stonewall nearby delineate our sacred space. The simple homemade buffet, plain banana sheet cake, and short guest list further downplayed the drama and ritual of the event.

We wrote our own ceremony, but borrowed heavily from Kahlil Gibran's *The Prophet*. Two years earlier I had quoted from the same book when separated from Doug on a trip to see my parents in Angola. I had been seized by a need to be independent and I had admonished Doug, in a letter, to live his own life without constantly worrying about me. Gibran's sentiment to allow "spaces in your togetherness" captured in a positive way that wish. "Love one another, but make not a bond of love. Let it rather be a moving sea between the shores of your spirits." Our wedding service, presided over by a local anti-war minister, expressed what was in our hearts without compromising our lack of religious belief. It lasted five minutes. Before the final guests had arrived, we were married.

Our wedding joined two enduring family philosophies: my Christian upbringing and Doug's dissenting one. His parents were not churchgoing. Maia, his mother in Brooklyn, was of Russian Jewish origin, but celebrated her Jewishness only in a cultural sense or with an occasional Passover Seder. His stepfather, Joe, was a lapsed Catholic. His father, Bud, had been raised by a Unitarian mother, but had found his faith in socialism and labor politics. His stepmother, Rita, raised in a New Hampshire Congregational Church, no longer was a believer. The diverse heritages of his parents had distilled, in Doug, into a skeptical humanism, with a decidedly materialistic bent. He argued long and often that thought, feeling, and mind derived solely from the chemical and biological processes going on in the body. The idea of a spirit independent, or even part of, the body made no sense to him. At that point in my life—age twenty-three and increasingly certain of my own political beliefs—Doug's family validated my growing religious doubt without forcing me to divorce from my Christian parents' values of social justice. Doug's full acceptance of me made him the man with whom I could imagine creating a new family.

Chapter 15 — "Make Love Not War"

Eteke tu lisanumula tu tandako; okaimbo ketu katito.
Numa guerra civil, um pais torna-se pequeno demais.
In a civil war, a country becomes too small.

Umbundu proverb

Two years before our marriage, in the summer of 1966 when I was twenty-one, I returned to Angola and to the continent I'd left so precipitously five years before. I hoped to reconnect with my family, disentangle my African roots, and say a more leisurely good-bye.

The previous summer, during my introductory correspondence with Doug, I had written, "I'm getting more and more wrapped up in the U.S. and her problems and potentials, but I still have that African blood in me asking for attention. Maybe going back to visit will appease the aching for Africa ... sometimes I feel like mother Africa has heaved me from her womb and I can feel her throbbing warmth calling me."

In the America I was leaving, the airports buzzed with American soldiers reporting for duty or going home on leave. The war in Vietnam suddenly involved hundreds of thousands of American troops, mostly my age and younger. Angry, scared students raged in the colleges, universities, and streets of America against a war that relentlessly sucked every young male who didn't have a draft deferment into the military. The black ghettoes of urban America rumbled with disturbances and calls for Black Power, justice, and equality. Forced to choose sides like every American, I was passionately anti-war and consumed with hatred for President Johnson and his cronies. I shouted out my loathing at street demonstrations, draft card burnings, and teach-ins. I even detested the soldiers themselves, whom I later was able to admit had little choice in the matter, unlike my more privileged friends. I ranted against an America whose values I despised. I couldn't wait to get back to Angola.

But when I got to Angola, it too was at war, in its sixth year of fighting for independence from Portugal, but still eerily calm and physically intact. The soldiers posted at the airport, in the city, and at roadblocks were ominous intrusions in the beautiful landscape. I stepped off the plane into the unmistakably African countryside—the coconut palms and sandy beaches of the coast, and the baobabs, cactuses, scrub brush, and grasslands of the interior highlands. The Africa deep in my bones stirred. I felt utterly at home.

My mother met me in Luanda at the end of June and we caught a bus and the train to Bela Vista where Dad and my brothers met us at the station. I was prepared for big changes in David since Mom had asked me to bring socks for him in the largest size available. I discovered his voice had changed. Mark had his usual goofy enthusiasm and a twelve-year-old's oversized nose, ears, and teeth, as if he hadn't quite grown into them yet. We drove into Dondi. A slew of emotions ambushed me; affection for my family tinged with anxiety left over from our parting the year before; the joy of returning to Dondi, my home away from home; sheer happiness with the amazing fact that I was back in Angola; *saudades* for my absent dorm friends; wonder that the tall eucalyptus groves lined the red dirt roads exactly as they had earlier, erasing the years I'd been gone. The greens of the lacy woods had darkened through the long rainy season. Now in the cold dry season, days were sunny and nights crisp. We passed the first buildings at the edge of the mission, the "new" school, completed after I left Dondi in 1957, and the dorm where I had lived for two years. They were empty. The war had scattered the missionary families to North America and countries in southern Africa. The red brick houses and the trees looked the same, the solid air of accomplishment felt the same, the dry season smell of wood smoke was the same, but without friends could it be home, I wondered. Across from the dorm, the solitary eucalyptus tree, massive enough to provide each of the sixteen dorm kids a perch, still stood. I breathed in its sharp aroma and my head cleared. Just beyond the dorm, we pulled in beside what I had known as the Knights' house, but it was now my family's home. During my dorm years, Aunt Eleanor had given me piano lessons in her living room and sometimes I had stayed on to play with her twins who were the same age as Mark.

The cook and laundry man came out to greet me, clapping their hellos. *Akombe veya* [the guest has come], *kalunga, ku ku* [hello, thank you], the men said. We milled around greeting each other and grinning. I felt a twinge of sadness that I might miss Tomás, Cipriano, and Mãe altogether, even if we visited Lobito. No one lived in our old house anymore. It only required a gardener-caretaker for the occasional guest.

"We're putting you out here in the guesthouse for the summer," Mom said. Before I could carry my bags in, a playful little goat bounded up to us. My brothers laughed and introduced me to their pet kid, affectionately named Nancy. She pranced around, compact, foot-and-a-half high amber bundle, butting her head into my hand and demanding attention. I knuckle-scrubbed her head, knobby with emerging horns, and patted her sleek sides. She walked right into the guesthouse with me.

The little one-story brick house behind the Knights had been my teacher Miss Neumann's house. I had the central room for my bedroom, the laundry man washed and ironed clothes in a room on the backside, and my parents used another room for storage. The coop, where Nancy the goat joined the chickens at night, was around back. The guesthouse lacked any sort of bathroom. Mom pointed out the tall chamber pot I'd be using, which made me wonder what Miss Neumann had done all those years she had lived there. My room was spacious and cool, with brick floors, and windows looking out toward the back of the main house.

The laundry man, whose name I no longer remember, took as his mission to reacquaint me with the little Umbundu I knew. Maybe he didn't realize that, being from the city of Lobito, I'd never known much Umbundu. We developed a morning ritual of greeting each other with all the varieties of Ovimbundu salutations.

He said, "*Akombe veya* [the guest has come]," and I responded "*Tueya* [I, the guest, have come]," and we followed with two sets of "*Kalunga* [Thank you] because I'd come from a very long distance.

Then he asked me if I was well. "*O kasi chiwa?*" and I said "*Ñasi chiwe* [I am well]."

"*Wa kolapo?*" [Are you strong?], he asked, and I replied, "*Nda kolapo* [I am strong]."

"*Wa lale chiwa?*" [Did you spend the night well?] I replied, "*Ocho muele, nda lale chiwa. Ove he?*" [Yes indeed, I spent the night very well. And you?]

Beyond our greetings, I couldn't converse with him in Umbundu. He laughed and appeared to take so much pleasure from our banter, as if I were paying him a personal compliment. Our daily exchange gave us a ritual, a playful liturgy, a joyful communion in which we both felt grateful for the chance to celebrate our Angolan-ness.

I settled in to my room and the life of my family, and began to roam the mission. I drank in all the landmarks I remembered from the last time I'd been in Dondi nine years earlier. The swimming pool looking a little neglected; the mango tree that I used to raid in front of the Child's house; the nespra tree near the Coelhos' house; the sprawling Institute campus dominated by the church tower; the seminary campus where I went to school when I was ten and eleven and the Collins' house where I lived when I was nine; the leopard's cave from which I could see the winding hill up to Means

School and Lutamo where Kathy lived one year; the hospital over the river, and up another hill on the opposite side of the mission; the orphanage where Tezinha came from, the *onjango*, and the leper colony beyond.

The buildings on the mission were still there but the uncertainty bred by war had taken its toll among the missionaries. Their houses were now home to the Angolan teachers, pastors, and nurses who had taken over mission duties. Only a handful of my childhood aunts and uncles were still around.

From my parents' house, I could look over toward the hospital compound, barely visible through the trees. Crossing the road, I found the narrow footpath that gradually descended toward the river and provided a shortcut to that side of the mission. Tall grasses along the path had browned in the dry air and the leaves of the trees were turning a gray-green. Acacias, the indigenous trees of the highlands, were delicate, with thin, flat layers of canopy. The shadows they cast were sparse and shot through with sunlight. I walked down the path until the landscape opened onto acres of flat gray rocks.

I greeted the half a dozen young women who had spread themselves out on the rocks under a perfect blue sky, singing as they worked. They were turning dried corn into meal, a familiar sight from my Dondi days. They sat with legs spread apart, their dresses hitched between their legs for modesty, and in unison they pounded the corn on the rock with L-shaped wooden clubs tapered to fit the hand. They scooped the meal into sifters to cull out the tougher parts of the kernels, swept the fine meal into piles with small hand-brooms made of grass cinched in the middle, and began pounding a new batch. Once all the kernels had been rendered into corn meal, they filled their enamel basins with it, hoisted them to their heads and walked home single-file across the rocks. I continued further down the hill to the river, with its small rapids, and there the path joined the road. Young women frequently squatted on the rocks and leaned over into the current to scrub their clothes clean. I had to pick my way carefully across the rocks to avoid stepping on the clothes that had been laid out to dry in the sun.

From the river, a short walk up the steep hill led me past Aunt Marie Crosby's house to the hospital compound. I walked around the *onjango* and headed for the orphanage, still full of infants lying in cribs or hospital-style bassinets, still tended lovingly, but hurriedly, by Angolan nurses stretched thin by the babies' needs. I offered to change diapers and rock a baby or two. The tiny babies swaddled in their bassinets reminded me of how small

Tezinha had been when I first held her at the Lobito train station, an eight-pound seven month old, as fragile as a newborn. If she were still living, if she and her family had survived the upheavals of the last five years, she'd be seven years old.

I lingered over every Dondi detail then to burn them more precisely into my memory, as I linger over them now because the landscape I remember, and the lives of the people, have been devastated. Though in 1966 the war hadn't yet taken much of a toll on the country, now, after four decades of colonial and civil wars, little of what I remember still exists. A video of Dondi my childhood friend had made showed that the eucalyptus trees, the mango tree, and all those trees whose names I never knew, had been cut down for fuel and to expose the enemy. The wonderful eucalyptus tree across from the dorm was a ghost of itself, partially hacked and burned. The tile roof and wood rafters of the dorm, and, in fact, of all the buildings, had been scavenged. With the roof of the church at the Institute gone, trees grew out of the building. All the buildings were in decay. Means School had been reduced to rubble. The red dirt road through the mission and the surrounding agricultural land had been sown with land mines, preventing the cultivation of corn and driving out the people who depended on it for their livelihood. Tall grasses covered the mission. Only the leper colony remained intact and functioning, ironic testament that fear of leprosy is stronger than the hatred that leads to war.

After exploring Dondi and seeing everyone I knew who was still around, I settled into an independent study of Angolan art. My father had obtained several books in Portuguese for me from the museum in Luanda. Most days I holed up in my room, reading about art and then writing. Nancy the goat jumped once too often onto my bed and tromped across the books and papers I'd strewn on the spread. I finally had to close my door. I made a couple of expeditions to Nova Lisboa and Silva Porto to buy carved wooden masks, stools, and animals and to visit some Portuguese friends I'd known in Lobito. I was glad to be slightly removed from the tension in the main house, where Mom, with sighs, threats, and offers to help, pushed David to complete his ninth grade correspondence course so he'd be ready for high school in Kinshasa in the fall. David pushed back, reluctantly doing his lessons, painfully drawing them out. He had a knack for silently slipping away and joining Mark to play soccer with the schoolboys down at the Institute.

As dusk gathered each late afternoon, I fell quite naturally into the habit of pulling out and lighting all the kerosene lamps. Lining them up on the kitchen counter, I replenished kerosene as necessary, washed the glass chimneys, lit the lamps, and distributed them about the house. Lamp lighting was a comforting ritual that led into dinner and evenings catching up with my parents and brothers and listening to the radio. In my earlier days in Angola, the only radio I recall hearing was local Portuguese news or BBC broadcasts from London. Most of the time, I was blissfully removed from news about America. That summer of 1966, as we were finishing dinner, Dad would tune his battery-run short wave radio to Armed Forces Radio and Voice of America. The news hammered us with one story after another about Black Power.

"In the latest news, Stokely Carmichael, the head of the Student Non-Violent Coordinating Committee has announced his organization's determination to pursue a policy of separate black institutions."

"H. Rap Brown, proponent of Black Power...."

"In a split with the Southern Christian Leadership Conference over its policy of Black Power, SNCC..."

"The NAACP and the Urban League responded to the challenge of Black Power..."

Black Power, as I understood it, meant that SNCC's black leaders and members wanted to determine their own destiny, to run black institutions without the interference of whites. Black Power was a direct challenge to the integrationist policies of NAACP, the Urban League, SCLC, and Martin Luther King, Jr. And a challenge to what I believed. Black power, though, essentially was the motivation for the war in Angola, and I didn't hesitate to cheer on the Angolans who wanted to throw off their Portuguese colonial masters.

In my correspondence with Doug that summer, I worried more about Vietnam and the draft than civil rights. We discussed whether he should refuse induction and go to jail if drafted, or if we should consider leaving the United States. I loved being in Angola. "I feel so much at home," I wrote Doug, and I wished he could join me. We both worried if leaving forever would be running away from America's problems rather than helping to solve them. I told Doug I'd just heard the rest of the phrase, "My country right or wrong." I said, "It makes all the difference. 'My country, right or wrong; when right to keep it right, when wrong to put it right.'"

Choosing another country presented a new puzzle. "All have their drawbacks," I wrote. I had known as I grew up that Angola was only a temporary home and that I'd eventually have to move to America. Now that I was back in Angola, I could see I no longer had a role to play there.

I was just a visitor. "There is nothing right here that could keep me happy for long." At twenty-one, I couldn't stay as an appendage of my parents forever. I could never have been a missionary; the Peace Corps didn't operate there; I couldn't see myself as an American diplomat; the war looked as though it would continue indefinitely. "Being here and not being able to say anything would be as good as supporting the [Portuguese] regime." Despite disagreeing with the Vietnam War and feeling alienated from an America that knew so little about the rest of the world, I was proud of its tolerance for dissenting opinions, at least of the peaceful nonviolent sort. The freedom of thought and movement I felt in America sharply contrasted with the atmosphere in Angola. Fear and censorship under the Portuguese made me tone down or even eliminate descriptions of the Angolan war and politics in my letters. As a precaution, I numbered each of my letters so Doug knew how many succeeded in getting through.

During our junior year, Doug and I had discussed getting married. Over the weeks in Angola, I increasingly questioned in my letters whether I was ready for marriage. "There are things I want to do and the question is whether I can get them done and still be married." As we approached our senior year, everything seemed unsettled. Would we marry after graduation? If not, would we go our separate ways for a year? Or forever? Would I work or go to graduate school? What work did I want to do? While my letters to Doug were heavily descriptive of my activities, Doug's to me were ardent expressions of love and dismay about my long absence.

In a letter I wrote at the end of July, I told him, "Please try not to think of me so much—keep busy with other things."

Doug wondered back if I were writing an oblique "Dear John" letter to him. As I remember, I was excited and preoccupied with being in Angola again but feeling increasingly detached from, and overwhelmed by, Doug's headlong, gushing letters. When he didn't receive any letters from me for two weeks, although I was writing at least three times a week, he said he was a nervous wreck, sure that I'd met a terrible end. I responded that I wished he were getting my letters, I was writing regularly, and I was O.K. I speculated that the censors found my writing hard to decipher.

"Please don't get so upset and worried," I pleaded with him. "Remember, you have to live your own life and enjoy yourself without always worrying over me, because we're two separate people with two separate lives. I do love you."

Although I was privately uncertain where my relationship with Doug would end, I couldn't bring myself to talk about it with my mother. That's why I felt ambushed one night when Dad came into my bedroom and said, "Mom is very upset about you and Doug."

"Why? What do you mean? About what?" I sputtered.

"The thing she holds most important in a woman's life—married love—you have violated and find meaningless," Dad said. He seemed to be implying Mom knew that Doug and I had a sexual relationship. I was confused and didn't know how to respond. Having dispatched his message to me, Dad said goodnight and left, but I was too edgy to fall asleep. My thoughts raced. How could she know anything about my sex life? Why was she so antagonistic toward Doug? What was wrong with loving him?

Suddenly I realized she must have been opening my letters to Doug, the letters Doug wasn't getting. The absent letters that had thrown him into nervous anxiety were held up, not by official government censors, but by my own snooping mother. I always placed my letters on the table in the living room with other outgoing mail to be driven into Bela Vista to the post office. They were easy marks.

Boiling with anger, I got out of bed and marched out to the tent where Mom was camping with my brother Mark. I demanded to know if she had been reading my letters. She admitted she had, "right at the beginning of summer."

Later she said, "Well, I might have read a couple letters."

I suspected she had read more than that. We settled in the living room and Dad joined us. Mom and I argued and yelled till 4 o'clock in the morning. Dad played the mediator role, as he had a year earlier when we'd argued about Janice Lee's wedding and my trip to New York. I was comforted to have him as my ally or at least not my antagonist. He was able to translate my wild rantings into something understandable. Meanwhile, Mom kept pressing me. She wanted to know how often we'd slept together and why.

"None of your business," I retorted.

She was particularly bothered that I was using the "pill." "This seems to be a studied affair," she said, implying that she'd more likely approve of unprotected spur-of-the-moment sex. How dare she think I'm that irresponsible, I fumed to myself.

"Do you love Doug?" she asked.

"Of course," I said quickly. I did love him, but my uncertainties about the future, with or without him, made me squirm under her cross-examination. I didn't want to feel pinned down by her. Nor did I want her to force me to lie.

"Are you planning to get married?" she asked.

"I don't know."

"Is Doug just getting what he likes out of you?" Mom asked. I didn't deign to answer her. How could she think I, *I*, would allow myself to be used?

"Are you engaging in sex only because everyone else is?" Did I look like a sheep to her?

"Can you give it up?" she asked.

By then I was too angry to speak. I was shocked that, in her view, I was deceitful, immoral, and selfish. I was upset that she couldn't see that I shared most of her values. I felt skewered right at a point when I'd been harboring many doubts about Doug. If anything, I wanted her reassurance that anyone could have doubts. I wanted my mother's understanding about the difficult life decisions looming ahead. But under her assault, I was unable to confide in her. I was crushed breathless between Doug's loving anxiety and my mother's obsessive disapproval of unmarried sex.

Anger never came easily in our family. When we did allow it to erupt, we were embarrassed to acknowledge that, yes, we were angry at each other. No one knew how to knead that anger into understanding. Instead, life carried on as if that lump of rage weren't gumming us up. For most of the next day, I stayed in my room, writing a letter to Doug about my mother's assault. Mom had invited to lunch an Angolan woman who wanted to see me, but I was in a daze from lack of sleep. My eyes were red and swollen from crying. I was still dizzy with anger. I refused to come out for lunch. I couldn't imagine trying to pretend everything was fine to our lunch guest, someone I barely knew.

Indeed, having left behind the war in Vietnam and sidestepped Angola's war for independence, I had landed squarely in another more personal war with my mother. It was a summer of wars.

The strained relations with Mom didn't prevent me from joining a missionary picnic at Kutatu Falls, as a farewell to Dondi. As a child, I had loved to watch the river, flat and quiet, round the bend upstream and gather speed as it charged toward the boulders and turned into froth. I used to leap easily from one boulder to the next, fearlessly crossing the river from one bank to the other and back. I never worried about losing my step.

In the summer of 1966, as we approached the falls, I imagined leaping across to the other side. My memories of Dondi were laden with images of my young, fearless self, the young girl who walked on stilts and climbed nespra and eucalyptus trees, who swam with a dolphin out beyond the breakers at Jomba, who traveled away to school at nine years old. We parked on a rise above the steep bank of the river. I jumped out of the car to look down. What a familiar scene! Not one rock was out of place. The water swirled and foamed exactly as it always had. I walked down the path to the flat rock at the edge of the water. It jutted into the river, like an arrow pointing the way. A fine spray, tossed up by the river, misted my bare arms and legs and made me shiver in the warm sun. I prepared to leap across the gap to the first boulder. But the boulder seemed impossibly far and high. The water plunged through the gap at such speed that I simply couldn't make myself jump. My fearlessness evaporated into the mist. I'd come up against an inner barrier that turned my legs to lead, as if all the turbulence about Doug and my life after Carleton, plus the anger I felt toward my mother had slammed into me and left me paralyzed.

A few days later, we packed up the car and drove down to Lobito for a short vacation before I had to leave Angola. We traveled the highway along the railway line, the line that had carried me back and forth to school so many times. Still a dirt road, it traversed a mostly empty plateau until, about three hundred kilometers after leaving Dondi, the road plunged down the escarpment onto the coastal strip and we were in Lobito. No one lived in our house anymore, only vacationers and those in transit like me.

I reclaimed my bright corner room with its views of the bay in two directions, where Kathy and I had lived with Tezinha when we were teenagers. Though the chilly cloudiness of the *cachimbo* season discouraged swimming, I walked along the beach and the water's edge to the end of the spit. Retracing the steps of my old Lobito life called out memories. I remembered Kathy, back from her ring-around-the-moon expedition to the spit with Dad, telling me that fairies and Santa were just pretend. Despite that sobering reality, I recalled other mysteries of my childhood. As I looked across the bay to the lighthouse high on the limestone hills, I remembered the magic dolphin dance. I thought about the miracle of Tezinha, growing from newborn to toddler as I watched. I remembered how languages had given me the codes for connection and home.

We made the rounds, visiting a few Portuguese families I'd grown up with. Several families had moved back to Portugal or to South Africa and most of the expatriate community of English, Belgians, and Americans had left when the war started. But on Sunday when we attended church in Canata, old and familiar faces gathered round, shaking my hand and welcoming me home. I'd left for six years, gone to Rhodesia and America, and when I returned, the three sisters I always associated with Canata were still there. I suppose they must have been in their thirties. They were tall and slim, with high cheekbones and fine lips. But their noses, flat across the bridges as if broken, and their smiles, unconsciously happy, at-peace-with-the-world-and-myself smiles marked them as family. The three always stood together after church to greet friends and talk. Three variations on a theme, I thought, two married sisters with sight, one unmarried sister blind. But the way they casually touched each other, the way they seemed to understand and tend to each other, broke my heart.

I felt somehow responsible for the rift in our family but unable to repair it in the little time I had left. I was feeling very much like the summer weather, cloudy and dreary. Life seemed flat and tasteless. After I left Angola, I wrote a letter to my mother telling her I loved her, because Dad had told me Mom thought I hated her. I explained to Doug, "You taught me that forgiving and loving even though you may be hurt is a much better healer, more constructive, than getting angry." Knowing what has since come to light about our family, I now understand my mother's obsession with my "despicable moral standards," as she called them. Mom's personal preoccupation that summer remained the single woman she had worried so much about back in 1961, when we left Dad in Angola. My father had quietly continued his relationship with her over the years. I became a handy receptacle for my mother's anxiety and anger.

I was not to see my parents again until after I had graduated from Carleton College, briefly attended graduate school at Indiana University, married Doug, and moved to a tiny farm community in southern Minnesota. And it would take me another thirty years to understand and give meaning to the events of that summer and indeed of my whole African life.

In that summer of 1966, when I stood at the Kutatu Falls, unable to jump, I was weighed down by worry and anger. I left Angola soon after, disappointed with myself and at odds with my family. For many years, it felt as though returning to Angola hadn't helped me separate from Africa nor brought me closer to my family. But now, as I look back from the vantage of forty years, I can see that, though it was a summer of conflicts and a time of great emotional turmoil, it launched me into a life of my own. Seeing Angola again after five years, I drank deep and long of its images and textures. The sand that gathered between my toes when I walked the beach in Lobito and the red dust that sprinkled on my sandals when I trod the paths in Dondi very tangibly relinked me to childhood. They were the salt and pepper of my memories, rendering them sharp and flavorful. Angola still lives deep in my core, but it's cushioned by my life here and now, with Doug and our children, with our families and friends. Today, I can picture myself again standing at the Falls. This time, I take a flying leap and land, sure-footed, on the boulder. The waters surge around me, yet I am confident. I know where I've come from and where I'm going.

Appendix: Favorite Portuguese Foods
   From Family Recipes

Canja (Chicken Soup with Mint, Rice, and Lemons)

4 to 6 servings

1 whole chicken, cut into pieces
1 medium yellow onion, peeled and chopped
1 handful of parsley sprigs
 lemon zest cut into strips from one lemon
1 sprig fresh mint
2 quarts chicken broth
1/3 cup raw rice
 juice of 1 lemon
¼ cup coarsely chopped mint
 salt to taste
1/8 teaspoon pepper

Garnish
4-6 lemon slices, each stuck with a small sprig of mint

   Simmer the chicken with the onion, parsley, lemon zest, and mint sprig in the chicken stock in a covered heavy saucepan over low heat 35-40 minutes until cooked through. Remove chicken and cool. Strain the broth and return to the pan. Cook the rice in the broth until done. Skin and bone the chicken, chop meat into large chunks, and add to the broth along with the lemon juice, chopped mint, salt, and pepper. Heat 2 to 3 minutes. Ladle into soup plates, float a mint-sprigged lemon slice in each portion, and serve.

Caldo Verde (Potato Kale Soup)

6 to 8 servings

1 large yellow onion, peeled and chopped
1 large garlic clove, peeled and minced
4 tablespoons olive oil
6 large potatoes, sliced thin
2 quarts cold water
2 ½ teaspoons salt
1 pound kale, washed, trimmed of coarse stems and veins,
    and sliced thin
6 ounces chouriço or other dry garlicky sausage, sliced thin (optional)

Sauté the onion and garlic in 3 tablespoons of the oil in a large heavy saucepan 2 to 3 minutes over moderate heat until they begin to color and become translucent. Add the potatoes and the water, cover, and boil gently over moderate heat 20 to 25 minutes until the potatoes are mushy. Meanwhile, fry the sausage in a medium-size heavy skillet over low heat 10 to 12 minutes until most of the fat has cooked out; drain well and reserve.

When the potatoes are soft, remove the pan from the stove and with a potato masher or stick blender, mash or blend the potatoes in the pan in the soup mixture. Add the sausage, salt and pepper, return to moderate heat, cover, and simmer 5 minutes. Add the kale and simmer uncovered 10 minutes until tender and the color of jade. Mix in the remaining tablespoon of olive oil, and taste the soup for salt and pepper. Ladle into large soup plates and serve as a main course accompanied by chunks of crunchy bread. Add more olive oil if desired.

Pescada Assada (Baked Fish with Tomatoes and Peppers)

4 servings

1 medium yellow onion, peeled and coarsely chopped
1 large garlic clove, peeled and minced
½ medium sweet green pepper, cored, seeded, and coarsely chopped
3 tablespoons olive oil
2 large bay leaves
2 tablespoons minced parsley
4 large ripe tomatoes, peeled, cored, seeded, and coarsely chopped
¼ cup dry white wine
2 tablespoons tomato paste
1 teaspoon salt
¼ teaspoon freshly ground pepper
4 slices of fine white fish

Saute the onion, garlic, and green pepper in the olive oil in a large Dutch oven over moderate heat 5 to 6 minutes until limp; add the bay leaves, parsley, tomatoes, wine, cloves, tomato paste, salt, and pepper; bring to a simmer; cover, and cook 30 minutes. Uncover and simmer, stirring often, 30 minutes more until the consistency of thick pasta sauce.

Preheat oven to 350°. Nestle fish into the tomato sauce, cover and bake for 15 minutes; uncover and bake 25 to 30 minutes longer or until the fish almost flakes at the touch of a fork.

Pasteis de Bacalhau (Cod balls)

Hors d'oeuvre for 6 to 8

½ pound dried salt cod
2 medium potatoes, peeled and cubed
1 large garlic clove, peeled and minced
4 teaspoons olive oil
2 tablespoons finely minced parsley
1 large egg, separated
1/8 teaspoon cayenne pepper
1/8 teaspoon freshly ground black pepper
Vegetable oil for deep-fat frying

Soak salt cod in cold water to cover for 24 hours, changing the water frequently. Drain the cod and place in saucepan with enough water to cover; bring to a simmer over moderate heat and cook 15 to 20 minutes until tender. Drain cod well, flake with a fork or fingers, removing bones and skin; mince fine and reserve. Meanwhile, boil the potatoes in water to cover until soft; drain well of all excess moisture.

Sauté the onions and garlic in olive oil about 5 minutes until limp; mix in parsley and remove from heat. In a meat grinder or food processor, grind the cod, potatoes, onion and garlic into a large bowl. Add the egg yolk, cayenne, and black pepper. Whisk the egg white into peaks and fold into the codfish mixture.

With 2 tablespoons, form the mixture into croquette forms and fry in hot oil until golden on all sides. Drain on absorbent paper towels. Delicious hot or at room temperature.

Bacalhau à Gomes de Sá (Cod Potato Casserole)

8 to 10 servings

2 pounds salt cod
8 cups water
¾ cup olive oil
8 garlic cloves, minced
4 medium onions, sliced thin
2 pounds medium Yukon or new potatoes, boiled, and sliced thin

Garnish:
4 eggs, hard boiled and sliced
1 cup whole small black pitted olives
¼ cup minced parsley

Rinse the salt cod in cold water; place in a large bowl, cover with cold water, and soak for 24 hours. Change the water several times. Drain the cod and place in a pot, cover with water, and simmer till it flakes. Remove bones and skin. Flake and return to a large bowl.

Preheat the oven to 350°. Heat olive oil in a large skillet and sauté garlic and onions. Stir occasionally and remove from heat when onions are transparent. In an oven-proof casserole place a third of the sliced potatoes, top with a third of the codfish, followed by a third of the onions. Repeat the layering, ending with the onions. You may sprinkle some olives and parsley between layers. Decorate with the egg slices, black olives, and parsley. Pour remaining olive oil mixed with some water over the eggs and olives. Cover and bake for 35 to 40 minutes until hissing hot and touched with brown. Serve slightly cooled.

Tastes even better if made a day or two before serving and then reheated.

About the Author

Nancy Henderson-James spent her early life until age sixteen in Portugal, Angola, and Rhodesia. She has published essays in newspapers and magazines and compiled *Africa Lives in My Soul: Responses to an African Childhood*, based on a survey of missionary kids and other global nomads. A chapter of *At Home Abroad* was published in *Unrooted Childhoods: Memoirs of Growing Up Global*. She has received honors from the Southern Women Writers Conference and the North Carolina Writers' Network. She lives in Durham, North Carolina with her husband.

Author photo by Alec Himwich